PHILIP ROLLINSON was born and raised in
Chattanooga, Tennessee. He did his under-
graduate work at the University of Chattanooga
and took an MA and PhD in English at the
University of Virginia. He served as a reserve
officer in the Navy and has taught at Vanderbilt
and the University of South Carolina, where
he is currently an associate professor of English.

PATRICIA PADEN MATSEN has taught Greek
at the University of South Carolina since 1969,
and is presently Associate Professor of Foreign
Languages and Chairman of the Program in
Classical Studies.

Duquesne Studies

LANGUAGE AND LITERATURE SERIES

VOLUME THREE

GENERAL EDITOR:

Foster Provost, *Department of English, Duquesne University*

EDITORIAL BOARD:

Classical Theories of Allegory

Classical Theories of Allegory and Christian Culture

by

Philip Rollinson

with an appendix on
primary Greek sources
by Patricia Matsen

DUQUESNE UNIVERSITY PRESS

HARVESTER PRESS

Published in the United States of America
by Duquesne University Press,
600 Forbes Avenue, Pittsburgh, Pa. 15219

Published in England
by the Harvester Press Ltd.
16 Ship Street, Brighton, Sussex BN1 1AD

First Edition

Library of Congress Cataloging in Publication Data

Rollinson Philip, 1939–
 Classical theories of allegory and Christian culture.

 (Duquesne studies in language and literature series; v.3)
 Includes index.
  1. Allegory. 2. Bible–Criticism, interpretation, etc.–History.
I. Title. II. Series.
PN56.A5R6   801'.95   81-4891
ISBN 0-391-01712-8   AACR2

Harvester Press Ltd., London
ISBN 0-7108-0386-9 (England)

Contents

Preface

This is a study of the development of theories of literary allegory in the Latin West in antiquity and the early Middle Ages. Additions and modifications were made to these theories in the later Middle Ages and Renaissance (the subject of another book in progress), but these early views continue their profound influence up through the Renaissance. I believe there are good reasons for undertaking such a study, both philosophically and practically. Philosophically there is a tendency to dismiss critical theory of the past and focus on the practices of allegorical interpretation. In his very important work on allegorical interpretation in the Renaissance Don Cameron Allen reflects this tendency when he remarks that "critical theory is never as interesting as practice."[1] Important as the study of the practices of interpretation is, it should never exclude the study of critical theory of the past, which really can tell us interesting and significant things about allegory. Primarily it tells us what allegorical interpreters as well as ordinary readers and writers in the Latin West may have thought they were doing or were taught to think they were doing in reading and writing allegorically. The philosophic validity of the study of theories of allegory reflects directly on the practical need of modern critics, scholars, and students in trying to understand late classical, medieval, and Renaissance poems.

It is my impression that interpreters of such poets as Dante, Chaucer, Langland, and Spenser, particularly interpreters of the past twenty or so years, who purport to be interpreting these poets under the auspices of some historically tuned sense of aesthetics, have a tendency to interpret on the bases of rather partial, incomplete understandings of classical, medieval, and Renaissance theories of interpretation. One consequently runs across very different notions of what medieval and

1. Don Cameron Allen, *Mysteriously Meant: The Rediscovery of Pagan Symbolism and Allegorical Interpretation in the Renaissance* (Baltimore: Johns Hopkins Press, 1970), pp. 282–83.

Renaissance literary allegory is all about. I am not setting out here to attack or defend any one of several currently popular conceptions of literary allegory, nor do I intend to plead for any special interpretation of any particular work. Rather, I want to examine the available evidence so as to provide a reasonably comprehensive, empirical survey of the nature and development of theories of allegory and allegorical literature. My hope is that this survey will become one starting point for the discussion of allegory and particular allegorical works.

The appendixes contain annotated translations of important theoretical works or parts of works which bear on the questions of allegory and which have not been available in English. I have translated and annotated the whole section on figurative language in Diomedes' *Ars Grammatica.* Allegory is one of the tropes Diomedes treats. Other figures, though, are also related to allegory, and I have translated the complete section so the reader will be able to grasp the entire context for the discussion of figures in one of the standard grammatical authorities for more than a thousand years in the Latin West. In Appendix II my colleague Patricia Matsen has translated all the pertinent grammatical and rhetorical passages in Spengel's *Rhetores Graeci,*[2] the standard collection of Greek rhetorical and grammatical writings. Her translation carefully gives the different definitions of allegory and related figures as they evolve. These Greek works parallel and in some cases directly influence the classical Latin grammarians and rhetoricians, and they again become available and directly known in their original form to the Latin West during the Renaissance.

I have been working on this project ever since graduate school. I am particularly indebted to two professors who taught me at the University of Virginia, Robert Kellogg and Stephen Manning. I have also been aided and encouraged by colleagues at Vanderbilt University and the University of South Carolina, particularly Jeffrey Helterman. I am deeply grateful, too, for the generous support, in direct aid and release time, from Vanderbilt and the University of South Carolina. The English Department, Dean of the College of Humanities and Social Sciences, and the Council for Research and Productive Scholarship at South Carolina have been especially supportive. My wife, too, has not only continued to support and encourage my work but has managed to treat a rather esoteric subject with extraordinary understanding and patient tolerance. Finally, the careful, thoughtful criticisms of the editor of this series, Foster Provost (himself an expert on allegory), and his readers have made this a much better work than it would have been.

2. Leonardi Spengel, ed., *Rhetores Graeci,* 3 vols. (1853–56; rpt. Frankfurt: Minerva, 1966).

Introduction

Allegory has distinct creative and interpretive aspects which are often confused. It may exist as a concept for the creative writer before and during the writing of what he imagines to be a piece of allegorical literature and certainly influences the resultant product. Allegory may also exist as a concept in the mind of the interpreter before and during the allegorical interpretation of a piece of literature and certainly influences such explication. Obviously these creative and interpretive aspects interact and influence each other—hence much of the disagreement and confusion about them and about allegory generally. But they are distinct and must not be confused.

Allegory also exists at or between poles of content and form, of meaning and method of expressing meaning, of *res* and *verba,* of what Wesley Trimpi in two penetrating articles on ancient critical theory calls respectively the philosophical and rhetorical.[1] The danger of misunderstanding and confusion is ever present in discussions of allegory because of these two poles. This condition has been particularly evident in the controversies surrounding the work of D. W. Robertson, Jr. Robertson, many of his students, and those medievalists who have been influenced by him, argue that beneath the literal sense of most medieval literary texts spiritual, Christian meanings are allegorically concealed. These meanings, it is claimed, will relate somehow to Augustinian (or biblical) *caritas.* This view of allegory is meaning oriented, for although the assumption that literary works have a literal and figurative sense (or husk and kernel, chaff and fruit) is necessary to it, the basic ingredient is its predetermination of a definite (albeit

---

1. Wesley Trimpi, "The Ancient Hypothesis of Fiction: An Essay on the Origins of Literary Theory," *Traditio,* 27 (1971), 1–78, and "The Quality of Fiction: The Rhetorical Transmisison of Literary Theory," *Traditio,* 30 (1974), 1–118. Together these articles amount to a book, and they represent a tremendously significant perception of the nature and evolution of ancient thinking about fiction.

broadly conceived) kind of meaning which will constitute the figurative sense of every text no matter what the literal sense. In an important recent study of Neoplatonic theories of allegory James A. Coulter points out that all the allegorical interpreters of antiquity (Jews, Christians, Stoics, and Neoplatonists) were "sectarian"[2] or, it might be said, doctrinaire. To these meaning-oriented interpreters literature, as Coulter perceptively observes, must first of all represent their own preconceived notions of what constitutes "certain and irrefutable truth about the nature of reality, whether physical, psychological, divine or metaphysical" (p. 19). Twentieth-century Marxist criticism suggests itself as an obvious modern counterpart to this kind of earlier allegoresis. It is not, however, the particular content or kind of meaning expected by this kind of interpreter which seems to create problems of simple communication among critics but the fact that such an overriding expectation exists.

A convenient example of the kind of problem such meaning-oriented theories can occasion may be found in the well-known scholarly debate before the English Institute, "Patristic Exegesis in the Criticism of Medieval Literature."[3] Speaking against the Robertsonian position in that debate, E. Talbot Donaldson attacks a patristic intrepretation of Chaucer's *Nun's Priest's Tale,* which identifies the poor widow as the Church, the fox as the Devil, and Chauntecleer as the alert Christian or priest.[4] Donaldson identifies this interpretation as "allegorical" (p. 19), but not his own interpretation of Chauntecleer as Everyman (p. 20). Methodologically speaking, however, a rooster as Everyman would seem to be just as allegorical as a rooster-priest. In either case the meaning is something other than what is literally presented, and indeed the Nun's Priest appropriately warns the Canterbury pilgrims to ignore the chaff of his tale and pay attention to the fruit.[5] Donaldson follows the Robertsonian lead and turns the question of allegory or no allegory into a question of content, entirely divorced from the question of allegory as expression of content or means of conveying it.

2. James A. Coulter, *The Literary Microcosm: Theories of Interpretation of the Later Neoplatonists* (Leiden: Brill, 1976), p. 19.

3. In *Critical Approaches to Medieval Literature: Selected Papers from the English Institute, 1958–1959,* ed. Dorothy Bethurum (New York: Columbia University Press, 1960), pp. 1–82.

4. E. Talbot Donaldson, "The Opposition," in Bethurum, pp. 1–26 and especially 17–20.

5. Line 622 (or Group VII. 3443) in *The Works of Geoffrey Chaucer,* 2nd ed., ed. F. N. Robinson (Boston: Houghton Mifflin, 1957). All subsequent citations from Chaucer are to this edition.

But the danger of confusing contentual and expressionistic aspects of allegory would seem to be equally great and ubiquitous. This is nowhere more true than in the matter of the well-known four (or sometimes three) levels of meaning to be found in the Bible, memorialized in this little medieval distich:

> *Littera gesta docet, quid credas allegoria,*
> *Moralis quid agas, quo tendas anagogia.*

[The letter teaches deeds, allegory what you are to believe, The moral what you are to do, anagogy where you should be going.]

It is frequently assumed that these lines imply that matters of Christian faith, behavior, and eschatology are always concealed allegorically (in the broader sense) under or in the literal meaning of any biblical text, which is limited to the expression of historical facts. The four levels are thus perceived as applying not only to kinds of content but also and especially to a nonliteral means of conveying content.[6] And so when a medieval or Renaissance writer or commentator indicates that a literary text can be read like the Bible, according to these four levels, it is sometimes assumed that he is indicating something about the method of expression in that literary text. Such an assumption, however, is not always necessary or even correct.

In the first place traditional Christian exegesis of the Bible works on the principle that the Bible is self-interpreting and self-consistent. Every passage in the Bible, as St. Augustine clearly points out in his *Christian Doctrine* (especially III. x. 14–16),[7] expresses Christian truth either literally or figuratively. One would never know the figurative truths concealed by some parts of the Bible *unless* they were literally expressed in some other part. And so, as far as the whole Bible is concerned, the letter not only teaches history but also matters of faith, behavior, and eschatology. In one basic sense, then, the distich above simply points out that there are four categories or kinds of content in the Bible. It reflects a method of conveying content figuratively only in the special (usually Old Testament) cases where literal, historical facts have additional figurative meanings (allegorical, moral, and/or anagogical). In these cases the literal text does not apparently treat

---

6. Beryl Smalley comments on the Alexandrian origin and long persistence of these levels and of their confused reference both to biblical subject matter and to a method of interpretation, *The Study of the Bible in the Middle Ages* (1952; rpt. Notre Dame: University of Notre Dame Press, 1964), p. 88.

7. A convenient modern translation is by D. W. Robertson, Jr.: St. Augustine, *On Christian Doctrine* (Indianapolis: Bobbs-Merrill, 1958), pp. 87–89.

Christian truths and so must be figuratively interpreted (since the assumption is that every passage in the Bible has something to say about Christian truth). St. Augustine discusses the example of the Old Testament patriarchs' having more than one wife (*Christian Doctrine* III. xii. 20). This account is to be construed, he writes, "not only historically and literally but also figuratively and prophetically, so that it is interpreted for the end of charity, either as it applies to God, to one's neighbor, or to both."[8] The four levels will be taken up later with reference to specific authors and texts. For the moment it will suffice to point out that even as a reflection of a kind or method of expression they do not refer to four kinds of expression but only two, literal and figurative, with four possible categories of meaning.

There is another problem related to the polarities of content and form, that of universality and particularity. The question of the truthfulness and reality of universals and/or particulars is central to an understanding of allegory. Wesley Trimpi has brilliantly demonstrated how crucial such questions are to the ancient conception of fiction.[9] Trimpi sees allegory as the general or universal and history as the particular, between which exists fiction ("Ancient Hypothesis" p. 63). He also observes that fiction is mimetic probability, hovering between truth and falsity.[10] It "reflects the very nature of language itself as analogy suspended in qualitative probability in constant danger of being resolved either into the true or the false," into history or fable ("Quality" p. 61). "The aim of literary theory," Trimpi writes, "has been to isolate and defend a type of discourse which could discover the significance of the particular in the immanence of the universal" ("Ancient Hypothesis" p. 61). Although Trimpi may be correct in associating allegory with the general and universal, it can also be said that certain kinds of expression, usually identified as allegorical, truly attempt to particularize the universal—in a kind of expression which tries to bridge the gap between universal and particular without stopping in between at the probable.

Underlying all these questions about allegory is the problem of terminology. It takes two forms. First, different meanings and extensions of meaning may be attached to the same term in different times, places, and writers. Secondly, the same concept or process may be identified in different times and places and by different people with

---

8. Robertson's translation, p. 91. For Augustine, of course, charity is the whole of Christian truth.

9. In the same two essays identified in note 1. See also Coulter's discussion of the Neoplatonic answer to this question (pp. 73–94).

10. See "Ancient Hypothesis," pp. 55ff. and "Quality of Fiction," pp. 49–61.

different terms. The terminological problem must be overcome for any really meaningful discussion of literary allegory to take place. It is for this reason that most scholar-critics, taking up questions of allegory or allegorical works, begin with comprehensive definitions of their own terms and concepts. The empirical survey of allegorical theories I am attempting here is intended to provide a common basis or starting point for future critics and criticism of allegorical poetry.

The writers and writings surveyed are philosophical, ethical, theological, doctrinal, rhetorical, and grammatical. Most of the issues of allegory are taken up by the rhetoricians and grammarians, both of whom taught the arts of language in antiquity. Although the grammarians treated the basics, their province included figurative language, schemes, and tropes. *Elocutio,* style or the stylistic manipulation of language, was also a major topic of rhetorical instruction and naturally included a full discussion of all the figures. Beginning rhetorical exercises, *progymnasmata,* also included practice in creating stories, fables, extended comparisons, and personifications.[11]

Aristotle's *Rhetoric* is important in the development of rhetorical theory in antiquity, but Cicero's theoretical works (1st cent. B.C.) dominated the Latin West, as did the examples of his speeches. Quintilian (1st cent. A.D.) was a famous teacher of rhetoric and his long Ciceronian *Institutio Oratoria* was also normative. The important Latin grammarians date from the fourth (Donatus, Diomedes) through the sixth centuries A.D. (Priscian). Their works are collected in Heinrich Keil's important eight-volume *Grammatici Latini.*[12] Several late classical encyclopedists treat all the liberal arts. Particularly important are Martianus Capella (5th cent. A.D.) and Isidore's *Etymologies* (7th cent. A.D.).

Since the number of works referred to is rather extensive and since many of the authors are relatively unknown (this will be particularly true for those interested primarily in the later Middle Ages and Renaissance), the following list records in alphabetical order authors, works, and in a few instances schools or positions which are significant in the subsequent discussion. Dates and a brief explanation for each

11. C. S. Baldwin has translated Hermogenes' *Progymnasmata* (2nd cent. A.D.) in *Medieval Rhetoric and Poetic* (1928); rpt. Gloucester, Mass.: Peter Smith, 1959), pp. 23–38. Ray Nadeau has translated the fourth-century Greek text of Aphthonius, "The Progymnasmata of Aphthonius in Translation," *Speech Monographs,* 19 (1952), 264–85. Priscian's sixth-century Latin *Praeexercitamina,* a considerably altered version of Hermogenes and the only Latin version prior to the sixteenth century, has been translated by Joseph M. Miller in *Readings in Medieval Rhetoric,* ed. Joseph M. Miller, Michael H. Prosser, and Thomas W. Benson (Bloomington: Indiana University Press, 1973), pp. 52–68.

12. Heinrich Keil, ed., *Grammatici Latini,* 8 vols. (1857–70; rpt. Hildesheim: Olms, 1961).

entry are given so that the reader will be able to remind himself of the identity or date of an unfamiliar reference. Following this list is a chart, organized chronologically, of rhetoricians, grammarians, philosophers, and churchmen, including those represented in Appendix II from Spengel's *Rhetores Graeci.*

ALDHELM (7th cent. A.D.). English churchman, scholar, writer, and teacher.

ALEXANDRIAN SCHOLARS. A group of learned men and writers who gathered around and developed the great library at Alexandria; they flourished in the 3rd and 2nd centuries B.C.

ARNOBIUS (3rd cent. A.D.). North African rhetorician, converted to Christianity, who attacks pagans and paganism in *Adversus Nationes.*

AUGUSTINE (4th–5th cents. A.D.). Prolific writer on all aspects of theology and doctrine, the most influential of the Fathers of the Church.

AVIANUS (4th–5th cents. A.D.). Important Latin writer of fables (like Aesop's), which were popular throughout the Middle Ages.

BALBUS. Spokesman for Stoic philosophy in Cicero's *De Natura Deorum.*

BEDE (7th–8th cents. A.D.). Great English churchman, historian of the church in England, scholar and teacher. His *Schemes and Tropes in Holy Scripture* adapts classical rhetoric and grammar to the Bible.

CHARISIUS (4th cent. A.D.). Latin grammarian in Keil, I.

CICERO (1st cent. B.C.). Greatest Roman orator and probably the most influential writer on theories of speaking and writing in Western Culture. Major theoretical works on rhetoric: *De Inventione, Orator, De Oratore,* [*Rhetorica ad Herennium* attributed to him throughout the Middle Ages]. *De Natura Deorum* contains extensive discussion of ancient philosophy, metaphysics, and religion.

CLEMENT OF ALEXANDRIA (2nd–3rd cents. A.D.). Learned early Greek churchman and teacher.

CLEMENT OF ROME (late 1st cent. A.D.). Early Greek churchman, to whom are attributed several later works from the 2nd to the 4th centuries. One of these, the *Recognitiones,* was available to the Latin West in a translation by Rufinus.

COTTA. Spokesman for the Academy in Cicero's *De Natura Deorum.*

DEMETRIUS (4th cent. B.C.). Athenian orator, writer, and public figure, traditionally (but no longer) thought to be the author of *On Style.*

DIOMEDES (4th cent. A.D.). Latin grammarian in Keil, I. Section on figures translated in Appendix I.

DONATUS (4th cent. A.D.). Most famous and best known of the Latin grammarians; in Keil, IV.

EUHEMERUS (4th–3rd cents. B.C.). Greek writer, responsible for idea that the gods were originally exceptional men, who were subsequently deified in legend. Only fragments of his work and of the Latin translation of it by Ennius survive.

GLOSSA ORDINARIA. A famous compilation of glosses, original and from the Fathers, on the Bible from the schools in Paris in the 12th and 13th centuries (*Patrologia Latina,* ed. J. P. Migne, CXIII–CXIV).

GNOSTICISM. Primarily a radical theology breaking away from mainstream Christianity in the 2nd cent. A.D. It stressed, among other teachings, the allegorical concealment of knowledge in various kinds of symbols.

HUGH OF ST. VICTOR (12th cent. A.D.). First of several famous and influential thinkers, theologians, commentators on the Bible, and teachers, associated with the Abbey of St. Victor in Paris.

ISIDORE (6th–7th cents. A.D.). Spanish bishop, historian, theologian, commentator on the Bible, and encyclopedist. His *Etymologies* was a definitive compilation of knowledge for the medieval West in its own right and continued its influence by being incorportaed into later and larger encyclopedic works, for example those by Rabanus Maurus and Vincent of Beauvais.

JEROME (4th–5th cents. A.D.). Great early scholar of the Church, prolific commentator on the Bible, and author of the standard Latin translation of the Bible (the Vulgate).

KING JAMES BIBLE (1611). Classic English translation of the Bible, the so-called Authorized Version.

LACTANTIUS (3rd–4th cents. A.D.). North African churchman, student of Arnobius and Christian apologist.

MACROBIUS (4th–5th cents. A.D.). Learned Latin Neoplatonist and commentator on Cicero and Virgil.

MANICHAEISM. A 3rd-century A.D. heresy influenced by Gnosticism, noted particularly for a dualistic view of the existences of good and evil. Augustine was a Manichaean for a time. After conversion to Christianity he inveighed against it.

MARIUS PLOTIUS (5th–6th cents. A.D.?). Latin grammarian in Keil, VI.

MARTIANUS CAPELLA (5th cent. A.D.). Author of Latin allegorical and encyclopedic survey of the seven liberal arts, *De Nuptiis Mercurii et Philologiae.*

NEOPLATONISM. The major philosophic (and religious) system of the pagan Roman Empire from the 3rd–6th centuries, primarily Greek and in the Eastern Empire. It ostensibly revived Platonism but combined with it aspects of other traditional philosophic schools such as the allegorical interpretation of the Stoics.

NICHOLAS OF LYRE (13th–14th cents. A.D.). Franciscan commentator on the Bible.

PHILO JUDAEUS (1st cents. B.C.–A.D.). Learned Alexandrian Jew, philosophic and allegorical commentator on the Old Testament, who exerted considerable influence on early Christian thought.

PLUTARCH (1st–2nd cents. A.D.). Famous Greek scholar, moralist, philosopher (Platonist), and biographer.

POMPEIUS (5th cent. A.D.). Grammarian and commentator on Donatus, Keil, V.

PRISCIAN (6th cent. A.D.). Influential grammarian, whose corpus is the most extensive of the Latin grammarians (Keil, II and III). His *Praeexercitamina* is an important Latin version of Hermogenes and until the Renaissance was the only text on early rhetorical exercises (*progymnasmata*) available to the Latin West.

PRUDENTIUS (4th cent. A.D.). Early Christian Latin poet. His well-known *Psychomachia* describes the battle of personified virtues and vices in heroic verse.

PSEUDO-HERACLITUS, *HOMERIC ALLEGORIES* (1st cent. A.D.). A treatise interpreting Homer allegorically in the tradition of the Stoics. The text was associated in the Renaissance with the philosopher and pupil of Plato, Heraclides Ponticus (4th cent.

B.C.), whose *Homeric Questions* had been arranged and published by the Neoplatonist Porphyry (3rd–4th cents. A.D.).

QUINTILIAN (1st cent. A.D.). A famous teacher and comprehensive theorist of rhetoric in the Ciceronian tradition. His great *Institutio Oratoria* was little known in the Middle Ages but was preferred to Cicero by some in the Renaissance.

RABANUS MAURUS (8th–9th cents. A.D.). Philosopher, teacher, and encyclopedist, a pupil of Alcuin, who brought systematic education based on the liberal arts to Germany.

REMIGIUS OF AUXERRE (9th cent. A.D.). French scholar and teacher, author of important commentaries on Martianus Capella, Bede, and others.

RHETORICA AD HERENNIUM (1st cent. B.C.). Vastly influential rhetorical treatise, believed in the Middle Ages and into the Renaissance to have been written by Cicero.

RUFINUS OF AQUILEIA (4th–5th cents. A.D.). Latin churchman, translator of many Greek works into Latin, including the Pseudo-Clementine *Recognitiones.*

SEPTUAGINT (3rd–1st cents. B.C.). Translation of the canonical Old Testament and Apocryphal books into Greek, so named from the reputed 70 (or 72) Hebrew scholars assembled at Alexandria to do it. It became the basic Old Testament text throughout the Greek-speaking world and was used by early Christians.

SERVIUS (4th–5th cents. A.D.). Grammarian and author of a famous commentary on Virgil.

VARRO (2nd–1st cents. B.C.). Great Roman scholar, philologist, and writer. His now-lost works include a history of pagan religion which was known and used by Augustine. Partly extant is a massive treatment of the Latin language.

VINCENT OF BEAUVAIS (13th cent. A.D.). Greatest of the medieval encyclopedists, author and compiler of *Specula* of all knowledge: *Naturale, Doctrinale, Morale,* and *Historiale.*

VULGATE (ca. 400 A.D.). The standard Latin translation of the Bible, completed early in the fifth century by Jerome.

Chronological Chart by Centuries*

CENTURY	GREEK	LATIN Pagan	LATIN Christian
B.C.			
4th	Aristotle Demetrius [but "On Style" much later] Euhemerus		
3rd	Alexandrian scholars Septuagint transla-		
2nd	tion of *OT*		
			Varro
1st	Trypho*		Cicero
		Rhetorica ad Herennium	
	Philo Judaeus		
A.D.			
1st	Pseudo-Heraclitus Aelius Theon*	Quintilian	Clement of Rome [in Latin by Rufinus]
	Plutarch		
2nd	Rufus* Hermogenes* Gnostics Aelius Herodianus*		
3rd	Longinus* Apsines*		Arnobius
	Neoplatonism		Manichaeism Lactantius
4th	Aphthonius*	Charisius Diomedes Donatus	Prudentius
	Georgius Choerobos- cus*		
		Servius Avianus Macrobius	Augustine Jerome Vulgate Rufinus of Aquileia
5th	Nicolaus*	Martianus Capella Pompeius	
	Phoebammon*	Marius Plotius	
6th		Priscian	
7th			Isidore Aldhelm
8th			Bede
9th			Rabanus Maurus

| CENTURY | GREEK | LATIN | |
		Pagan	Christian
10th			Remigius of Auxerre
11th			
12th	Gregorius Corin-thius*		Hugh of St. Victor
			Glossa Ordinaria
13th			Vincent of Beauvais
14th			Nicholas of Lyre

*Writers included in Appendix II are identified with an asterisk.

The first of the following two chapters describes the various elements which essentially determine ideas about allegorical creation and interpretation down through the Middle Ages and Renaissance. The second chapter attempts to outline how these elements came to be assimilated into Christian consciousness and expectation in the Latin West. Classical theory seems to recognize two basic kinds of allegory: the allegory of implied application and the allegory of partial or concealed reference. Each of these involves a number of different, explicitly identified tropes, figures, and techniques. In the first basic kind an expression with literal reference to one context is used with reference to a quite different context, and the reader or listener is expected to make the necessary analogical leap, applying the meaning of the literal context mutatis mutandis to the other. Various hints may be employed to alert the reader that such a leap in reference is necessary. Virgil concludes Book II of his *Georgics* with the remark that now is the time to unhitch the steaming horses. He means for the reader to guess, from simple proximity, that he is analogically referring to the concluded subject matter he has labored to present in Book II. The second basic kind of allegory makes a partial (as in allusion) or concealed (riddle) reference to some fact, person, event, or statement, which it is assumed is known by the reader already or can be known by him using the limited expression presented to him.

The Christian response to and use of this classical tradition is complex, beginning with the Septuagint translation of the Old Testament (3rd cent. B.C.) and continuing in the Greek New Testament and early Fathers. The Bible presented itself as a special text to which Christian writers, translators, and interpreters brought classical expectations about allegory, but expectations with a broader scope which included the meanings even of history. The complete assimilation of one classical tradition of allegory, as a figure, into an explicitly Christian context and the broader application of it as well is nicely illustrated by Bede's *Schemes and Tropes in Holy Scripture.* This broader scope also modifies the classical tradition in important ways. One is the development of a rather sharp distinction between (1) allegory which has essentially two meanings, a satisfactory literal sense and some additional other meaning, and (2) allegory conceived as involving only one level of hidden meaning, which is to be inferred from the obscure or literally impossible text. A related, commonplace development posits that allegory may be factual (based on *res*) or verbal (based on *verba*). Christian theorists and commentators exhibit a marked predilection for factual allegory. But it is through one-meaning allegory, factual (story, parable) or verbal (riddle), that nonbiblical literary techniques, similar or identical to biblical ones, are endorsed and legitimized, as long as there exists a strong didactic intention. This is explicitly the case in Augustine, who is a key figure in the development of theories relating to secular literature.

Some of the important results of his speculations are not widely realized, however, until Dante and Boccaccio. And in general the broadened scope of Christian allegorical theory, which expands the potential for allegory in literature, does not bear fruit until the later Middle Ages and Renaissance, long after paganism, pagan religions, and pagan fables had ceased to be a problem demanding a hostile, polemical response. These later medieval and Renaissance developments in the area of literary allegory are not the subject of this book, but the attempt has been made here to lay a proper systematic foundation for describing, understanding, and evaluating them.

Classical Theories
of
Allegory

CHAPTER ONE

The Classical Background

Allegory is a Greek term meaning "other-speaking" (in Latin, *alia oratio*). Its basic function is a grammatical/rhetorical one of designating a trope or figure of speech with seven species, a designation which Diomedes still reflects in the fourth century A.D. Other associations of allegory with literature and philosophy, however, gradually developed in ancient Greece. The principal one, which evolved very late, is that of *allegoria* with *hyponoia* (ὑπόνοια). *Hyponoia* is the hidden, underlying meaning of a story or myth, or a conjecture or guess about such a meaning. Finding *hyponoiai* was a pre-Socratic practice of rhapsodes, who not only recited but also interpreted Homer.[1] This sort of interpretation of Homer and ancient myths was rejected by Plato, by Aristotle, and by the Alexandrian scholars (3rd–2nd cents. B.C.) but was adopted, legitimized, and perpetuated by the Stoic school of philosophy.[2] In later antiquity Greek Neoplatonic philosophers (3rd–6th cents. A.D.) also adopted this method of interpreting, and so appropriated Homer and ancient mythology.[3]

The nonphilosophic tradition of finding hidden meanings seems to have been motivated by the desire to maintain the primacy of Homer as the basis of ancient Greek education. This purpose is meaning oriented

1. See Rudolf Pfeiffer, *History of Classical Scholarship from the Beginnings to the End of the Hellenistic Age* (Oxford: Clarendon Press, 1968), pp. 10–11 and 35. In a published University of Chicago dissertation, Anne Bates Hersman briefly but with comprehensive annotation surveys "Allegorical Interpretation before Plutarch," *Studies in Greek Allegorical Interpretation* (Chicago: Blue Sky Press, 1906), pp. 7–23.

2. See Pfeiffer, pp. 237–42 and 259.

3. The most notable extant example is Proclus's *Commentary on The Republic*. This Commentary takes the form of a number of essays on separate questions or problems. The sixth essay, in dialogue form, is wholly devoted to defending Homer and poetic representations of ancient myth against the objections of Plato. Proclus's *Commentary* is available in a modern French translation: Proclus, *Commentaire sur la République*, trans. A. J. Festugière, 3 vols. (Paris: Vrin, 1970). Coulter's *Literary Microcosm* fully discusses Proclus's and other Neoplatonic interpretations and theories of interpretation.

insofar as the interpreter is committed to the assumption that there are significant meanings in Homeric story and myth, whether such meanings appear to be there or not. Stoic interpretation was also meaning oriented but with narrower assumptions about what kind of meaning was hidden. Rudolf Pfieffer puts it: "As the λόγος (reason) is the fundamental principle of everything, it must manifest itself in poetry also, though hidden behind the veil of mythical and legendary tales and pure fiction."[4]

In the Latin West during late antiquity, the Middle Ages, and the early Renaissance, one major source of knowledge about this sort of literary/philosophic interpretation was Cicero's *De Natura Deorum* (1st cent. B.C.). The *De Natura* is cast by Cicero in the form of a dialogue, in which three important schools of ancient Greek philosophy are represented by spokesmen: Velleius for the Epicureans, Balbus for the Stoics, and Cotta for the Academy. Cotta's principal role is to rebut the Epicurean and Stoic positions. But Velleius also summarizes and criticizes the Stoic view of the gods (I. xiv–xv. 36–41). On the Epicurean behalf he construes the poetic representations of the gods literally and so rejects them as impious or absurd (I. xvi. 42–43). Balbus's presentation is extensive and revealing (II. xxiii. 60–xxviii. 71). According to him the gods may first of all be what springs from them: Ceres as grain or Liber as wine. Forces or powers (faith, virtue, mind, concord, or victory) and other abstractions (desire, pleasure) are deified. So, too, are certain human benefactors (Hercules, Aesculapius). Ancient poetic myths reflect physical, scientific truths. Saturn devouring his sons means that time eats up the years. Etymology is important here. Saturn's Greek name, Balbus points out, is Kronos (*chronos,* a period of time), and Saturn, he says, etymologically means saturated or filled up with years. The lower air is Juno, the upper air, or ether, Jupiter. Neptune, the sea, is etymologically derived from *nare,* to swim. Balbus rejects the myths themselves in their literal implications but insists that what they represent (earth, sea, powers, and so forth) must be worshipped (II. xxviii. 71).

Balbus's comments on deified humans are closely allied to another ancient treatment of myth, that of Euhemerus and known by his name, euhemerization. Velleius also touches briefly on the Stoic theory of

4. *History of Classical Scholarship,* p. 238. Substitute *caritas* for *logos* and you have the modern position of D. W Robertson, Jr., about medieval literature. The Stoic explanation might be classified as historical-metaphysical/physical and Robertson's historical/sociological, since in the latter view Christian meanings occur in medieval literature because medieval readers are supposed to have expected such meanings to be there and medieval writers are supposed to have expected to write them in.

deification of humans who have made great contributions (1. xv. 38), but in euhemerization the principal gods and goddesses themselves are rationalized as being originally only talented and important humans whose memory had been so exaggerated that ultimately they were represented as being divine.

Cotta rejects both the mythical representations of the gods and their Stoic interpretations (III. xv. 38–xxv. 64) without employing the euhemeristic rationalization which was later to become a favorite tool used by Christian apologists against the pagan gods. He observes again and again that myths and their Stoic interpretations cannot be worked out consistently and so proves that the meanings are not inherent in the myths but that they have been arbitrarily and selectively foisted off on them by the ingenuity of the Stoics. Cotta also ridicules the Stoics' etymologizing as phony and arbitrary (III. xxiv. 62). He rejects, too, the idea of deifying abstractions (see especially III. xxiv. 61) and points out that what is involved in grain/Ceres and wine/Liber is simply a figure of speech (III. xvi. 41)—as it still is considered to be in Diomedes (under metonymy). In a philosophic, but not necessarily a literary sense, then, Cotta rejects the idea of what we call allegorical personification.

It is important to note that Cicero's interlocutors do not use the word *allegoria* (the word does not appear in its Greek or Latin form in the philosophical writings of Cicero—although it does in his rhetorical works). The extension of the term *allegoria* to include philosophic categories of hidden meaning occurs earlier in the Greek tradition than in the Latin, although not nearly as early as some English translations of classical Greek works appear to indicate. For example, in a well-known passage in *Republic* II Plato insists that young people should not be exposed to poetical tales, even if they do have (in many English translations) "allegorical" meanings (378D). Plato does not use the term allegory here but *hyponoia.* However, the title of the Pseudo-Heraclitus's *Homeric Allegories* (1st cent. A.D.) is self-explanatory, and by the early second century A.D. Plutarch observes that hyponoiai are now called *allēgoriai.*[5]

Plutarch's essay "Isis and Osiris," an extensive excursus into allegorization, is itself significant for the terms it employs and as a classical expression of ideas somewhat different from those in Cicero's *De Natura Deorum.*[6] Plutarch's basic position is that Stoic allegorization of

5. "How to Study Poetry," *Moralia* 19 E–F. I have used the 14-volume Loeb translation by Frank Cole Babbitt.

6. The second part of Ann Bates Hersman's *Studies in Greek Allegorical Interpretation* extensively analyzes "Isis and Osiris" (pp. 25–57).

the gods into forces of nature and moral qualities is atheistic, leaving no gods at all, and he felt strongly that popular religion should be maintained. For the same reason he also explicitly rejects the related use of the gods (Ceres/grain, Liber/wine) as mere figures of speech (*Moralia* 377D–78A). On the other hand the literal presentation of much traditional mythology was filled with ridiculous absurdities and improprieties, leading to the grossest kind of superstition. Between atheism and such superstition Plutarch wants to see the gods as symbolic — not losing their deity but not being bound literally to the absurdities and improprieties of their myths. The gods then are literally gods, but many of the stories about them are to be symbolically construed.

Most of this essay illustrates how to go about such symbolic interpretation, but there is at least one important theoretical statement of method. In this passage Plutarch emphasizes that myths are not to be construed as if they were openly true accounts (λόγοι), but, as Frank Babbitt translates in the Loeb text, "we should adopt that which is appropriate in each legend in accordance with its verisimilitude" (374E). Thus, the truth symbolically conveyed is already known to the interpreter, and the practice of symbolic interpretation involves not the understanding of new meanings but the appropriate adjustment of mythic details to truths already understood and known — leaving literal what is consonant with truth and symbolically construing what is not, so that it too will appropriately witness to what is already known to be true. Coulter's study shows that this principle remains a cardinal theoretical assumption for Neoplatonic interpreters (pp. 41–60).

It should be remembered that Plutarch was not nearly so tolerant of poetic fiction itself as separate from myths about the gods. A moderate Platonist, but Platonist nonetheless, he is deeply suspicious of the potentially bad influence of poetic fictions on the young. Like Plato, he does not endorse the discovery of *hyponoiai* or allegories as a justification for young people being exposed to fictions ("How to Study Poetry" 19E–F). In fact he states that such interpretation is deliberate distortion. He sees fiction as primarily conveying an imitative-exemplary meaning and, like Plato, thinks that for the most part traditional poetic fiction contained bad examples. These bad examples are to be ignored, rejected outright, or identified as bad examples; they do not have to be construed symbolically because, unlike the gods, neither their sanctity nor their existence need be maintained. And so the utility of reading or teaching poetic fictions lies in applying their exemplary implications to as many analogous situations as come to mind (34B–F). Examples are not symbolic or allegorical.

"Isis and Osiris" is especially interesting because of its development of a theory of symbolic understanding of the gods. Plutarch's favorite terms are *symbol* (378A, 381F), *symbolic* (354F, 363F, 370F, 380F), *enigma* (riddle) and *riddling* (354C, 354F, 368D), and αἰνίττομαι, to speak darkly, hint at, or shadow forth (366C, 368A, 373E, 376E). These terms are all applied to Plutarch's symbolic interpretation of myths, as is the verb *allēgoreō* (to speak or interpret allegorically), but only twice (362B and 363D), and the noun *allegory* is not used at all. Nonetheless no clear distinctions appear to differentiate allegorical, symbolic, or enigmatic readings.

The late-Hellenistic rhetorical treatise *On Style,* attributed to Demetrius, does separately discuss allegory and symbol (99–102 and 243 respectively), but the same example is used to illustrate both. Philo Judaeus (1st cents. B.C.–A.D.), however, who died about the time of Plutarch's birth, provides an interesting parallel to Plutarch in both the brief theoretical statements and terminology of his commentaries on the Pentateuch, and like Plutarch, Philo's writings influenced the Latin West in late antiquity and the Renaissance. A highly educated Alexandrian Jew, Philo came to the Old Testament with a point of view greatly influenced by Greek learning and philosophy. His attitude toward the text of the Old Testament is remarkably similar to Plutarch's attitude toward accounts of the pagan gods. There is, however, at least one important difference. Plutarch sees the gods as entities described and sometimes misrepresented in various texts and seems to assume a clear distinction between the subject matter and the written representation of that subject matter in these texts. Philo, on the other hand, has only one text, the Bible, to which he is committed, and except for a God and a physical universe — including man — which clearly in his view transcend the text representing and describing them,[7] he consistently blurs any distinction between subject matter and expression of it by subordinating the former to the latter. He focuses almost entirely on what the text of the Bible says without worrying much about whether the content, particularly historical data, is accurate or even true in any sense, implying a separate existence divorced from the truth and reality of the text itself. Philo's overwhelming allegiance is to his text and what it says.

Moreover, his text is full of meaning, down to the smallest phrase

---

7. This is particularly and appropriately obvious for God and the physical universe in the first parts of "On the Account of the World's Creation Given by Moses" (I–XLV). I have concentrated on Volume 1 of the Loeb translation, which contains not only "On Creation" but also the long "Allegorical Interpretation of Genesis II, III." For man, see "On Creation" and "Allegorical Interpretation" II. 13.

and word ("Allegorical Interpretation" III. xlix. 147), and this meaning usually says more than—or other than—what is indicated by the
literal text (although the literal text is for all intents and purposes
sacred and may not be tampered with, even when it appears to be in
error). Philo applies the terms *symbol, symbolic, allegory, to interpret*
allegorically, αἰνίττομαι, *hyponoiai, figurative* and *figuratively* (τροπικός
and τροπικῶς), and *sign* (σημεῖον) to the nonliteral meanings he finds
and to the process of finding them.[8] These terms are applied indis-
criminately and appear to be roughly equivalent. *Symbol* and *symbolic*
are most frequently used and after them *allegory* and *to interpret*
allegorically.

The kind of meaning to which these terms refer involves basically
two different relationships to the literal text. In most cases the allegorical or symbolic meaning is an addition to a perfectly satisfactory and
meaningful literal sense of the literal text. Occasionally this duality of
meaning is made explicitly clear. For example, Philo affirms explicitly
the literal and figurative senses of Adam's naming the creatures
("Allegorical Interpretation" II. 14). Many historical characters are
also described as both typical beings (their literal sense) and as symbols
of some abstraction: e.g. Laban as a sensual man and symbolically as
inclination or friendship toward the senses (III.20); or Abraham as a
typical man of wisdom and allegorically the soul inclined to virtue and
so searching for God ("On Abraham" 68). And, of course, Adam is the
first man, who also symbolizes the mind throughout the comments on
Genesis.

The other relationship of allegorical to literal meaning involves a
literal text which is puzzling, inadequate, or erroneous, and which
consequently must be construed allegorically or symbolically in order
for any meaning at all to be elicited from it. In a number of cases Philo
makes this point explicit. The description of the Garden is explicitly
symbolic rather than (not in addition to) literal ("On Creation" 154).
The River Euphrates, the fourth of the Edenic rivers, is erroneously
described; Moses, however (Philo assures us), is not talking about rivers
anyway but about the correction of moral character ("Allegorical
Interpretation" I. 85–86). Eve's answer to God (Genesis 3:13) is puzzling literally but makes good allegorical sense (III. 59–60). Literalists

---

8. For *symbol* and *symbolic,* see "On Creation" 154, 157, and 164, and "Allegorical
Interpretation" I. 1, 21, 72, 80, 97, and II. 27, 72; for αινιττομαυ, "On Creation" 154;
allegory or *to interpret allegorically* occurs in "On Creation" 157 (with *hyponoiai*), "Allegorical Interpretation" III. 4, 59–60, and 236, and "On Abraham" 68 (Loeb, Vol. 6);
figurative is in "Allegorical Interpretation" II. 14 and *figuratively,* I. 44; and σημειν (with
symbolic), I. 21.

will be bothered by the eunuch Potiphar's having a wife, but the passage is no problem for those who, like Philo, read allegorically (III. 236).

Coulter's study reveals that the Neoplatonic theorists emphasize the necessity of a text's hinting at the existence of its hidden meaning. The surface will point to added symbolic implications by means of, as Coulter felicitously puts it, the "suggestive incompleteness" of its literal text.[9] In the case of Philo, however, although such hints occasionally are noted, they are clearly not a prerequisite for symbolic interpretation.

In two instances — one a major theoretical statement — Philo, with an attitude mutatis mutandis much like Plutarch's, importantly separates and distinguishes his text and the meanings he elucidates from myth and poetry. The major theoretical statement ("On Creation" 154–57) begins, as noted above, with the assertion that the description of paradise is symbolic rather than literal. This passage continues to use the verb *to speak darkly* and the nouns *allegory* and *hyponoia*, along with the adverb *symbolically*, to indicate that paradise is the governing power of the soul, the tree of life respect and reverence for God, and the other tree moral wisdom. Philo insists that the text here does not involve the imitations or fabrications of myth ("μῦθον πλάσματα") such as poets customarily create (157). Rather, the biblical accounts are "modes of making ideas visible" so that we will "resort to allegorical interpretation guided in our renderings by what lies beneath the surface" (Loeb translation). In "Allegorical Interpretation" Philo interestingly observes that were we to imagine that the text literally means that God literally planted the Garden (an impious impossibility), it would then be on the order of a mythical fabrication or invention (μυθοποιία, I. 43–44). The meaning here is figurative, but the literal text is not a myth. Philo does find the literal words of at least one passage (that describing God making Eve from a rib out of Adam's side) literally untenable and thus on the order of myth ("Τὸ ῥητὸν ἐπὶ τούτου μυθῶδές εστι," II. 19).

Plutarch feels that mythic accounts of the gods need to be purified, where necessary, through symbolic interpretation, but that poetic fictions and fables do not need to be so treated, clearly because he is committed to the gods and the necessity of popular religion, but not to poets and poetic fictions. Philo is similarly committed to defending and

---

9. P. 61 and see pp. 39–60, 66, and 72. The same point is strongly made by the Neoplatonic emperor Julian, *Orations* V. 170A–B and VII. 222C, as Michael Murrin points out in *The Veil of Allegory* (Chicago: University of Chicago Press, 1969), p. 147.

purifying, where necessary, the text of the Bible, because he is openly committed to the sacredness and validity of that text. He is not similarly committed to details of pagan mythology or poetic inventions, and so rejects them and presumably the symbolic interpretations of them. He implies that they are empty of truth and do not, as the Bible does, actually visualize, symbolize, or imagize abstract ideas.

The concept of visualizing abstractions or embodying them in images explains a creative rather than an interpretive process, although in this Platonizing view of God's word as the visualization of ideas, Philo is justifying his own practice of interpretation. Plutarch does not seem to worry about how the truths of the gods came to be embodied in their various symbolic forms, and indeed he emphatically approves the passages of the poets which, in the manner of Pope or Dr. Johnson, treat abstract ideas and generalizations abstractly and generally in the manner of the philosophers ("How to Study Poetry" 35F–36E). Such statements of general truth mixed in with the myths of the poets will prepare a youth for the study of philosophy (36D). In this same passage Plutarch characterizes poetry as containing myth and impersonation (προσωπεῖον, literally "a mask"), and these differ from general statements of truth (36D). Plutarch probably means here the impersonation in fictitious characters and speakers, rather than the personification of abstract ideas, since elsewhere he identifies Diotima's account of Plenty, Poverty, and Love in the "Symposium" as myth ("Isis and Osiris" 374C).

The great classical scholar Rudolf Pfeiffer considers those passages in Homer which personify abstractions to be pure or true allegory.[10] The evolution of ideas about allegory and personification in Greek and Latin antiquity and their transmission in the Latin West are not, however, simple matters. The connection of fable or myth with personification and with allegory is gradual and occasional, and it involves many concepts which in our day are not thought of as involving allegory. Certainly Philo's explanation of God's creative embodying of incorporeal ideas in concrete, albeit verbal, symbols is a significant development, although Plato himself identified his story of the cave as an illustrative image or likeness (εἰκών, Republic VII. 517A and D). The concept of visualized idea is elaborated by the Greek Neoplatonists and becomes, as Coulter demonstrates, central to their theory of symbolic representation.[11]

10. *History of Classical Scholarship*, p. 5.
11. In chapter 2 Coulter elaborates the two Proclean concepts of simpler eiconic (or imagistic) and more complex symbolic visualization (pp. 39–60).

In the Latin West the heir of some of these Greek Neoplatonists, especially Porphyry, is the commentator and polymath, Macrobius (4th–5th cents. A.D.), whose works exerted a continuing influence throughout the Middle Ages and into the Renaissance. Chapters 1 and 2 of Book I of Macrobius's *Commentary on the Dream of Scipio* thoroughly discuss the theory and use of fables as vehicles of philosophic truth. These chapters and subsequent remarks in the *Commentary* and Macrobius's other extant work, *The Saturnalia,* constitute a full and important introduction to the development of theories of the allegory of literature in the Latin West, although Macrobius never uses the term *allegoria.*[12]

In *Commentary* I. 1 and 2 Macrobius is at pains to defend Cicero's *Dream of Scipio* (Book VI of *De Re Publica*) from the indirect attack against it implied by the Epicurean attack on Plato's vision of Er at the end of *Republic* X. In I. 1 he refers to Plato's vision as a *somnium* and a *commentum* (something invented or fabricated, a fiction) and then observes that some people call it a *fabula.*[13] He seems to accept the term *fabula* himself at the end of I. 1, only to qualify and elaborate it extensively in I. 2 and develop a new term, *figmentum.* Macrobius's care in using the term *fabula* would seem to be warranted by its extensive and sometimes varied use up to his day (early fifth century A.D.) in Roman rhetorical manuals. Martianus Capella, a fifth-century contemporary of Macrobius, sees *fabula*, as does Priscian (6th cent. A.D.), as one of four kinds of narrative, the other three being fiction (*argumentum* in Martianus, *narratio fictilis* in Priscian), history, and civic or judicial narrative, used by orators pleading cases (V. 550).[14] Priscian's account of the fable and that by Macrobius are the fullest in Latin. For Capella the fable is simply "neither true nor like the truth," while fiction "contains not what happened but what could have happened." The triad *historia, argumentum, fabula,* had been introduced as early as

---

12. He does use the definition of the trope allegory to define the figure of *scomma,* the agreeable rebuke. *Scomma,* he writes in *The Saturnalia,* conceals its meaning under refined wit, "so that it says one thing, but you understand something else," (*ut aliud sonet, aliud intelligas,* VII. 3.3). I have used the recent Teubner text, ed. Jacob Willis (Leipzig, 1963). There is an English translation of the *Commentary* by William Harris Stahl (New York: Columbia University Press, 1952). *The Saturnalia* has also been translated into English by Percival Vaughan Davies (New York: Columbia University Press, 1969).

13. Plato himself identifies the vision of Er as an ἀπόλογος (*Republic* 614B, translated directly as *apologus* in Ficino's Renaissance Latin). Plato refers to Aesop's fables as μῦθοι ("Phaedo" 60C, 61B, and elsewhere).

14. All citations from Capella are to the edition of Adolf Dick, cor. ed. (1925; rpt. Stuttgart: Teubner, 1969). See Priscian's *Praeexercitamina,* a reworking of Hermogenes, in Keil, *Grammatici Latini* III, 431.

the first-century B.C. *Rhetorica ad Herennium* (I. viii. 13) as three basic kinds of narrative, and the definitions there generally remain standard. History recounts events which actually happened. Fiction recounts events which did not actually happen but could have (i.e., they are like real events), and, of course, fables recount events which did not and could not have happened. Cicero's *De Inventione* offers the same distinction (I. xix. 27), as does Quintilian (II. iv. 2) and another contemporary of Macrobius, the commentator Servius (in the note to *Aeneid* I. 235).

However, some variation arises in the application of the terms. Capella properly equates Greek *mythos* and Latin *fabula* and uses these terms to refer to his own work (e.g., II. 219, 220, and IX. 997) and to such stories as those about Dionysus being born out of the thigh of Zeus (VI. 695) or Daphne being turned into a tree (V. 550). In another passage Capella refers to Aesop's stories as apologues (V. 558). The *Ad Herennium* associates tragedy with fable (apparently underscoring the marvelous, unrealistic events in tragedies) and comedy with fiction. Quintilian (1st cent. A.D.) follows this lead, including poems with tragedies.

But Macrobius is primarily interested in the fable and he generates a new term, *figmentum* (something invented or made, especially a fictitious creation), not used in the classical Latin of Cicero and Quintilian, to encompass all kinds of fabulous discourse. According to Macrobius some species of fable are appropriate in philosophic writing and others are not. He first distinguishes two purposes in fables: to entertain and to encourage the reader in areas of moral improvement. Three examples, all literary, are given of fables fulfilling the first, entertaining purpose, and each one represents a different meaning of the word *fabula*: Menander's comedies (*fabula* as drama); Petronius's *Satyricon* (*fabula* as fiction); and Apuleius's *The Golden Ass* (*fabula* not only as fiction but also as story involving impossible unrealities). The second variety of morally encouraging fables is subdivided into two distinct species. In the first "the subject matter is established in fabrication, and even the arrangement of the telling [of it] is constructed according to falsehood" (*argumentum ex ficto locatur et per mendacia ipse relationis ordo contexitur*).[15] He elaborates by noting that in this kind of fable "what is conceived out of feigning is narrated by means of feigning" (*quae concepta de falso per falsum narratur*). Macrobius offers Aesop's fables as

15. A difficult passage, as are many in Macrobius, for pinning down the precise meaning. I have translated literally and awkwardly but a little more accurately than Stahl's "both the setting and plot are fictitious" (p. 85).

examples, differing by implication from *The Golden Ass* only in their morally encouraging purpose but not differing in form and technique.

The second species of morally encouraging fable, given the distinguishing name *narratio fabulosa* ("fabulous narrative"), does differ in form and technique, and only it is acceptable in philosophy. In it the subject matter (*argumentum*) "rests on a solid foundation of truth" (Stahl, p. 85), and "this truth is itself expressed in fabricated arrangements" (*haec ipsa veritas per quaedam composita et ficta profertur*). Put slightly differently, "truth is inherent in the subject matter [or plot, *argumentum*]." Here the examples are religious rituals, Hesiodic and Orphic accounts of the gods, and "the mystical notions of the Pythagoreans." Of course, the visible externals of religious ritual reflect incorporeal truths. The gods themselves are similar visualizations, as is the numerical symbolism of Pythagoras so important to Neoplatonic metaphysics and discussed extensively by Macrobius and Philo. Fabulous narrative tells about truths in the visualized form of invented stories; it narrates truth.

Morally encouraging fables (*narrationes fabulosae*) have religious and philosophic uses. The invisible gods have always preferred, Macrobius says, to be worshipped in the traditional way representing them as visible and physical images and likenesses (*imagines* and *simulacra*, *Commentary* I. ii. 20). The visible, concrete *figurae* of the traditional pantheon conceal invisible, immaterial truths from the masses, who must be satisfied with the limited truths of externals. The visible likenesses are also man-made and thus within the intentional, arbitrary control of religious leaders, fabulists, and philosophers. The images themselves are frequently presented or represented in stories (*figmenta*, or more narrowly *narrationes fabulosae*). Offensive or indecorous *figmenta* (for example, Saturn castrating his father, Caelus) are to be rejected (I. ii. 11). Fabulous narratives should always be chaste and restrained.

These stories are also limited in function. Fabulous narratives serve for lower truths about the soul, the spirits of the lower world, and the traditional gods (I. ii. 13). But when the highest matters of philosophy are to be discussed, questions of the mind and of the greatest good, then even fabulous stories are inadequate and inappropriate. These ultimate truths, incomprehensible to the human mind, can only be approached with simple analogies or patterns (*similitudines* or *exempla*, I. ii. 14); they cannot be treated narratively or discursively. And so Plato chose the sun as a similitude for the Good (I. ii. 15), and the Good was never represented as a god, nor were fabulous narratives ever written about it (I. ii. 16).

Following his Neoplatonic teachers, Macrobius uses this theory of fabulous creation in religion and philosophy as a basis for interpreting poetry, especially Homer and Virgil. Homer, "the fountain and source of all divine invention," concealed truths of natural philosophy "under a cloud of poetic fiction [*figmentum*]" or by means of a fabulous image (*imago fabulosa*), when he described Zeus and the other gods, invited to a feast by the Ethiopians, going off to Oceanus (meaning that the planets draw the water up from the ocean, *Commentary* II. 10). In *The Saturnalia* Macrobius treats myth, divorced from any poetic account of it, in precisely the same way and with the same term, *imago,* and the corresponding *efficies* (see especially I. 20 and 21). His interpretations also fluctuate between a strong emphasis on the interpretive process of discovering hidden meaning and a focus which implicitly emphasizes the creative aspect of such images as visualized, concretized abstractions. This latter emphasis is particularly apparent in Macrobius's discussion of Virgil's use of the figures of *exemplum, parabola* (comparison), and *imago* (*Saturnalia* IV. 5). *Imago,* he says, may involve simply the vivid description of a bodily form which is known but absent and thus needs description, or it may involve the vivid description of something purely imaginary (a possibility ignored in Diomedes' account of icon mentioned below), where the details of the description must be invented in the same manner by which any abstract idea is given concrete form. Three of his four examples here of the latter kind of *imago* are significantly what we now call personifications: *Furor* (*Aeneid* I. 294–96), *Fama* (*Aeneid* IV. 173–97), and *Discordia* (VIII. 702).

In Diomedes icon (= *imago*), parable, and paradigm constitute three species of likeness (homoeosis): vivid description, comparative illustration, and exemplary pattern. Macrobius introduces a feature for *imago* derived from his basic definition of fabulous narrative and fabulous imagery as visualizing and concretizing of the invisible and the abstract (this kind of personifying is also reflected in Priscian). *Imago* then, as personification, has possible connections with allegory, but *exemplum* (paradigm in Diomedes) would seem to involve a different process. Here the person or event is well known and is mentioned as an illustration or proof of some argument or declaration. Macrobius cites Aeneas's remark to the Sibyl that, since Orpheus, Pollux, Theseus, and Hercules had visited Hades, he should be able to do the same thing (*Aeneid* VI. 119–23). Orpheus here does not embody or concretize an abstraction or idea. He simply provides a known precedent or pattern which, Aeneas argues, can be imitated by him. Macrobius also gives exemplary interpretations not only of Scipio as presented in Cicero's *De Re Publica* (e.g., *Commentary* I. 10) but also of legendary and mythical personages, euhemeristically transformed into real, historical people such as Orpheus and Amphion (*Commentary* II. 3) and the Giants (*Saturnalia* I. 20).

The relationships which example, paradigm, comparison, similitude, analogy, and parable bear to each other in classical rhetorical tradition are significant here,[16] particularly in the ways each might be considered allegorical. Quintilian's discussion of argument or proof by example and comparative illustration (V. xi) is the most comprehensive in Latin antiquity (see also Cicero, *De Inventione* I. xxx. 49) and establishes connections retained by later theorists and commentators. Servius explicitly equates *exemplum, parabola,* and *comparatio* in his note to *Aeneid* I. 497, but what is especially interesting in this respect is Quintilian's inclusion of the fable (*fabula, fabella,* or apologue) as a species of comparative illustration or example (V. xi. 17–21). Capella similarly includes the fable as one species of argument by analogy (V. 558), and the Latin fabulist Avianus in his brief dedication (to Macrobius) remarks that fables contain exemplary (*pro exemplo*) comments about life and living. For Quintilian the only thing explicitly allegorical about proof by example or comparison or about the fabulous species of such proof occurs in the use of an abridged form of a fable, which proverbially alludes to the meaning of the whole story (V. xi. 21). Allusion, then, is allegorical, but in his dedication Avianus also comments on the representation of impossibilities (animals speaking, and so forth) and thus emphasizes the traditional rhetorical distinction of fable as untrue and improbable narrative—another potentially allegorical aspect, differing from Macrobius's Neoplatonic concept of fabulous narrative and fabulous imagery as visualizations and concretizations of the invisible and abstract.

Macrobius's idea of concretization would seem to relate naturally to the concept of personification. In earlier Latin rhetorical tradition, the *Rhetorica ad Herennium* defines personification (*conformatio*) as (1) the impersonation by a speaker of an absent person, and (2) the attribution of speech, form, and appropriate action to mute or inanimate things (IV. liii. 66). Quintilian discusses impersonation (προσωποποιία) as interior monologue and as the giving of speech to gods, the dead, cities, and absent people, including imaginary conversations (IX. ii. 29–37 and VI. i. 25). In none of these cases is personification or impersonation asociated with allegory.

16. Marsh H. McCall, Jr., has made a comprehensive and very useful study of *Ancient Rhetorical Theories of Simile and Comparison* (Cambridge, Mass.: Harvard University Press, 1969).

But potential associations of allegory with impersonation and with different kinds of stories construed as having underlying meanings are implicit in the earliest definitions and comments on the figure of speech, allegory. These definitions are rhetorical and Ciceronian. In the *Orator* Cicero notes that a succession of metaphors (*translationes*) produces a wholly different kind of speaking (an *alia oratio*), which the Greeks call allegory but which might just as well simply be called metaphors (XXVII. 94). Elsewhere in *De Oratore* Cicero uses the phrase *inversio verborum* for allegory (II. lxv. 261). Cicero also refers in *De Oratore* to a kind of speaking which joins a succession of metaphors "so that one thing is said, but something else has to be understood" (*ut aliud dicatur, aliud intellegendum sit*), III. xli. 166. Saying one thing but meaning something else remains the basic definition of allegory, usually in some version close to this Ciceronian phrasing. (That allegory is a succession of metaphors is also common, for example, as late as Martianus Capella, V. 512, but it is not as pervasive.) In this same passage Cicero warns that there is a potential obscurity in allegorical speaking which must be avoided. This obscurity is the obscurity of riddles (*aenigmata*) which, he observes, are constructed the same way (III. xlii. 167). He also identifies the substitution of the abstract names of virtues and vices for the people who possess them as metonymy (III. xlii. 168).

The *Rhetorica ad Herennium* uses the term *permutatio* (alteration or substitution) for the technique of having words say one thing and mean something else (IV. xxiv. 46). One kind of *permutatio* involves the similitude of a succession of metaphors. Another involves allusion (*per argumentum; argumentum* here as sign or token), as in calling Drusus a poor copy of the Gracchi (or as we might call Napoleon III a mere shadow of Napoleon I). We do not name Drusus but allude to him covertly as a poor copy of the Gracchi. Thirdly, *permutatio* may use ironic contrast. The *Ad Herennium* continues to point out that *permutatio* of both similitude and contrast can use allusion.

These early Latin authorities, then, introduce the basic definition of allegory and associate it with the riddle, with irony, and with allusion. Quintilian, using the terms *allegoria* and the pure Latin *inversio,* repeats the Ciceronian definition of saying one thing and meaning something else in a succession of metaphors (VIII. vi. 44), but immediately adds that some allegorical other-saying does not involve metaphor at all (VIII. vi. 46). As an example he quotes lines 7–10 of Virgil's "Ninth Eclogue." This poem is a dialogue between Moeris and Lycidas. The exemplary lines are spoken by Lycidas and refer to another pastoral character, Menalcas. Quintilian points out that nothing in these lines is other than literal in reference except the name, Menalcas, which allegorically refers to Virgil himself (vi. 47). Quintilian's comprehensive discussion here also warns against riddling obscurity (as he does earlier discussing metaphors in succession, vi. 14), points out that allusions—examples cited but not explained—are allegorical (vi. 52), and to irony adds antiphrasis, sarcasm, proverb, and astismos (refined wit), although he notes that some have questioned whether these are species of allegory or separate tropes (vi. 54–59). He thus mentions in one way or another all of the seven species of allegory except charientismos (more or less equivalent to euphemism but with sarcastic possibilities) and importantly includes as allegory the concealed reference to real, historical people under fictitious names.

The part of this passage on the proverb is corrupt, but Quintilian probably explained how the proverb (παροιμία) is allegorical. Earlier, discussing fables as exemplary or comparative arguments, he adds, as has already been noted, that one kind of proverb is a shortened, little fable (fabella brevior), which must be construed allegorically (V. xi. 21). In the example Quintilian gives here the basic allegorical aspect of such a proverb is obviously its allusive quality, since, if the listener is not familiar with the whole fable, he will completely miss the import of its shortened form. An important alteration has also occurred in Diomedes and other late-classical grammarians. The allegory of paroemia is no longer inherent in the proverb itself. Rather the allegory consists of the application of the proverb to some specific circumstances, thus emphasizing another kind of other saying.

All of the examples of other-saying adduced by the various Latin authorities on the trope allegory are of considerable interest, particularly those examples of the trope in general as opposed to its species. Aside from Quintilian's allegorical name (Menalcas/Virgil), the commonest and the most repeated example is the first one cited by Diomedes, which is also used by Quintilian and is the only example offered by the grammarians (4th–6th cents. A.D.) Marius Plotius (Keil, VI, 461), Pompeius, commenting on Donatus (Keil V, 310), Donatus (Keil IV, 401), and Charisius (Keil I, 276). The example, of course, is the last two lines (541–42) of Georgics II, in which Virgil refers to his poetic course in Book II as a journey over a plain, a journey which, now finished, requires the unhitching of his poetic steeds (implying a poetical chariot). The analogy of chariot, steeds, and plain to the poetic course through Book II is only implied and not directly stated or explained. The other examples are: (1) Georgics II. 41–46 in Diomedes, in which the context for all practical purposes indicates the analogy of a sea voyage to reading the poet's verse; (2) Horace's Odes I. xiv, the famous ship-of-state poem, in Quintilian (VIII. vi. 44); (3) Lucretius, *De Rerum Natura* IV. 1–5 in Quintilian (vi. 45), lines very much like *Georgics* II. 41–46; and (4) Quintilian's citation of Cicero's remark that Marcus Caelius had a good right arm but a weak left one—meaning that, as a pleader in court, he was better at prosecuting (sword) than defending (shield on left arm) (VI. iii. 69).

[Conclusions]

This empirical survey presents a formidable but not really bewildering array of possibilities. The significant elements in ancient thought relating to allegory, or possibly relating to allegory, include: (1) other-speaking (by similarity or contrast); (2) a succession of metaphors; (3) seven species—irony, antiphrasis, riddle, charientismos, astismos, sarcasm, and proverb or proverb and application; (4) visualizing and concretizing the invisible and abstract; (5) symbolic gods and events; (6) personification; (7) allusion; (8) literal, external concealment of a hidden, inner meaning; (9) fable as impossible story; (10) concealed biographical reference; and (11) analogy as in comparison, parable, example, and fable. Clearly these elements are all interrelated and in some cases subordinted to each other.

All of them, of course, involve the intention of conveying or construing meaning,[17] and this conveyance or construction implies some means of accomplishment, some expression of meaning. If we look at these factors from the writer's point of view, from a creative perspective, we must necessarily focus on the method or means of expression rather than the content of the meaning to be conveyed. The creative aspect of writing allegory emphasizes method and technique of expression. Just the opposite is true of the interpretive point of view, which naturally tends to concentrate on the meaning, the content of whatever text or expressions are being construed. It is true that the interpreter must assume some method of expression, however fuzzily or precisely conceived, but he obviously wants to see through the method to the meaning allegorically conveyed. The interpreter of an allusion looks through the partial reference to the whole meaning, but the writer of it concentrates on finding an appropriate partial reference to hint at his already conceived whole meaning.

Beyond the intentional attitude of creating allegory or interpreting

17. Coulter emphasizes the importance of authorial intentionality in Neoplatonic theories of interpretation, p. 19 et passim.

allegorically lies the question of purpose. All of these allegorical or potentially allegorical elements involve some kind of purposiveness. Diomedes observes that the basic purpose of all figurative language is embellishment or adornment. Metaphors, he adds, provide beauty, polish, emphasis, and sometimes the necessary means of conveying meaning, when no denotative term is available. Macrobius points out that the invisible gods have always desired to be visibly represented and that some abstract truths need to be concretely presented. The Christian interpreter of the Bible and the Stoic interpreter of Homer both want to discover their versions of the truth. And, of course, one writes fables, creates personifications, proposes riddles, or cites proverbs for some purpose or purposes.

The dual considertions of purpose and intentionality must always be brought to bear on any question of literary allegory, but these two alone will not discriminate among the numerous factors relating to allegory and allegorical possibilities articulated in antiquity. These factors do, however, lend themselves to several groupings. One obvious grouping contains the trope allegory as generally conceived, five of its species (irony, antiphrasis, astismos, sarcasm, and charientismos) and possibly a sixth, paroemia, and concealed biographical reference under a fictitious (pastoral) name. In all these the meaning of the words depends on and varies with their application, implicit or explicit. Irony, for example, depends on the context of application. When one says, "You are the most beautiful girl I know," to a truly attractive girl, there is no irony, only simple declaration. But when this same declaration is applied to a plain or conspicuously unattractive girl, then the meaning of the same words changes accordingly and ironically (and, as Diomedes notes, this contextual antithesis may have to be pointed up by emphasis in pronunciation). Although antiphrasis is defined as occurring in the word itself, it still depends on conceptual application for meaning, otherwise there would be no point in it. If we did not know or imagine that some people and deities were indeed gracious and kindly, it would be pointless to apply the epithet "gracious ones" to the Fates. Sarcasm and its urbane variety, astismos, would also seem to depend on application. In the famous example of sarcasm quoted from the *Aeneid* by Diomedes, Mezentius tells a Trojan he has just killed to measure out with his corpse the fields which he had intended to measure out in a victorious division of spoils. The sarcastic meaning of the words depends on the context in which they are used and the object to which they are applied. The same is true of charientismos, which uses graceful words to avoid a blunt declaration of some unpleasant information or fact. It is the unpleasant information to which they are applied that determines their meaning rather than the meaning normally implied by the words themselves.

The trope allegory, as generally defined and as exemplified by Diomedes and other theorists, is similarly controlled by context of application. Take the sustained metaphorical statement about racing headlong across a field in a chariot and stopping to unhitch the steaming horses at the end of the ride with which Virgil concludes *Georgics* II and which applies to the completion of that book. Clearly the particular allegorical meaning Virgil wants to convey depends on the particular application of the literal designation of his phrasing. Finally, and similarly, in the case of concealed biographical reference there is no intrinsic association of the fictitious, pastoral names Menalcas or Tityrus (another name used for Virgil) with the poet Virgil. That particular application must be made, and only then are the subtleties of meaning which depend on that application developed.

This dependency of allegorical meaning on application involves what is still and will always remain an essential question of allegory. How does one know that a particular application is being made or has been made for any particular verbal expression? How do we know that Menalcas is not just Menalcas but also Virgil or that Caelius's good right arm, in Quintilian's example, refers to his ability as a prosecutor in court? This question is, of course, an interpretive one and posed from the interpreter's point of view. The creator of such an allegorical expression knows what he is talking about. Cicero knows that Caelius is a better prosecutor than pleader for the defense. He tries to think of a clever way of expressing this fact, and so he says, "Caelius, you have a good right arm but a weak left one." But now look at Cicero's remark from Caelius's or some other auditor's hypothetical perspective. Caelius may or may not know that he is a better prosecutor, but whether he knows it or not, what is there in Cicero's words to indicate to him that Cicero is talking about his rhetorical/legal skills rather than the literal, physical condition of his arms or even, in terms of the figure, rather than his respective abilities with sword and shield? There is nothing in the words themselves or their syntactical arrangement to indicate that Cicero is referring to a particular legal skill. The same is true of Virgil's remark about unhitching the steaming horses. There is nothing in these two lines at the end of *Georgics* II which indicates their reference to the poetic progress of composition and reading through Book II. So, too, with irony. When we call an ugly person handsome, we mean to emphasize just how ugly and far from handsome he is. But nothing in our words indicates that he is in fact ugly.

The success of communication, of course, does not involve merely a speaker or writer intending to convey meaning by some expression. Successful communication demands that the auditor or reader be able to construe the expression he hears or reads in the proper way in order to recover the intended meaning. Normally this successful construction or reconstruction of intended meaning is basically a question of both writer and reader or speaker and hearer sharing the same conventions of language (and assuming, of course, they are both trying to communicate). That, however, is not sufficient for successful communication with this kind of allegorical expression. For successful communication to take place the allegorical expression *must* be assisted by some means other than, and beyond, its own verbal expression. This means may be simply some other verbal expression which indicates the application intended for the allegorical one. Cicero may have had to tell a dumbfounded Caelius, "I am referring to your legal abilities as prosecutor and defender." We hope that our auditor will realize that the person we refer to as beautiful is in fact ugly and so will understand our meaning. But our auditor may not and may have to be told explicitly. Virgil undoubtedly assumed that his readers would guess his meaning at the end of *Georgics* II from sheer proximity of his expression to its referent, from closeness of the analogy, and possibly from his readers' assumed acquaintance with similar literary usage. Some of the rural details in *Eclogues* IX are apparently not fictitious, and the reader must recognize these allusive elements in order to guess that Menalcas is not simply Menalcas but Menalcas/Virgil from their explicit similarity to details in Virgil's own rural experiences with his ancestral farm.

It would seem in fact that there are numbers of ways in which the creator of an allegorical expression could hint at the proper application of his expression and that the particular reasons which might lead him to expect his reader to guess correctly the application he intends, and so his meaning, could also vary tremendously. It is this potential variation and its cause, the lack of immediate association of verbal/syntactical expression with meaning (a normal association in verbal communication), which characterize this kind of allegorical expression as intrinsically indeterminate and unpredictable. Not inappropriately, then, we find allegorical meaning described as hidden or concealed.

From an interpreter's point of view this characteristic indeterminacy and unpredictability is a persistent problem—and, in the case of the literature of certain cultures and periods, a constant irritant. Scholarly interpreters have frequently tended to respond to this vexing characteristic in one of two extreme ways (extreme in the sense that both provide an apparent intellectual cover of determinacy and predictability where none in fact probably exists). One of these extreme responses has been simply to deny that this kind of verbal expression exists or normally exists in most literary texts. The other extreme predetermines a specific context of application to which, it is assumed, most literary texts allegorically refer. In both cases the interpreter's task has been made considerably, if unrealistically and inaccurately, easier, because he has already avoided the problem of dealing with what is the basic question of any allegorical expression of this kind — determination of some context of reference to which the verbal expression being interpreted was probably intended to apply.

This question of application or context of application also bears on the grammarians' alteration of the definition of paroemia or proverb as allegory. In Diomedes' example of paroemia from Terence's *Phormio,* a slave, Geta, is recounting to another slave, Davus, how his master and his master's brother, off on an extended trip, have left him to look after their respective sons, Antipho and Phaedria. Geta observes that at first he really tried to control the sons responsibly, but that in so doing he met severe and physically painful resistance. Davus replies that "it is indeed stupid to kick against the pricks." Pricks or goads were used to herd cattle (and sometimes slaves), and the proverb itself means that it is not only stupid, because unavailing and painfully counterproductive, for cattle or slaves to kick back at the sharp goads used to herd and direct them, but that by analogy it is foolish to resist any inevitable pressure of direction applied to one. The application Davus makes in the context of this passage is that Geta was indeed stupid in trying to curb and resist the irresistible force of the two sons' pursuing their own incorrigible direction of behavior. Davus manages to indicate the particular application of the proverbial wisdom by simple proximity, by inserting his remark into the context of a particular topic of discussion, just as Virgil does with his remark at the end of *Georgics* II about unhitching the steaming horses. Nevertheless, it is left to Geta's own understanding to construe the application Davus intends, just as it is left to the reader to figure out what the steaming horses have to do with the end of *Georgics* II. Geta, however, might not have gotten the point, especially since it ironically and cleverly inverts the analogy to apply to someone who intended or had been trying to use the goads of direction himself on two subjects who instead ended up irresistibly directing him.

The issue over paroemia is significant for some other possible categories of allegory. In the earlier rhetorical view the proverb itself is allegorical. Its specific reference, literally stated, and its implicitly analogous general truth, which can be potentially (and is intended to be) applied to other specific circumstances and events, these two characteristics themselves involve or imply allegory. The grammarians, however, insist that some specific application must be made in order for the allegorical potential to be fulfilled. Quintilian notes the possible association of fable with proverb by observing that some proverbial statements of wisdom are in effect simply shortened fables. Fables, of course, commonly have a moral appended, the *epimythios* or *affabulatio*, "in which," as Priscian points out, "the utility of the fable is uncovered" (p. 430). Frequently this moral is itself a proverbial statement. Thus the bird, faced with the prospect of getting a drink from shallow water at the bottom of a tall, narrow-mouthed vase, patiently fills the vase up with pebbles until he can get at the water. The moral here is that little by little does the trick. But whether or not the *affabulatio* takes the form of a proverbial statement, it does, like the proverb, imply a general truth about life tied to the fable it interprets which, also like the proverb, is susceptible of many different applications.

In this perspective the fable is any story with a general implication about life, a story told primarily to illustrate just that general truth, and the occurrence of talking animals and other impossibilities is merely incidental. The animals are clever, unusual, and entertaining imitations of humans, and this kind of fabulous story does not really differ from the historical or fictionally probable anecdote which is told to illustrate or establish a general principle of living. Quintilian, Capella, and the fabulist Avianus all remark on the fable in this sense. But note this important difference. The proverb exists because it intrinsically contains a general implication about life. As Macrobius observes, the same cannot be said of all fables, nor is it true for all history or all fiction per se.

Clearly the exemplary or paradigmatic use of an anecdote or episode which is historical, fictional, or fabulous involves a specific application of the analogy intended being explicitly indicated in the text itself. Homoeosis involves explicit comparison, as Diomedes points out, in all three of its species, icon, parable, and example. It is true that of these three, parable would seem to be most in need of explicit application because it involves, as Diomedes says, "comparison of things or managements different in kind." In this important sense of application of meaning it would seem that from a rhetorical/grammatical perspective figures involving explicitly indicated analogies are not allegorical, and indeed they are never identified as such.

Both the riddle and allusion are, however, identified as allegorical in this rhetorical/grammatical tradition. They are different from the general trope allegory and from the proverb (in either sense) in that their meaning involves no application at all, potential, implicit, or explicit. In both, meaning implies specifically matters not explicitly indicated but intrinsically tied to them. The riddle deliberately makes an obscure reference to a specific, perfectly clear explanation. In allusion partial reference is made to specific material, which is not explicitly discussed or elaborated. In both cases the full meaning may be said to be hidden or concealed — and truly is, from the person who cannot figure out the answer to the riddle or who is not familiar with the explicitly unelaborated material alluded to. But this concealment is of a different order than the concealment of the indeterminate, verbally unpredictable kind of allegorical statement whose meaning depends on its application.

A final category would seem to be that of visualizing and concretizing the invisible and abstract. In Philo, Macrobius, the Neoplatonists, and some of the rhetoricians and grammarians, this process or its product is described as symbolism, allegory, figure, personification, fabulous narrative, riddle, and fabulous image or icon. The basic problem with this category is that it would on one hand seem to involve the most obvious kind of implication and on the other the most intrinsically indeterminate. This difficulty is partly explained by the fact that some treatments of these strongly emphasize creative invention and others interpretive understanding of a given text. For example, Priscian looks at the fable, understandably, from a creative perspective, and so focuses on the writer's finding appropriate visualizations for abstract qualities (the peacock, for example, for beauty or the fox for cunning, p. 430). Macrobius, too, frequently emphasizes that philosophers have chosen certain visualizations to embody and represent abstract truths and that part of the institution of human religion involves the invisible, immaterial gods' desire to be represented to humans in visible, material forms. At the same time he uses these creative explanations to justify interpretations of literary or other texts, interpretations which discover the abstract and invisible by reading about the visible and concrete.

However, in only two of these kinds of visualizing the invisible is the meaning clear and obvious — that is, from an interpretive point of view is the creative intention of visualizing a specific abstraction apparent, and the identity of the particular abstraction visualized. These two are personification and what seems to be just like personification in Macrobius, the species of *imago* which invents a body for an abstract idea. Crucial here, of course, is the naming. A lady, identified as Justice, described with a long flowing dress and holding a sword in one hand and scales in the other, is obviously a visualized and personified abstraction. (It would not seem necessary to personify every abstraction, but most visualizations seem to have fallen under an irresistible humanistic desire to anthropomorphize.) Closely related to this obvious concretization is the metonymy of referring to grain by naming Ceres, and it is clear that Cicero's understanding of Stoic interpretation was that it was based on such personification. Balbus not only mentions the grain/Ceres connection (not as metonymy), but many of his gods are simply personified abstractions. And it is the Stoic emphasis on etymology and etymologically-based interpretation of those traditional gods and goddesses, whose names do not indicate their abstract identity, which clearly reveals this assumption. Saturn, etymologically "saturated" in Latin, and Kronos, his Greek name (in Balbus's view) meaning *chronos*, "time," lead Balbus to interpret the story of Saturn's eating up his sons as meaning that Saturn, the god, really means the concept of being filled up with passing years. For the Stoics etymology and pseudoetymology, along with numerical symbolism, provided a degree of rational, predictable control in the interpretation of mythical and fictional characters and events whose abstract (physical or scientific) identity was not overtly obvious. Their intention of grounding such interpretation in some sort of predictability was certainly not foolish (however foolish some of their interpretations seem), because the interpretive problem becomes acute when the concrete visualization does not in some overt way indicate first of all that it is a concretization and secondly what its abstract identity is. How do we really know that Homer was concealing abstract, scientific or philosophic truths in some (or all) of the concrete details of his story, and if some, which details are concrete visualizations and which are not? How do we know with any assurance of probability that Homer meant to visualize ether or the upper air as Zeus? How do we know that Adam is more than just Man, that he is also a concrete representation of Mind? How do we know who a lady with sword and scales is meant to be, if her name does not indicate her abstract identity? It would seem that Cotta, one of Balbus's opponents in Cicero's *De Natura Deorum,* is right, that there is an inherent and inevitable tendency for such interpretation to be capricious and arbitrary, and not to reflect authorial intention to any significant degree but rather to reflect the ingenuity of the interpreter in inventing likely abstractions for the preexistent concrete visualizations at hand to represent. Moreover, Cotta is judging what is probably the best theoretical attempt in antiquity to establish a predictable, determinate means of interpreting myth, the etymological personification of the Stoics.

One measure of the difficulty of construing such concrete representations, which are not named and their abstractions clearly identified as personifications are, is seen in the fact that they may be a verbal image, a fabulous story, or a fictional episode. It is tempting from a modern perspective to see the fabulous tale, with its defining impossibilities, as the cue to or indicator of the likely presence of some abstract meaning, as opposed to fictional verisimilitude, which indicates that no such concretization of abstract truth is being represented. Although the former indicator usually is valid, judging from ancient (and later) interpreters, and is strongly supported by Neoplatonic theory, the latter assumption is not sound. In Philo, for example, literal impossibilities do seem to demand allegorical interpretation, but at the same time perfectly satisfactory literal passages in no way seem to inhibit the same kind of interpretation. Although Philo's text is special, other interpretations of Homer and Virgil illustrate allegorical interpretation of the fabulously impossible and the fictitiously probable as well.

From a creative rather than an interpretive perspective, however, the assumption that a perfectly satisfactory literal text will never indicate on its own anything beyond its obvious literal implications seems sound, if not inevitable. From the author's point of view there must be some means of at least hinting that an image or motif is actually intended as a visualization or concretization of an abstraction, just as in the allegory of verbal application there must be some means of indicating the application intended. Obviously, on the other hand, the interpreter can easily substitute for such hinting or indication the arbitrary assumption that covert, abstract meanings are in fact being imagized and symbolized in the text he is construing. Indeed this possibility has been repeatedly actualized. An empirical survey of allegorizers, early and late, philosophic and literary, unequivocally shows that, while they all assume that the text(s) or stories they are construing do conceal abstract meanings, few of them ever bother about explaining precisely how they know such meanings are present or about indicating by what precise means these covert meanings are conveyed. Although frequently there is a general area or kind of meaning which is assumed to be hidden, that assumption provides only a slightly smaller domain of truth (as opposed to the whole undifferentiated domain of all truth) from which to choose particular meanings. It thus establishes only the illusion of predictability and determinacy and in no way helps to indicate how or why a particular meaning is probably being covertly conveyed in a particular passage or story.

From an interpretive perspective, then, ancient allegorical theory provides very little explanation in this area of visualized abstractions, except in the cases where such deliberate image making is obvious, as in the naming of a personification by its abstract identity. Stoic etymologizing is a real attempt at providing a predictable method of allegorizing images and motifs which are not, overtly at least, obvious. Certainly there are many ways of hinting at the presence of visualized abstractions in a text, and there is one further area, not mentioned by ancient theorists but perhaps assumed by some of them, which does indeed provide some predictable determinacy in allegorical interpretation of images and motifs in texts. This area is the traditional accretion of commonplace details relating to certain images and motifs, the area of iconology. The study of traditional iconographic equations might indicate that a lady with scales and sword and otherwise unidentified is probably Justice, depending, of course, on other evidence about the author, his milieu, and the nature of his text. In this iconographic case, the representation and the interpretation of the imagized abstraction depend on allusion, the traditional iconographic details providing a partial reference metonymically to the whole imagized abstraction.

Indeed, the ambiguity and obscurity involved with the interpretation of concrete visualizations of ideas or symbols are actually always a question of the obscurity either of allusion or of application. Ultimately the only sure way to know that a particular concrete manifestation is meant to refer to, visualize, or symbolize a particular idea or concept is to be told so explicitly by the author. Adam is not intrinsically or inevitably Mind. A peacock is not intrinsically beauty. These applications must be arbitrarily made, as not only Cicero's Cotta but even Macrobius observes. The naming of personifications accomplishes this specific application or explicit joining of idea and concrete embodiment very nicely. In the absence of such unequivocal direction, the interpreter is simply put to the task of making guesses, constructing hypotheses, not only about what particular abstractions or ideas may be symbolized in his text but also about whether such concrete visualizations even occur. Except for the original Greek naming, *hyponoia* (emphasizing the obscurity of meaning and the fact that interpreting such meaning is guesswork), and Stoic etymologizing, ancient theory is not much help to the modern scholar-critic in determining when such symbolic concretizations are likely to be occurring. However, all the various lines of theoretical investigation taken by the ancients are extremely useful in showing that the interpretive problem of allegorical expression fundamentally involves either an obscurity of intended application of the expression or the deliberate incompleteness or obscurity of reference in the riddle and allusion.

These two questions of application and reference indicate first of all that each text must be construed individually and the evidence weighed and evaluated on its own merits. Although similar evidence may understandably occur for more than one text, nonetheless each text must be interpreted from the evidence available for it. The fact that we might judge an unidentified lady with sword and scales in one text to be an embodiment of Justice will in no way mean that every lady we come across with scales and sword is Justice. Secondly, the modern interpreter to a considerable extent can predict the kind of evidence he needs to gather. The question of application is always one of extrinsic propriety, as far as the verbal expression is concerned. This is true of the trope allegory, of concealed biographical reference, of potential proverbial application, of irony, and even of particular concrete embodiments of particular ideas (more than a peacock can stand for beauty, and a mirror can stand for more than vanity). The interpretive answer is not in the words alone or what their normal literal and figurative implications convey, but in the combination or conjunction of verbal expression and the intended application of that expression. The question of inaequate or obscure reference on the other hand is a question of intrinsic implication and involves a wholly different kind of concealment, a concealment of knowledge (for allusion) and intellectual ingenuity (for the riddle). Sometimes, of course, a well-defined iconographic tradition will be used in an allusive or riddling manner to indicate a particular application of symbol to idea, and judging from contemporary historical criticism, particularly of medieval and renaissance texts, this kind of riddling or allusive guide is currently the principally recognized tool for the construction or reconstruction of allegorical meanings in literary texts.

CHAPTER TWO

The Christian Response

[The Bible]

It seems clear that during the Middle Ages and Renaissance in the Latin West there is a mutual influence and interaction of ideas about allegory in the Bible and in other kinds of texts. One constant in this relational influence is the Bible itself. Although biblical interpreters and theologians could and did differ in their ideas about the presence and nature of allegory in the Bible, the text of Scripture itself remained a familiar, unchanging source. The Septuagint Old Testament (3rd–1st cents. B.C.) and Greek New Testament (1st cent. A.D.) incorporate many terms and concepts relating to allegory from grammar, rhetoric, and philosophy. These are naturally reflected in the Latin Vulgate (ca. 400 A.D.), as is St. Jerome's perception of them, a perception which may be taken as typical of early Christian attitudes in the Latin West and which continued to exert a normative influence throughout the Middle Ages and Renaissance.

Jerome, of course, knew Hebrew, and it is easy to see his translation of the Old Testament going through the Septuagint to the Hebrew, especially in those cases where the Septuagint will use one Greek word for more than one Hebrew word.[1] The Septuagint translators, for example, use *eikon* to translate five different Hebrew words. In Genesis

---

1. I have used *A Concordance to the Septuagint and the Other Greek Versions of the Old Testament (Including the Apocryphal Books)* by Edwin Hatch and Harry A. Redpath, 2 vols. (1897; facs. rpt. Graz: Akademische Druck, 1954). For the New Testament I have relied on *A Greek-English Lexicon of the New Testament, Being Grimm's Wikke's Clavis Novi Testamenti,* trans., rev. and enl. by Joseph Henry Thayer, cor. ed. (New York: Harper, 1889). I have also used *The New Testament, Greek and English,* ed. Kurt Aland et al., 2nd ed. (New York: American Bible Society, 1968); *The Apocrypha and Pseudepigrapha of the Old Testament in English,* ed. R. H. Charles, 2 vols. (Oxford: Clarendon Press, 1913); and *Biblia Sacra Iuxta Vulgatam Clementinam,* ed. Alberto Colunga and Laurentio Turrado, 4th ed. (Madrid: Library of Christian Authors, 1965).

1:26,27 Jerome follows the Septuagint's *eikon* with the direct Latin equivalent, *imago*. But although a few chapters later (Genesis 5:1) the Septuagint translates another Hebrew word *eikon*, Jerome prefers the Latin *similitudo* as closer to the original Hebrew. No such problem existed, of course, for the Greek New Testament.

Some terms used in the Greek allegorical tradition do not relate at all to that tradition, when they occur in the Bible. The single New Testament use of *hyponoiai* (I Timothy 6:4) has nothing to do with guesses about texts but means (evil) suspicions about people. Jerome translates *suspiciones* here and in other Septuagint passages (e.g., Sirach or Ecclesiasticus 3:26; 3:24 in Charles). Furthermore such important terms as *antiphrasis, irony,* and *symbol* are not used in either Testament. The significance, however, of the one instance of the verb *allēgoreō*, "to speak allegorically," probably cannot be overemphasized. It is the only form of this word for "other-speaking" in the Bible. Paul uses it in the context of an extended nonliteral interpretation of an Old Testament event (Galatians 4:21-31) and unquestionably sets a formative example for subsequent Christian exegesis.

The Galatian church to which Paul wrote was beset by a Judaizing, legalizing group which was perverting the gospel of liberty in Christ by demanding ritual and legal observances from the Old Law as prerequisites to salvation. Paul's letter argues against this legalizing perversion. One of his arguments occurs in this passage and is based on a nonliteral reading of some historical events described in Genesis. The substance of the argument is this. The Bible says that Abraham had two sons, one by a slave woman, Hagar, the other by a free woman, Sarah. The child born of the former was natural and of the earth, but the latter was born according to God's promise. This is allegorically spoken to refer to the two covenants, the one of the Old Law, the other the New Covenant of grace. Hagar [using etymology] is the Arabic name for Mount Sinai and corresponds to present-day Jerusalem. She brings forth slavery. But the freewoman, the heavenly Jerusalem, is the mother of all believers who have faith in the promise of God's grace. And so all believers, like Isaac, are children of the promise. Just as Ishmael, the natural child, persecuted the spiritual child of the promise, so it is today (the modern legalizers persecuting the true believers in Christ). But the Bible says [actually, God says to Abraham in the account in Genesis] to throw out the slavewoman and her child, for her son will not be an heir with the free son. Therefore throw out the legalizers, because we believers are not children of the slavewoman but of the freewoman, that is, we are not slaves to the Law but free in Christ.

Here is the archetypal Christian reading of the spiritual sense of an Old Testament text. Paul has not denied the historicity of Abraham, Sarah, Hagar, Ishmael, and Isaac. He has simply asserted that the spiritual reason for these events being written down in the book of Genesis is to make a comment to Christians about the Old and New Covenants. He does so on the basis of analogous correspondences. Hagar was a slave; her name is Arabic for Mount Sinai, the location of the giving of the Mosaic Law; and her child by Abraham did reflect an attempt by Abraham to help God fulfill His promise of a son and heir in a natural, ordinary, fleshly way. Jerusalem had long been used metonymically to stand for all the Jews. Paul draws a contrasting analogue of that earthly, fleshly, unbelieving Jerusalem to the other heavenly, spiritual Jerusalem, and works out the rest of the corresponding details to suit his argument.

Paul's methodology here will not support the sharp distinction between so-called Hebraic and Hellenic allegoresis familiar to students of medieval literary allegory.[2] Paul's interpretation is Hellenic and allegorical, and yet it is potentially Hebraic and typological. The literal sense of the Old Testament passage is separated from the historical status of the events described. As far as what the Genesis text says, the letter is useless and must be discarded for the spiritual, Christological meaning articulated by Paul. On the other hand Paul in no way implies that Abraham, Hagar, and the rest are mere fictions whose existence is dissolved by the spiritual solvent of an argument about bondage to the law and freedom in grace. It would seem to have been a very short leap indeed for Paul to have added or substituted the idea that Ishmael is a type of all those bound to the Old Law and Isaac a type of those freed in God's grace in Christ.

As for this interpretation's rhetorical and possible literary relationships, it is obvious that Paul is working out a sustained metaphor or analogy. If we assume, as the Church assumed and continues to assume, that Paul was not interpreting arbitrarily out of his own natural understanding but that the Holy Spirit inspired him to see the proper spiritual significance of the words in Genesis (also inspired by the same Holy Spirit), then it becomes apparent that the Holy Spirit is the creator and interpreter of an allegory, using Moses and Paul as

2. Particularly in the "Summation" by Charles Donahue to the English Institute Debate "Patristic Exegesis in the Criticism of Medieval Literature" in *Critical Approaches to Medieval Literature: Selected Papers from the English Institute 1958–59,* ed. Dorothy Bethurum (New York and London: Columbia University Press, 1960, pp. 61–82, and restated and used by Donahue in a long article, *"Beowulf* and Christian Tradition: A Reconsideration from a Celtic Stance," *Traditio* 21 (1965), 55–116.

amanuenses. Typologically, the result is quite similar. God ordains certain events in the lives of Abraham, Hagar, and the others (in such a way, of course, so as not to limit their free will). These events actually happened but are in themselves incomplete in the pattern or context of their full significance established by God. This pattern is completed when the New Covenant of grace and promise actually comes to pass in historical time. Working in the actual events, in Moses' account of them, and in Paul's understanding of them, God completes the full meaning.

St. Jerome renders Paul's Greek directly into Latin, using the noun form of allegory in a prepositional phrase, so that those Old Testament events "sunt per allegoriam dicta" (are spoken of allegorically). The Vulgate does not similarly bring the Greek words for type, antitype, and undertype over into the Latin. *Typos* is frequently used in the New Testament to mean a model, example, or exemplary pattern of behavior. The Vulgate translates these instances either with *exemplum* (Titus 2:7, I Timothy 4:12) or *forma* (Philippians 3:17, II Thessalonians 3:9, I Peter 5:3). These are all examples of current human beings (Titus, Timothy, Paul, and elders). When used for the example set by men and historical events of the past Jerome translates *figura* (I Corinthians 10:6, and for the adjective in 10:11). However, Jerome uses *forma* in Romans 5:14, where *typos* definitely means a prefiguration (Adam of Christ), and he uses *figura* in Acts 7:43, where the Greek word refers to idols. When the model is impersonal, he uses *exemplar* (in reference to the plan of the tabernacle, Hebrews 8:5).

As with type, when *antitypos* is used to refer to a prefiguration in I Peter 3:21 (baptism prefigured by Noah and the ark) Jerome renders *forma*. But in concrete, impersonal usage (the holy places in the tabernacle built by Moses as figures of Heaven itself, Hebrews 9:24) antitype becomes *exemplar* in Latin. *Hypotypōsis* in one instance is translated *informatio* (I Timothy 1:16) in reference to the example of Paul's suffering. Referring to the style and content of one's language (Timothy's and Paul's) in II Timothy 1:13 it becomes *forma* in Latin. Other Greek words for pattern, model, or example show Jerome relying on *exemplum* and *exemplar*. Christ is our example (*hypogrammos-exemplum*, I Peter 2:21). The fate of Sodom and Gomorrah gives us a warning pattern or example of God's judgment (*deigma-exemplum*, Jude 7). The priests under the Mosaic Law were patterns of heavenly things (*hypodeigma-exemplar*, Hebrews 9:23), and their services are prefigurations of Christ (idem, Hebrews 8:5). But in examples of unbelief, suffering, and the example of Christ, *hypodeigma* becomes *exemplum* (Hebrews 4:11, James 5:10, and John 13:15 respectively). *Paradeigma,* not used in the New Testament, occurs frequently in the Septaugint for two Hebrew words. In Latin it becomes *exemplum* (Nahum 3:6), *exemplar* (I Chronicles 28:19), *descriptio* (I Chronicles 28:11,12), and even *similitudo* (the pattern for the tabernacle and its instruments which God reveals to Moses, Exodus 25:9).

Greek words for likeness, resemblance, similarity, or analogy usually and understandably become *similitudo* (e.g., *homoiōsis*, James 3:9, Ezekiel 10:22; *homoiōma*, Romans 6:5, Exodus 20:4; *homoiotēs*, Hebrews 4:15) or the adjective *similis* (e.g., Matthew 13:31, Genesis 2:20). At least once Jerome uses *forma* for *homoiōma*, appropriately with reference to the appearance of God (Deuteronomy 4:12). *Homoiōsis* never seems to be used in its grammatical or rhetorical sense, but *parabolē* (analogous comparison) is in both Old and New Testaments with varying implications and nuances. In Jerome's translation it is linked not only to *paroimia*, as in the classical rhetoricians and grammarians, but also to *ainigma*.

The verb *paraballō* (to liken or compare) appropriately becomes *comparo* (Mark 4:30), but *comparatio* is seldom used for the noun (as in Sirach 47:17). The noun itself is used in a number of related but different contexts, all established in the Old Testament. In the story of Balaam (Numbers 22–24) the phrase "and he took up his parable" (KJV literally translating the Septaugint) introduces statements the prophet Balaam makes when in his formal, prophetic capacity he is being led by God to speak particular words (23:7,18 and 24:3 and 15). In Jerome's Vulgate this is rendered *assumpta* (or *sumpta*) *parabola*. Here *parabola* is a divinely guided utterance containing prophetic truth. But these prophetic utterances are not particularly obscure or unclear in this case. King Balak wished Balaam to curse Israel, but Balaam's prophetic parables are plain, unmistakable blessings. In Ezekiel 20:49 *parabolē-parabola* is similarly used for a prophetic utterance, but one whose meaning is veiled by comparative analogy and partial, incomplete statement. Here is the King James:

> Moreover the word of the Lord came unto me, saying, son of man, set thy face toward the south, and drop thy word toward the south, and prophesy against the forest of the south field; and say to the forest of the south, Hear the word of the Lord; Thus saith the Lord God; Behold, I will kindle a fire in thee, and it shall devour every green tree in thee, and every dry tree: the flaming flame shall not be quenched, and all faces from the south to the north shall be burned therein. And all flesh shall see that I the Lord have kindled it: it shall not be quenched. Then said I, Ah Lord God! they say of me, Doth he not speak parables? (Ezekiel 20:45–49)

A similar analogy, prophetically judging Jerusalem, is identified as a *parabola* and *proverbium* in Ezekiel 24:3–5. Here God ironically elaborates the boast of the citizens of Jerusalem that they were as safe as flesh in a pot (Ezekiel 11:3). The analogy is explained in detail (24:6–14).

In I Samuel 10:12 the Greek word parable is also used for a byword or proverb (although in the context of prophesying); Jerome translates *proverbium* instead of *parabola*. After Saul has been anointed by Samuel (10:1) the Spirit of God falls on the king to be. He meets some prophets and begins to prophesy with them (10: 10–12), an event which is the origin of the parable-proverb, "Is Saul also among the prophets?" The use of parable in Ezekiel 12:22,23 is similar. Here God through Ezekiel notes that there is a commonplace saying (parable — again *proverbium* in the Vulgate) going around the southern kingdom of Judah and Jerusalem that time keeps passing as it has and that every prophetic vision of God's destructive judgment has failed to materialize. God ironically observes that this parable-proverb is itself going to cease, because He is getting ready to fulfill those prophetic visions of destruction. Later in an even more vivid passage (chapter 16) God refers to the kingdom of Judah as the whoring daughter of a Hittite mother and Amorite father with similarly inclined sisters, Samaria (the destroyed northern kingdom) and Sodom. In this context God observes through Ezekiel that everyone who likes bywords (again parable-proverb 16:44), will begin using this one of the Jews: like mother like daughter. Here the parable is a well-known example, which will be frequently repeated. The Septuagint also refers to a commonplace saying as a parable in Ezekiel 18:2,3 (Vulgate again translates *proverbium*). God indicates here that a current saying going around among the Jews states a misconception about His punishment of one generation carrying on into the next: "the fathers have eaten sour grapes, and the children's teeth are set on edge" (18:2, KJV). In this case the elements of the parable/*proverbium* are a barely developed analogy with typical implications making up a commonplace saying.

A very well developed prophetic analogy without any commonplace aspect is proposed and then interpreted in Ezekiel 17 (1–10 and 11–24). Two great eagles are used along with cedars of Lebanon to judge Jerusalem's rebellious alliance with Egypt. The account of the eagles is obscure as it stands (3–10) and needs explication, contrary to the prophetic utterances of Balaam. And so it is appropriately identified not only as a *parabola* but also *aenigma* (2). The same pair, *ainigma* and *parabolē*, occur in the Septuagint version of Moses' prophecy of blessing and cursing in Deuteronomy 27–30. In this great discourse Moses basically outlines the conditions for the Israelites being blessed in the Promised Land and those for incurring God's curse. In the midst of a long catalogue of specific examples of typical results of disobedience (28:15–68) Moses observes that wherever the Jews are dispersed this curse will be evident and known to other nations and that consequently they will be to other peoples an enigma and a parable (37). Jerome translates *proverbium* for *ainigma* here and *fabula* for *parabolē*. *Proverbium* emphasizes the fact that the riddling aspect of the Jews' history under God's punishment will become a byword among the nations. *Fabula* also exaggerates the aspect of parable as well-known story. The Jews will not only be a parable of God's justice and treatment, but that treatment itself will become a commonplace story among other people of the world.

Parable is also used in conjunction with another common Septuagint word for riddle, *problēma*, in Psalm 78:2. Jerome either Latinizes *problema* or uses the Latin equivalent, *propositio*, without any distinction between them (e.g., in the several references to Samson's famous riddle or problem, Judges 14:12,13,14,15,16,18, and 19). In Psalm 78:2 *propositio* is used with *parabola* to describe the long poem which follows, summarizing the history of the Israelites up to God's selection of the tribe of Judah and from it David to be king. The psalmist calls the people to listen to his words (1) and then says that he is going to speak parables and problems about ancient matters. The description that follows is richly figurative and very poetic, but it is not like the parable of the two eagles in Ezekiel, obscure or particularly riddling — except possibly in suspending the sense of Israel's failures having been finally amended by David until the very end. A similar rhetorical formula begins Psalm 49. Here the poet claims to speak about wisdom and things of understanding (4). In so doing he will listen to a parable (*parabola* in the Vulgate) and open up or reveal a *problēma* (*propositio*). The poem which follows is personal, moderately figurative, and very aphoristic — and so authentically full of wisdom with a proverbial flavor.

Parable is associated with enigma and proverb in other significant ways. In Sirach or Ecclesiasticus Solomon is said to have composed parables, enigmas, songs, proverbs, and interpretations (47:17–18).[3] The Septuagint *parabolē* becomes *comparatio* this time, emphasizing the original and basic sense of parable as a comparative placing of one thing beside another. *Ainigma* is Latinized to *aenigma*, and *paroimia* becomes the normal Latin *proverbium*. Rather than confusing terms,

---

3. The passage has great textual problems. See Charles's notes to verses 15 and 17 in his text (I, 497). Judging from Charles and Hatch/Redpath, Jerome used what Charles believes are corrupt readings of 15 and 17.

this passage seems to distinguish parables, enigmas, and proverbs. Parables and proverbs also seem to be distinguished in 39:3 (*parabola* and *proverbium* in Vulgate). Such distinction is, however, not the rule. Jerome not only translates *parabolē* with *proverbium* but also renders the Greek *paroimia* with Latin *parabola*.

In the very first verse of Proverbs Jerome has *parabolae* for *paroimiai* in the expression "the proverbs of Solomon." The same occurs again in 25:1. But there is a method and consistency here. Jerome invariably translates *paroimia* with *proverbium* in Ecclesiasticus (6:35, 8:9, and 18:29 in addition to the other passages already cited). In the two passages in Proverbs (the only occurrences of the word *paroimia* in the book aside from the title) Jerome seems to feel that *parabola* is the preferable translation of the Hebrew word (only one) behind the Septuagint *paroimia*. The reason seems to be that the Septuagint translates this same Hebrew word in Proverbs and elsewhere sometimes with *paroimia* but more often with *parabolē*. This is true in Proverbs 1:6 where the Septuagint renders *parabolē* and Jerome follows with *parabola*. The reference here is not just to parables but also to their interpretation and to the words of wise men as being *aenigmata*. From a Latin perspective, then, the boundaries separating proverb, parable, and enigma tend to be blurred here insofar as it is implied that something proverbial, parabolic, and enigmatic characterizes the sayings of the wise. This sense corresponds to the sense of Psalm 49, because Solomon's parabolic sayings are much more of the nature of aphoristic maxims.

These, of course, may be said to employ comparisons in several ways. Probably the most important way that these or any wise sayings may be said to be parabolic is in their implications, the relational aspect of their teaching which is, after all, their point. It is true that there are also parabolic stories in Proverbs with explicitly articulated lessons (e.g., in chapters 7–9). But the stories and lessons are intended to apply meaningfully to the reader. The staples of Solomon's proverbs are two kinds of generalizations: undirected general statements of truth ("the fear of the Lord is the beginning of knowledge," 1:7) and general truths directed to specific types or categories of people ("a wise son makes a glad father," 10:1). Readers or hearers of these truths may or may not be related to them in the proper way. A reader may be a wise son and so make his particular father glad, and he may fear the Lord so as to have a foundation for knowledge. On the other hand he may not, but in either case he illustrates the teaching—and so stands beside it in a parabolic way. It is also this possibility of standing in a negative

relationship to truth that may well justify the classification of proverbial, aphoristic teaching as enigmatic. Wisdom is concealed from the
simple and foolish, even though she cries out from the housetops
(8:1-2 and ff.).

Problēma-aenigma is also linked with *parabolē-parabola* in Habakkuk
2:6. Habakkuk says that when the Babylonian Empire falls, all the
nations conquered by and included in it will "take up a parable" against
the Babylonian leadership and speak enigmatic words against it. The
parable/enigma is then quoted:

> Woe to him that increaseth that which is not his! how long? and to him
> that ladeth himself with thick clay! Shall they not rise up suddenly that
> shall bite thee, and awake that shall vex thee, and thou shalt be for booties
> unto them? Because thou hast spoiled many nations, all the remnant of
> the people shall spoil thee; because of men's blood, and for the violence
> of the land, of the city, and of all that dwell therein. (Habakkuk 2:6-8)

Habakkuk continues with more "woes to him:" who evilly covets
(9-11); who establishes government by bloodshed (12-14); who makes
his neighbor drunk for lascivious purposes (15-17); and who makes
and worships idols (18-20). This continuation expands from specific
Babylonian leadership (although it is implied) to these kinds of activities typically and generally. And so the parabolic content is like
Solomon's proverbs, and the first lines of the taunt against the Babylo-
nians is indeed enigmatic, especially the reference to thick clay.

Parabolē-parabola occurs alone in the same context and expression
("take up a parable") in Micah 2:4, which describes the evildoing
(2:1-2) that is going to incur God's judgment (2:3). "In that day [of
judgment]," the Vulgate reads (my translation), "a parable will be taken
up on you [the evildoers]." The parable is rather enigmatic. It will be a
song (*canticum*) of lament, sung apparently by the evildoers suffering
their judgment: "we have been laid desolate of people; the portion of
my people has been changed; how He will withdraw from me, when He
turns back, Who breaks up our lands" (2:4). Parable here becomes
appropriate generalizations, poetically put, about the condition of
judged peoples, and it has the overtone of a proverbial truism.

Ainigma by itself is also significant. The Queen of Sheba comes to test
Solomon with enigmas (I Kings 10:1). Reproving Aaron and Miriam
for presuming to speak for God in addition to Moses, God says that
although He normally speaks to and through a prophet in a vision
(*visio*) or a dream (*somnium*), to Moses He reveals Himself openly, not
through enigmas and figures (*per aenigmata et figuras*, Numbers 12:6-

8).[4] The dreams Joseph and Daniel interpret and the visions and dreams Daniel has, which are interpreted for him by an angelic being, all come to mind. These are truly enigmatic, until interpreted. In the Septuagint Book of Wisdom Lady Wisdom is said to know the past and the future and to understand "subtleties of speeches and interpretations of dark sayings" (8:8, Charles). The dark sayings are *ainigmata.* But Jerome translates *argumenta* (signs, evidences, tokens, or the interesting and frequent meaning of theme, content, or subject of written or other artistic representation) and has Lady Wisdom knowing how to destroy or break down such signs (*scit . . . dissolutiones argumentorum*).

In another interesting passage (Ecclesiasticus 39:2–3) Jerome translates *ainigmata* with *abscondita* (hidden or concealed things). Here in addition to other virtues the wise scribe is said "to enter into the subtleties of parables, to search out the hidden things of proverbs, and to keep company with the concealed things of parables" (*Et in versutias parabolarum simul introibit. Occulta proverbiorum exquiret, Et in absconditis parabolarum conversabitur*). Not only does the Septuagint read "in the enigmas of parables" here but it joins *paroimiai* with parables and enigmas by emphasizing a common trait of concealment and darkness.

Problēma does not occur in the New Testament, but *ainigma, paroimia,* and *parabolē* do. In the well-known thirteenth chapter of I Corinthians Paul refers to the obscured understanding of spiritual things in this life. "For now we see through a glass, darkly," the King James puts it. But the Greek, and the Latin following it more literally, has humans seeing "in a riddle" (*in aenigmate,* I Corinthians 13:12). St. Augustine's discussion of this phrase (to be examined a little later in this chapter) is highly significant. For the moment Paul seems to be alluding to the inherent obscurity of riddles as commonplace. The much more frequent use of *paroimia* and *parabolē* in the New Testament also often involves an implication of obscurity or concealment.

John identifies a generalized story with typical implications as a proverb (*paroimia,* John 10:6—here and elsewhere in the New Testament translated *proverbium*). Jesus points out that he who enters the sheepfold by the gate is the shepherd and that he who enters by some other way is an interloping thief; the sheep know and follow only the shepherd (John 10:1–5). John observes that the Pharisees and others who heard Him say this proverb did not understand it (10:6), and so

---

4. The translation of verse 8 is disputed. KJV renders "With him . . . I will speak . . . apparently, and not in dark speeches; and the similitude of the Lord shall he behold." Jerome reads "he sees God openly, not through enigmas and figures."

Jesus interpreted it for them, pointing out that He is the door to the sheepfold and the good shepherd who lays down his life for his sheep (7–18). Later in John Jesus refers to His teachings generally as proverbial, as *paroimiai* (16:25), saying that in the future He will teach the disciples plainly and not in proverbs. Jesus immediately remarks in this context that He came from God and is going to return to Him (16:28), and the disciples respond that now He is speaking plainly and not in proverbs (29). John then definitely seems to associate fictional, typical, exemplary stories with proverbs and also to see the proverb as a synecdoche for all teaching which is not openly and readily understandable.

Peter quotes and identifies as proverbs two statements which by their brevity are more recognizably proverbial. He gives the general import of each proverb explicit, particular application. Jesus does that, too, of course, by identifying Himself as the good shepherd. Peter remarks of those who after gaining some knowledge of Christ and the gospel return to their evil, sinful lives that the proverb applies to them which says that the dog returns to its vomit (quoting Proverbs 26:11) and the washed sow goes right back to wallowing in the mud (II Peter 2:20–22). In both cases, of Jesus as good shepherd and backsliding sinner as dog, a parabolic quality of placing one thing beside another for comparative or illustrative purposes is quite evident in the particular application of a general statement of truth or story (indeed KJV renders *paroimia* in John 10:6 as "parable").

Parabolē itself frequently occurs in the New Testament. Matthew 13, filled with Jesus' illustrative stories, frequently identifies these accounts as parables (e.g., verses 10, 13, 31, 34, 36, and 53). The same is true of similar gospel passages (Luke 8:4,9,10, and 11). The comparative aspect of a parable, the putting of two things side by side for illustrative purposes, is frequently made explicit. In Luke 12:36 Jesus tells His disciples that they are just like servants waiting for their master to return from a wedding. He explicitly indicates that He and His second coming are like the return of that fictional master from the wedding (40). Peter then identifies this analogous illustration as a parable (41), but significantly he wonders about the extent of its application, to the disciples alone or to everyone.

Peter's question points up the inherent potential for ambiguity in this kind of parabolic discourse. The relative precision, clarity, or ambiguity of application depends on the teller of the parable. He indicates the application and can make it as vague or as pointed as he wishes. The first two parables in Matthew 13 illustrate this problem. Matthew describes Jesus, sitting in a boat, teaching a huge crowd

(13:2). Jesus tells them a story without any indication at all of its intended application (3–8). The story is about a sower whose seed falls respectively on the road, on stony ground, among thorns, and on good ground. Jesus then calls on those who have ears (which can understand) to hear and pay attention to his story (9). The disciples are puzzled, as obviously the crowd must have been, and ask Jesus why he speaks in parables — presumably meaning those for which some application is not given (10). Jesus responds by quoting Isaiah and pointing out that these people's hearing (understanding) has grown dull and their eyes (perception) are closed; and so He speaks to them in parables to be sure that they continue not to understand and are not converted from their ways (13–15). Thus, uninterpreted parabolic teaching takes away even what dulled understanding and perception are left to these dull, unperceiving people (12). Jesus goes on to observe how blessed the disciples are because they do perceive and understand (16–17). However, they have not perceived or understood at that point any better than the crowd, because Jesus immediately explains the application of His story in detail to them (18–23) and not to the crowd. Understanding, then, comes only with some kind of explicit application; technically, until some application was indicated there was no parable anyway, only a story. The disciples' question (10) only points out that they imagined the story Jesus told must have some intended comparative application. Thus parables may or may not be ambiguous or inexplicable, depending on the intention of the teller.

The next parable Matthew records in this discourse, instead of being completely incomprehensible, is tantalizingly ambiguous. Jesus begins this story by saying, "The kingdom of heaven is like . . ." The story is about another sower who sows his field with good seed, only to have his enemy sneak into the field that night and sow it with weeds. This deed creates a problem in tending the field, since the weeds grow up with the grain. The problem will only be resolved at the harvest, when the grain will be taken in and the weeds cast out and burned (24–30). Jesus gives no indication of the parabolic application of His story other than His opening comment about the kingdom of heaven. Here is ambiguity rather than total incomprehensibility, but the effect is the same. Clearly the crowd could not guess what application was intended (and anything more specific than the kingdom of heaven would be simply a guess), because the disciples themselves did not understand the story. Immediately after Jesus dismisses the crowd, the disciples ask Him what that story meant (36), and He tells them the application He had in mind in detail (38–43).

The parabolic story, then, is only parabolic if it is linked with some application, explicit or implied. This application may be vague, general, or highly detailed and precise, but there must be some analogous application indicated. Jerome's translation of *parabolē* in the New Testament seems to reflect this. In addition to *parabola* he frequently alternates the Latin *similitudo,* analogous likeness or resemblance—for example in Luke's account of the parables in Matthew 13 (Luke 8:4) or again in Luke 12:16. Jerome never translates *parabolē* with *similitudo* in the Old Testament, where there is not this rather more restricted sense of story with analogous application.

However, the use of the Greek term parable is not limited in the New Testament to the well-developed, fictional story/analogy. It may involve only a brief, almost storyless comparison, as in Jesus' reference to the leaves and branches of the fig tree (Matthew 24:32–33). Just as one recognizes the advent of summer when the fig tree sprouts new leaves, so one will be able to recognize the approach of the second coming of the Son when one sees all the signs described by Jesus in the Olivet discourse. Such aphoristic, even proverbial sayings as that about the blind not being able to lead the blind (Luke 6:39) or patching an old garment with a new piece of cloth (Luke 5:36), or about what goes into the mouth not defiling a man but rather what comes out of it (Matthew 15:11–20) are identified as parables. The last example is aphoristic without being proverbial, but the unmistakably proverbial saying, "physician, heal yourself," in Luke 4:23 is also identified as a parable. Jerome translates the Greek with the Latin *parabola* in the aphoristic passage (Matthew 15:15) but uses the Latin *similitudo* for the other three. Both the Greek and Latin point up the fact that proverbial wisdom or any general aphorism is created for the sake of application. Obviously there would be no point in saying a stitch in time saves nine (stitches) if this proverb could not be applied to many specific, analogous experiences of life. Neither would there be any point in saying that a wise son pleases his father if there were not particular wise sons to whom the general truth of the saying could be applied. Proverb and aphorism are intrinsically designed for parabolic application. This fact seems to be overwhelmingly attested in both Old and New Testaments by the use of the terms *parable* and *proverb.* The parabolic putting of analogous things side by side can even include symbols or types. The writer of Hebrews points out that the furnishings of the tabernacle and the ritual sacrifices under the Old Law were a parable, for those people at that time, of the nature and sacrifice of the Messiah (Hebrews 9:9).

The parables of Jesus illustrate one enigmatic aspect of parables. The Old Testament and Apocrypha frequently associate parables and any kind of wisdom with enigmas and enigmatic concealment. As Jesus' use of parables demonstrates, uninterpreted parables are in fact story/enigmas, about which the hearer must simply guess what the teller had in mind when he told them. It is true, as Jesus also indicates, that some people will be better equipped to guess than others. But even though Lady Wisdom knows how to interpret enigmas, there are conceivably some parables which even she would have to have interpreted and applied. For the Christian, of course, as with Paul construing the allegory of Abraham, Hagar, and Sarah, the Holy Spirit makes a decisive difference. Although the Christian may not write inspired Scripture, he does, as Paul emphatically teaches, have the mind of Christ (I Corinthians 2:16). The Christian has divine access to true spiritual understanding through the gift of the Holy Spirit. Jesus remarks to the disciples (implicitly explaining their lack of understanding of his parables) that although he speaks to them in proverbs now He will speak to them plainly in the future (John 16:25–29). In this same discourse He explains to them that they will understand everything from the beginning of their knowledge of Him as soon as He sends them the Holy Spirit (John 15:26–27 and, earlier, John 14:26). Of course, they had to wait until after he had ascended into Heaven in His resurrected body for the Spirit to descend on them.

While riddles, parables, and proverbs are particularly prominent and are legitimized in the Bible, fables are not. The Septuagint does not use the word *mythos* in the canonical books of the Old Testament, and in every instance of its appearance in the New Testament (always translated *fabula* by Jerome) it invariably has bad connotations and associations (I Timothy 1:4 and 4:7, II Timothy 4:4, Titus 1:14, and II Peter 1:16). In all these cases fables, whatever their origin, are pitfalls obscuring the truth and must be avoided.

[St. Augustine (4th–5th cents. A.D.)]

The Bible, inspired by the Holy Spirit, is a special text, and the Christian interpreter, guided by that same Spirit, is a special reader. In this sense none of St. Augustine's many theoretical remarks about Biblical interpretation apply to any texts beyond the Bible. However, Augustine's ideas about biblical interpretation were developed not only out of the Bible but also out of pagan philosophy, grammar, and rhetoric, so that there is a significant relationship of his theories of biblical interpretation to received theories of interpretation of uninspired texts. There is also the relational aspect of the influence of Augustine's theoretical remarks on later European ideas about the interpretation of texts other than the Bible. This latter influence has been strongly argued, particularly by D. W. Robertson, Jr., and others in the past thirty years.[5] Such a view is not at all unlikely insofar as Augustine is unquestionably the most influential Christian writer in the Western Church from his own day to ours. Augustine, however, has much more to say about interpretation than Robertson or any other writer interested in literary-critical theory has to my knowledge ever discussed. This is particularly and ironically true for Augustine's many comments about poetry, its utility and value, about pagan mythlogy, and about the interpretation of fables and poetic inventions. But it is also true about Augustine's numerous theoretical positions on the allegory of the Bible.

Basic to all of Augustine's ideas about interpretation are some related concepts about things (*res*) and words (*verba*) and signs (*signa*). The little treatise *Concerning the Teacher* and Book II of *On Christian Doctrine* develop these concepts.[6] From these two sources it is clear that words mean nothing intrinsically except as signs for things. And so speech signifies. Words are conventional, must be learned, and without signs nothing can be taught. Consequently the reader of the Bible must be as educated as possible in verbal and other—for instance musical or numerological—signs (*Christian Doctrine* II. xii–xviii). Difficult signs are either unknown or ambiguous. Verbal signs are literal or transferred from their literal to some other designation. Frequently the sequence of reference goes: word to thing to real meaning, as in ox→animal→St. Luke the Evangelist (*Christ. Doc.* II. x. 15).

After this set of ideas a whole series of fundamental principles of interpretation appears in the writings of Augustine. Some of these are well known, but others are not. Robertson, of course, emphasizes the Augustinian insistence that meanings which are difficult to discover are the more pleasurably found and that things are actually understood better when they are conveyed indirectly through similitudes (*Christ. Doc.* II. vi. 8). Augustine faces squarely and fully the problems

5. A convenient, concise view is argued by Robertson in the "Introduction" to his felicitous translation of Augustine's *On Christian Doctrine* (Indianapolis and New York: Bobbs-Merrill, 1958), pp. ix–xxi. Other books and articles by Robertson and an early collaborator, Bernard Huppé, are well known. Many of these are conveniently listed in John H. Fisher's *The Medieval Literature of Western Europe: A Review of Research, Mainly 1930–1960* (New York: NYU Press for MLA, 1966). Too late for that review but very important is Robertson's *A Preface to Chaucer* (Princeton University Press, 1963).

6. *Concerning the Teacher* conveniently appears in an English translation in that useful collection, *Basic Writings of Saint Augustine*, ed. Whitney J. Oates (New York: Random House, 1948), I, 361–95. The Latin text appears in J. P. Migne's *Patrologiae Cursus Completus . . . Series Latina* (Paris, 1844–1903), XXXII, cols. 1193–1220. Robertson's translation of the *Christian Doctrine* is good. The Latin text is available in the excellent edition in the *Corpus Christianorum Series Latina* (Turnhout: Brepols, 1962), XXXII.

of literal and figurative meanings (figurative generally is equivalent to allegorical and to a signification or signifying by similitude). He warns not to take the literal figuratively or the figurative literally (*Christ. Doc.* III. v. 9 and x. 14). But the crucial question is, How does the reader know when to read literally and when not to? The various answers Augustine provides for this question constitute most of the fundamentals of his hermeneutics.

The simplest of these fundamentals is that "almost everything" in the Old Testament, historical events as well as prophetic and poetic passages, is figurative or allegorical.[7] A text meant to be read figuratively will also contain some kind of hint or hints (Augustine calls them traces, tracks, or vestiges—*vestigia, Christ. Doc.* "Proemium" 9) that it is to be read figuratively. For example, any text which in its literal import is improper or indecent in the Bible is always figurative (*Christ. Doc.* III. xii. 18). In fact any problem at all with the literal text is almost always a hint or direction to read figuratively. An extreme example is discussed in the *City of God* (*CD* hereafter), where Augustine observes that the original Hebrew and the Septuagint differ markedly in the account of Jonah's preaching to Ninevah. The Hebrew has Jonah warning the Ninevites that in forty days their city will be destroyed. The Septuagint translators, however, have a warning of only three days. But what appears to be a contradiction in the textual tradition is really a hint to read allegorically for another sense: both the forty and the three refer to Christ (*CD* XVIII. xliv).[8] Parables similarly hint at their meaning subtly or obviously ("by insinuation or necessity") according to similitude or dissimilitude (as in Diomedes).[9] Augustine also adds that what appear to be deliberate ambiguities (ambiguous signs) in the Bible are put there by God to conquer human pride as well as to hint at figurative meanings.

But Augustine knew that some real control of interpretive results was needed if the soundness and purity of Christian doctrine were to be maintained in the face of heresies and perverse readings of Scripture. And so he mandates that every meaning interpreted must con-

---

7. In the essay *Lying* XV. 26: "sicuti sunt fere omnia in libris ueteris testamenti; quis enim ibi aliquid audeat adfirmare non pertinere ad figuratam praenuntiationem?" *Lying* and the companion treatise, *Against Lying,* are discussed later. See note 25.

8. I have used the Loeb Library *The City of God against the Pagans,* 7 vols. (Cambridge, Mass.: Harvard University Press, 1957–72) with various translators and convenient Latin text facing the English.

9. Discussing parables at length in the context of Luke 18:1–8 (parable of the widow and the unjust judge), Augustine observes, "ducitur intellectus ejus rei, cui adhibentur, insinuandae aut requirendae," *Quaestionum Evangeliorum* II. xlv, *PL,* XXXV, col. 1358.

form to known Christian truth (*Christ. Doc.* II. vii. 10). He refers to this whole domain of Christian truth variously as the rule of faith (*Christ. Doc.* III. ii. 2 and x. 14) or, in the aspect of Augustinian hermeneutics most emphasized by Robertson, as the rule of charity (*Christ. Doc.* III. xv. 23). Every passage of the Bible, then, expresses some aspect of Christian truth, either literally or figuratively (*Christ. Doc.* III. x. 14–16). In another variation of the rule of faith or charity based on epideictic rhetorical theory Augustine posits that whatever does not literally praise virtue or condemn vice is to be read figuratively so that it does praise virtue or condemn vice (*Christ. Doc.* III. xvi. 24).

Not just any allegorical meaning is warranted, however, by this contentual mandate. Allegorical meanings suitable or appropriate to the literal text in question must be construed. It is true that for Augustine any interpretation which is suitable is a valid interpretation (a point frequently made, e.g., *Christ. Doc.* III. ii. 2, *CD* XVIII. xliv). Intentionality seems to be irrelevant. Even if the original intended meaning is never known, any interpretation which is suitable and which conforms to the standards of orthodox Christian truth is an acceptable interpretation. Augustine make this point emphatically and explicitly (*Christ. Doc.* III. xxvii). It might be said that even though the human author's specific intention may not be known, the Holy Spirit, who explicitly inspires the allegory of Scripture,[10] intends some meaning or meanings conforming to Christian truth. This broad intentionality might even govern non-Scriptural texts where there is textual suitability but contradiction of authorial intention. Augustine invokes suitability to accept a Messianic interpretation of Virgil's *Fourth Eclogue* (*CD* X. xxvii). Even though he knows Virgil intends this poem to refer to another human being, Augustine will accept a Messianic interpretation simply because, if one applies the sentiments to Christ, they do fit, they are suitable and appropriate. But this propriety is obviously governed by what are accidental and partial similarities taken out of intentional context. The principle of suitability, then, is not arbitrary, but it does involve a rather unrestrained kind of interpretation.

The divorce of interpreted meaning from authorial intention opens the door to multiple interpretations. But these cannot be contradictory, and there are limitations. Augustine allows explicitly for many different interpretations of one biblical passage (*CD* XV. xxvii), that is, many figurative, allegorical interpretations, but they must all conform

10. In *De Vera Religione (On True Religion)* L. 99: "allegory, which is believed to have been spoken through the wisdom in the Holy Spirit" (*allegoriae, quae per sapientiam dicta creditur in spiritu sancto*). In *Corpus Christianorum, Series Latina,* XXXII, 251.

to the defined body of orthodox Christian truth. Another constraint is that no allegorical interpretation may ever deny or question the historical accuracy of facts indicated in the literal sense of biblical passages. Augustine decries both those interpreters who insist that everything in the Bible is figurative and allegorical and those who insist that everything is literal. The ability to read both literally and allegorically is mandatory, not only in the sense discussed above of accurately identifying a particular passage as either literal or figurative and reading it accordingly, but also in the allegorical interpretation of the perfectly satisfactory historical account, where the interpreter must read literally *and* figuratively together (*CD* XV. xxvii and XVII. iii). Thus some passages are to be read purely figuratively, some purely literally, but others which contain historical information in their literal sense must be read allegorically in addition to being read for their historical content. And so, as long as the historical data of any passage are accepted as true, any number of spiritual or allegorical interpretations may be formulated as long as they are all suitable and conform to the truth (*CD* XV. xxvii).

The crucial assumption in Augustine's thinking on this question is that the recording of historical events must have some purpose greater than the mere recording of historical events. Put another way, historical events are not important or significant enough on their own account to merit being recorded. Consequently the written account of historical events (at least in sacred history) will naturally convey some meaning beyond or different from the relatively insignificant knowledge of those historical facts. Augustine frequently makes this point (*CD* XIII. xxi, XV. xxvi and xxvii, XVIII. xliv, and *On the Profit of Believing* III. 8[11]). Allegory of a historical passage therefore operates wholly independently of the account of the historical facts, which are not at all jeopardized by the existence of figurative meanings in the written account of those facts (*CD* XIII. xxi and XV. xxvii). Augustine takes his cue from St. Paul in Galatians 4:24 where, as Augustine affirms, Paul's assertion that the child of Hagar is the Old Covenant and the child of Sarah the New in no way impugns the historical validity of Hagar, Sarah, and the rest, and he makes the same point about spiritual symbolism in the description of the Garden of Eden (*CD* XIII. xxi).

This view of the nature and importance of history may explain a curious definition of history in *On the Profit of Believing* (III. 5). Here Augustine says that history teaches what has been written or done in

---

11. I have used the text of *De Utilate Credendi* in *PL,* XLII, and the English translation in Oates, I.

the past *or* what has not really been done but what is recorded as if it had. This definition of history obviously combines the rhetorical definitions of history and fiction and is quite close to Priscian's subsequent definition of narrative in *Praeexercitamina*. The key for Augustine is not whether a historical-looking account indeed records bona fide factual information, but the purpose informing the narrative. Real meaning comes from the written account, whether it records history or a parable. And so, although one must not question the historical validity of facts presented in the Bible as historical facts, one must also recognize that the real import rests not in the bare facts but in the writing down, the recording of those facts. Whatever the content of narrative, it is narrated for purposes beyond the mere details of its account, whether fictional or historical.

The interpretive restraints in discovering those meanings in historical accounts which are really significant are the same for other purely figurative passages and are grounded in classical rhetorical theory. The overriding constraint is that every meaning interpreted must conform to the standard of acknowledged orthodox Christian truth. Meanings must also be appropriate or suitable. One is reminded of Priscian's subsequent insistence on a standard of suitability and propriety in the creation of fables. Indeed the supporting limitations of suitable interpretations which Augustine articulates have a definite basis in classical rhetoric and grammar. A related limitation seems to reflect the figure of homoeosis, defined by Diomedes as "the vivid delineation of something less known by its similitude to something which is better known and the representation of something unknown by its similitude to what is better known." For Augustine the interpreter of the Bible is, mutatis mutandis, to coordinate the obscure point with the obvious one, to learn the unknown by its suitable, appropriate relationship with the known (*CD* XVII. xvi and *Christ. Doc.* III. xxvi. 37).

Another related guideline, which insists that suitable meanings must be similar and not unlike the text they interpret, seems to limit the extent to which irony may be inferred in Biblical allegory. Augustine emphatically asserts this rule of similitude in a comment on Psalm 8. "And this rule," he writes, "ought to be maintained in every allegory to consider in the place of the immediate [obvious] meaning what is said by means of similitude." "This," he adds, "is in fact the Lord's teaching and the apostles'."[12] This rule would seem to militate against irony as a

12. "Et haec regula in omni allegoria retinenda est, ut pro sententia praesentis loci consideretur quod per similitudinem dicitur; haec est enim dominica et apostolica disciplina." *Enarrationes in Psalmos* VIII, para. 13, in *Corpus Christianorum*, XXXVIII, 57. See also *Christ. Doc.* III. xxv. 34.

primary aspect of biblical allegory and interpretation. Similitude, of course, grammatically and rhetorically includes dissimilitude in, say, negative comparisons (see Diomedes on parables), but that is different from the implicit contradiction of irony. Figurative meanings are different from and other than the literal meanings, but they are not directly contradictory in implication. It is true, however, that when the occasion demands (as it does in the treatise *Against Lying,* discussed later in this chapter), Augustine will push the rule of suitable similitude right up to the point of ironic contradiction.

Finally Augustine offers the important view that, since Scripture itself uses the same figure or image in radically different senses (Jesus as the lion of the tribe of Judah, and the Devil as that roaring lion, seeking to devour the faithful; or the leaven of the pharisees and the leaven of the Kingdom of God), the interpreter must be guided to the suitably appropriate figurative interpretation, construing the unknown from the known through similitude, by the immediate context of the passage in question.[13] The literal context of a passage determines whether a figure is construed as having a good or a bad sense. Here is an early stage of the ubiquitous habit of interpreting images *in malo* and *in bono* so familiar to modern students of medieval and Renaissance iconography.

Within all these constraints and limitations the biblical interpreter still had enormous leeway in construing passages not embodying direct, literal statements about faith or life. Further refinements are suggested in the several passages where Augustine tries to categorize and sometimes explain more specifically the different kinds of meanings in the Bible. These categories seldom speak directly about the interpretive methods involved in construing such meanings, but they do contain important implications about methodology. Generally speaking Augustine, like the Stoics, is prone to use etymology in construing figurative or allegorical meanings, particularly of historical characters (see on Cain and Abel, *CD* XV. xviii, and for many others, *CD* XVI). When attacking Stoic and other allegorizations of the pagan gods Augustine uses their own method of etymologizing to ridicule and demolish the validity of their rationalizations (see especially *CD* IV. xxi and xxiv).

For biblical meanings three and fourfold distinctions are made. There are several articulations of this. In one set of threes Old Testament prophecy from the time of the Israelite kings is said to refer

---

13. See *Christ. Doc.* III. xxv. 35 and 37 and *Enarrationes in Psalmos* CIII, para. 22, *Corpus Christianorum,* XL, 1519.

either to (1) the natural descendants of Abraham and the physical, historical Jerusalem; (2) the spiritual descendants of Abraham in the New Covenant of Christ and the true, heavenly Jerusalem; or (3) a combination of both (*CD* XVII. iii). Another, focusing on the means of expressing content rather than on content itself, establishes that prophetic statments but not historical figures in the Old Testament (the context of discussion is the Psalms) are either (1) plainly clear in import; (2) figurative; or (3) a combination of both (*CD* XVII. xiv and xv).

A different and intriguing categorizing in *On True Religion* divides the figurative into four kinds of allegory in the Bible. Discussing the learning of matters related to true faith in a context of things historical and temporal and spiritual and eternal, Augustine refers only in passing to the different allegories of (1) history; (2) a deed (*factum*); (3) speech (*sermo*); and (4) a sacrament or mystery (*sacramentum*).[14] Another better-known and extremely important passage in *On the Profit of Believing* asserts that the whole Old Testament has been transmitted fourfold (*quadrifaria*), according to (1) history, (2) etiology, (3) analogy, and (4) allegory.[15] History here, as noted earlier, is defined as occurring when the reader is taught what actually happened (deeds or words) or what did not actually happen but is recorded as if it had. Augustine's examples of these categories are all taken from the New Testament. For history the passage in Matthew 12 is cited, where Jesus, rebuked by the Pharisees for allowing his disciples to eat grain from the fields on the sabbath, refers His critics to the written account of David and his men (in Samuel), also hungry, entering the tabernacle and eating the shewbread. Etiology shows the cause for something being said or done, and etiological significance is demonstrated in Jesus' severe restriction of divorce, which He defends by explaining the cause of the more liberal provisions in the Mosaic Law (Matthew 19:8). Analogy, "whereby the agreement of both Testaments is plainly seen" (Oates), is not demonstrated by example.

Of great interest are the examples of allegory. Allegory, Augustine says, occurs when one is directed not to receive what is written accord-

14. "in quibus haec omnia [the visible, the intellectual, and eternal laws] vestiganda sint, et quae sit stabilis fides siue historica et temporalis siue spiritalis et aeterna, ad quam omnis interpretatio auctoritatis dirigenda est, et quid prosit ad intellegenda et obtinenda aeterna, ubi finis est omnium bonarum actionum, fides rerum temporalium, et quid intersit inter allegoriam historiae et allegoriam facti et allegoriam sermonis et allegoriam sacramenti. . . ." *De Vera Religione* L. 99.

15. Augustine discusses these categories in four long paragraphs (5–8), to which my survey here refers.

ing to the letter but to understand figuratively: "secundum allegoriam, cum docetur non ad litteram esse accipienda quaedam quae scripta sunt, sed figurate intelligenda." The familiar Galatians passage (4:22–24) is quoted without explanation, but another Pauline observation in I Corinthians 10:1–11 is quoted and explained. Here is the King James:

> Moreover, brethren, I would not that ye should be ignorant, how that all our fathers were under the cloud, and all passed through the sea; and were all baptized unto Moses in the cloud and in the sea; and did all eat the same spiritual meat; and did all drink the same spiritual drink: for they drank of that spiritual Rock that followed them: and that Rock was Christ. But with many of them God was not well pleased: for they were overthrown in the wilderness. Now these things were our examples, to the intent we should not lust after evil things, as they also lusted. Neither be ye idolaters, as were some of them; as it is written, The people sat down to eat and drink, and rose up to play. Neither let us commit fornication, as some of them committed, and fell in one day three and twenty thousand. Neither let us tempt Christ, as some of them also tempted, and were destroyed of serpents. Neither murmur ye, as some of them also murmured, and were destroyed of the destroyer. Now all these things happened unto them for examples: and they are written for our admonition, upon whom the ends of the world are come.

The passage itself is very significant. As in the Galatians passage Paul construes historical events allegorically. Not only was the account recorded for their admonitory significance, but the events themselves happened for that reason. The rock from which water gushed forth when Moses struck it is Christ, and the experiences of the Israelites led by Moses had the same spiritual significance for them that Christ and the gospel have for Paul, the Corinthian church, and other believers under the New Covenant. The Israelites obviously did not know the true nature of their baptism nor the true identity of that Rock. They did not know about the Trinity or that they had tempted Christ specifically. All those visible, actual experiences were for them an as-yet incomplete or unfulfilled figure. The Vulgate verse 11 reads: "Haec autem omnia in figura contingebant illis" (all these things happened to them in a figure).[16] But these same things were also done, Paul says, in a figure for the contemporary believer under the New Covenant ("Haec autem in figura facta sunt nostri," verse 6), and they were written down and recorded for the modern believer's correction, discipline, or admonition ("scripta sunt autem ad correptionem nostram," verse 11).

16. Augustine regularly uses *figura* and *allegoria* in the sense of type or foreshadowing or prefiguration.

It is clear that the corrective warning here for Christians is exemplary. Christians are to take warning from the bad example of the response to Christ of the Israelites under Moses and not do as the Israelites did. Again the Pauline and Augustinian point is being made that history is recorded for some reason greater than the mere knowledge of historical facts. Here the reason is to provide exemplary figures of behavior to avoid. Furthermore the historical deeds themselves were figures to the very participants in the sense of the shape of things as yet incomplete and unfulfilled for them. Prefacing his quotation of I Corinthians 10:1–11, Augustine explains that Paul "signifies that the history itself of the Exodus was an allegory of future Christian people" (*ipsam Exodi hisotriam futurae christianae plebis allegoriam fuisse significat*). Augustine is not confusing the Pauline distinction between historical facts and the historical record of them here, because history is the narrative record and not the deeds themselves. It is significant, though, that Augustine sees the historical record as an allegory *of*, not *for*, Christians. The Christian may, of course, not take warning from the example of the Israelites — the point of Paul's warning explicitly articulated in verse 12. Whether of or for, a parabolic quality of putting incomplete or unfulfilled Christian/Israelites beside Christians is definitely suggested, and figuratively or figurally the Israelites were mutatis mutandis Christians. The ultimate, completed significance of the Israelites' experiences was figurally hidden from their understanding, but it is revealed to the Christian by Paul (and the Holy Spirit) in the time of their completion and fulfillment (the Christian era).

The other example of allegory offered by Augustine also demonstrates hidden and open aspects. Augustine identifies as allegory the use Jesus makes of the story of Jonah in Matthew 12:39–40, which he quotes:

> But he [Jesus] answered and said unto them, An evil and adulterous generation seeketh after a sign; and there shall no sign be given to it, but the sign of the prophet Jonas: For as Jonas was three days and three nights in the whale's belly; so shall the Son of man be three days and three nights in the heart of the earth. (KJV)

Again a historical event and the record of it have an incomplete, hidden meaning to the participants. Jonah clearly did not know why he was in the belly of the whale for three days. It remained for Jesus, toward whom the whole Old Testament points, to reveal the completed or full significance, His own burial for three days and nights. After the interpretation the analogous connection according to similitude, the allegorical implication, is revealed.

The question of obscurity in connection with allegory is taken up in
On the Trinity XV. ix, another very important chapter on biblical
allegory.[17] Here Augustine considers the questions of schemes and
tropes in conjunction with the Pauline remark in I Corinthians 13:12:
"Videmus nunc per speculum in aenigmate" (Now we see through a
glass in a riddle). Augustine notes the allusive character of the phrase
"in a riddle" and observes that those who are not educated in schemes
and tropes will not understand the phrase. This fact leads him to
explain briefly that enigma is a species of allegory. Citing Paul's use of
the term allegory in Galatians 4:24, he explains the etymology of the
Greek (signifying one thing by another) and gives the common
grammatical/rhetorical definition discussed in chapter one:

> Quid est ergo allegoria nisi tropus ubi ex alio aliud intellegitur (What
> then is allegory except the trope in which one thing is understood by
> means of something else).

He thus mentions both the creative and interpretive sides of allegorical
expression (signifying and construing signification).

In accordance with the logical relationship of species with genus
Augustine observes that while every enigma is allegory not every
allegory is enigma. He quotes I Thessalonians 5:6–8 as an example of
allegory which is not enigmatic, not obscure:

> Therefore let us not sleep, as do others; but let us watch and be sober. For
> they that sleep sleep in the night; and they that be drunken are drunken
> in the night. But let us, who are of the day, be sober. (KJV)

This passage is allegorical but obvious to all, he says, except the most
dull of spiritual understanding. Enigma, however, is "obscure allegory." Augustine's example is the cryptic "The horseleach hath two
daughters . . ." (KJV) of Proverbs 30:15.[18]

The climax to this interesting paragraph is a discussion of the
Galatians 4 passage. Before Paul explained that Hagar's child was the
bondage of the Old Law and Sarah's the freedom of the New Covenant, this meaning, Augustine says, was obscure and so technically an
enigma. The implications of this distinction are not pursued, but it

---

17. This chapter appears in a translation of selections from *On the Trinity* in Oates, vol.
2. I have used the Latin text in *Corpus Christianorum*, La.

18. There is a textual problem here. Augustine's Bible had "three" daughters, not two.
The Vulgate has two, as does the *Glossa Ordinaria*, *PL*, CXIII, col. 1113, which explains
the allegory as follows: the horseleach is the devil and his two daughters are Debauchery
and Avarice. Two daughters, though, are just as obscure allegorically as three.

would appear that according to this thinking not only is enigma obscure allegory but that once an enigma has been definitively and authoritatively (i.e., accurately) interpreted, it is no longer enigmatic. Augustine brings up another problem here, too, when he asserts that, since the basis of Paul's allegorical exposition was not just words but events, the allegory was found in and based on these events (*facti*) and not just words (*verbi*):

> Sed ubi allegoriam nominauit apostolus non in uerbis eam reperit sed in facto . . . quod non dictum sed etiam factum fuit . . .

Augustine seems to be saying, as Bede and Hugh of St. Victor after him definitely say (to be discussed later), that allegory based on or in real events is thereby sounder and more authoritative. And yet it is just as enigmatic (until explained) as the cryptic verbal (factlessly based) remark about the horseleach's daughters. This assertion also seems to question the implication in the Galatians passage itself and elsewhere in Augustine that allegory operates wholly aside from the validity of facts in historical narrative and that the key to allegorical purpose in such narrative is the writing of it.

In at least one other passage Augustine uses the grammatical/ rhetorical definition of allegory as a jumping-off point for discussing biblical allegory. Commenting on the phrase in Psalm 103 (104):3, "Qui ambulat super pennas uentorum" (Who walks on the wings of the winds)[19] Augustine argues that the winds are to be understood as souls (*animae*) in an allegory or figure (*in allegoria, in figura*), and he makes a point of distinguishing the allegory of dramatic pantomime on the secular stage from the allegory of the Bible. As if to defend the legitimacy of an allegorical reading here, he again refers to Paul's identification of the two children in Galatians 4:24 as an allegory and then gives a full definition of the trope allegory:

> Allegoria dicitur, cum aliquid uidetur sonare in uerbis, et aliud in intellectu significare (Allegory is spoken when something seems to mean one thing in the words and signifies another thing in the meaning).

He immediately continues:

> How is Christ called the Lamb: not [meaning] a sheep? Or the Lion: not a beast? Or the Rock: not hardness? Or the Mountain: not an elevated piece of earth? And so, many things seem to mean one thing and signify something else, and this is called allegory.

19. *Corpus Christianorum*, XL, 1486.

But, of course, as Augustine explains elsewhere, not every lion is Christ, either.

Augustine is typically opposed here to the stage and theatrical spectacles of any sort. He attacks the influence of secular allegory of theatrical spectacle, preferring the country to the evil influences of city life (*"Videtis quid faciat ciuitas ubi abundant spectacula: in agro securius loquerer"*). He then remarkably adds that perhaps the only place where allegory can really be learned anyway is in the Bible, and he proceeds to redefine the grammatical/rhetorical trope as a Christian sacrament:

> Quid sit enim allegoria, non ibi forte didicissent homines, nisi in scrip-
> turis Dei. Ergo quod dicimus allegoriam figuram esse, sacramentum
> figuratum allegoria est (In this respect perhaps men would not have
> learned what allegory really is except in God's scriptures. Therefore
> insofar as we say allegory is a figure, it is a figured sacrament).

Augustine also refers in this passage to one of Jesus' parables as implicitly allegorical. The Bible, then, as opposed to other secular forms of literary, dramatic, and spectacular allegory, is more fully and completely allegorical.

The position here, claiming complete actualization of allegorical potential only for the Bible, is consistent with Augustine's many remarks about the various practices of allegorization of the pagan gods and about poetic expressions of myth and the interpretation of myth. Books IV through VII of *The City of God* take up the whole question of the pagan religions. Book V discusses astrology, augury, and fate, but Books IV and VII are particularly interesting for their discussion of the rationalization, allegorization, and interpretation of pagan myth. Augustine takes a qualifiedly euhemeristic view of the nature of the gods in order to destroy any potential divinity in them (VII. xviii and VIII. xxvi). But he is even more interested in attacking their utility in any sense whatever. Consequently, his long treatment of various means of utilizing myth allegorically is rather like the discussion in Cicero's *De Natura Deorum* and expresses an attitude very close indeed to Cotta's in Cicero. Like Cotta, Augustine rejects not only the surface myths but also the allegorization of them, especially physical interpretations. He uses Cotta's technique, even more extensively, of ridiculing the inconsistencies of the relationships of the fables about the gods to the interpretations of hidden meanings (see IV. x). Augustine characteristically takes up an interpretation and pushes it to an absurd point of inconsistency (see especially IV. xi). Frequently this process involves his using the pagan etymologizing against itself (e.g., IV. xxi and xxiv). He includes an attack on the gods as personified abstractions which are also inconsistent and logically absurd (IV. xiv), and says that the use of divinities to represent allegorically parts of the physical creation is irreligious and simply unnecessary (IV. xii and VII. v).

Physical allegoresis, approved by the pagan scholar Varro, whose now-lost work on the gods and religion Augustine uses, is emphatically rejected and the myths branded as "empty and pernicious figments" (VII. v). The gods as allegorizations of physical reality or as personified abstractions are thoroughly reviewed but completely rejected (VII. vii–xv). In these chapters in Book VII and importantly in the *Christian Doctrine* (III. vii) Augustine consistently denies for pagan myth the concept of an outer husk concealing an inner kernel of useful meaning, a concept central to Augustine's biblical hermeneutics. Augustine's main argument is Cotta's: the pagan interpreters have arbitrarily and selectively invented meanings which have no necessary or intrinsic relationship to the myths they purport to explain (*CD* VII. xxvi and xxvii). The pagan interpretations are willful, arbitrary, after the fact, and extrinsic. To know or learn that Neptune is a sign of the entire sea is useless. Such a husk as Neptune has no useful kernel and "is not food for men but for swine" (*Christ. Doc.* III. vii, Robertson). And so Augustine sharply distinguishes the truth of the Old Testament signs from these useless signs of pagan false religion (III. ix).

One important reason for this distinction is articulated in the polemic *Against Faustus the Manichean.*[20] In passing Augustine points out that the pagans must understand and be in awe of the figurative understanding of Scripture in Christianity (XII. xxxix–xli). The pagans understand the allegorical interpretation of the Bible because it involves the same kind of sequential relationship between image and meaning as is claimed in their own allegorization of myth. Myth predates and precedes interpretation. In the same way prophecies and prefigurations in the Old Testament precede their fulfillment in Christ and the New Testament. However, for pagan myth there is only that arbitrary, extrinsic, after-the-fact relationship between myth and interpretation; whereas the prophecies and prefigurations in the Old Testament have actually and truly and demonstrably been fulfilled in a relationship which is necessary and intrinsic.

Precisely how such an intrinsic, necessary relationship may also be reflected in the figurative interpretations made by Christians outside the New Testament is unclear, since any suitable figurative reading which conforms to Christian truth is acceptable even if the original intention of the Old Testament passage is never known. This question

---

20. I have used the text of *Contra Faustum Manicheum* in *PL,* XLII, cols. 207–518.

notwithstanding, sequence seems to remain an important aspect of the relationship of image to meaning in the medieval Christian understanding of allegory. Isidore's first example of the trope allegory in his *Etymologiarum Libri XX* is interesting in this respect. Immediately after defining allegory in the customary grammatical/rhetorical way, Isidore quotes the *Aeneid* I. 184, " 'He [Aeneas] saw three deer wandering on the shore.' "[21] Isidore explains that by these three deer Virgil meant three leaders of the Punic Wars or the three Punic Wars themseves (I. xxxvii. 22). I do not know whether this allegorization is original with Isidore (it is not in Servius), but that is immaterial, since it is presented as a prime example of allegory. The ingredients might even suit Augustine, particularly if they are seen from Virgil's point of view as creative artist. There is sequence and from Virgil's perspective a necessary, intrinsic relationship between image and meaning. The historical/fictional Aeneas of Virgil's poem, of course, founds a Trojan colony in Italy which ultimately becomes Rome. Rome defeated the Carthaginians in the three Punic Wars, a defeat essential to the rise of Roman hegemony in the western Mediterranean. Virgil, writing long after the Punic Wars and celebrating the origins of Rome, has his epic hero driven by a storm onto what will become the Carthaginian coast of North Africa. There he sights three deer (an animal which Servius notes is not indigenous to North Africa and so is poetically but not ecologically appropriate) and kills them—thus prefiguring the Roman slaying of the Carthaginians in the three Punic Wars. Isidore's other example of the general trope allegory is also oriented toward the creative control of the writer and his intentions.

But for Augustine the arbitrary, extrinsic, after-the-fact nature of pagan interpretations of the gods is distinctly inferior to and different from the intrinsic, necessary relationship of prefiguring image and Christian fulfillment of meaning in the Bible. However, although the images of the pagan gods are not at all necessary to the different kinds of meaning they are supposed to represent or personify and are not even useful to an understanding of those meanings, they are nonetheless better than the Manichean mythology, dichotomizing the forces of good and evil and giving to evil an ontological status equal to good. Augustine makes this point strongly in a later chapter in *Against Faustus* (XX. ix). Here he gives an extensive catalogue of physical and moral interpretations of the chief pagan gods. At least, he says, the pagans tried to convey some instruction about virtues and vices in these

21. I have used W. M. Lindsay's edition of Isidore's *Etymologies*, 2 vols. (Oxford: Clarendon Press, 1911).

god/meanings. And, although it was damnable to worship such gods, the temptation was certainly not great to worship a moral quality or physical part of the universe. These gods were religiously harmless, and the rationalizing interpretations made them rather laughable as gods. Manichean doctrine, however, is worse in two respects. First, it seriously tempts and invites people to worship as gods the forces of evil. Second, since evil actually implies the absence of being, Faustus and the Manicheans are really worshipping nothing. The pagans simply worshipped false gods, which were not gods but at least were something in the phyiscal and moral interpretations of them.

Augustine also regularly separates the poets and their fabulous accounts of the gods from pagan religion and its worship and explanation of the gods. In the *Against Faustus* passage he does combine them to the disadvantage of the Manicheans (since the poets are writing nothing more than fables), and in the *Confessions* he focuses completely and understandably on the fables of the grammarians and the poets which were not religiously dangerous to him because he knew they were just fables, as opposed to the dangerous Manichean mythology (*Conf.* III. vi).[22] But religion and poetry are separated in Augustine's discussion of the question of who is responsible for the myths about the gods. Augustine invariably answers this question by shifting any blame away from the poets, who simply wrote down the myths as they received them from the organizers and purveyors of the pagan cults (*CD* II. viii and IV. x, xxvi, and xxvii). Understandably for Augustine poetic fables were not the kind of enemy that pagan religions were, but this favorable comparison on the question of responsibility for the origin of myths would appear to be only a mildly ameliorative aspect of a generally bad view of poets, poetry, and drama. Since poetry is empty (*vana*), it is not recommended for education in grammar, vocabulary, or syntax. Homer's fictions represent and endorse bad moral examples, and the Bible is a better pedagogical tool (*Conf.* I. xv–xvii). All kinds of dramatic performances and spectacles (*ludi scaenici*), including tragedy, are bad, as are actors and the profession of acting (*Conf.* III. ii and *CD* I. xxxii). Plato's exclusion of poets and all poetic inventions (*figmenta poetica*) from his ideal commonwealth is to be applauded, as is the similar position of the early Roman republic on poetic fictions (*CD* II. xiv). The pagan theological poets write empty, vain, childish, trifling *fabulae* and *figmenta* (*CD* XVIII. xiv and *On True Religion* I. 1. 99), and

22. My text is the two-volume Loeb *Confessions*, trans. William Watts (London: Heineman, 1912).

all "theatrical and poetic trifles" are to be repudiated in the treatment of the Bible (*True Religion* I. li. 100).

Augustine characteristically casts a highly literal eye on pagan myth and poetry, as opposed to his allegorical eye on Scripture. In agreeing with Varro that the poets misrepresent the true nature of the gods in their fables Augustine applies a strictly literal view which assumes that no allegorical rationalization could possibly be useful or appropriate anyway (*CD* VI. v). Discussing the metamorphoses in the Circe episode in Homer and those in *The Golden Ass,* Augustine takes an excessively literal view which refuses even to consider allegorical or figurative readings and finds the explanation of such phenomena to be literal, actual trickery of demons (*CD* XVIII. xvii–xviii). This literalism, which refuses to see any redeeming truth behind the obscene, the morally improper, or the fabulously impossible in pagan drama and poetry pervades Augustine's writings. The inspiration of the Holy Spirit in the Bible and the Bible's consequently unfailing truthfulness would seem to make the crucial difference in the treatment of biblical as opposed to pagan poetic texts. Only in contrast to the religiously vicious fables of the Manicheans do the rationalizing, allegorical explications of pagan myth have any redeeming features. Even here, however, there is no necessary connection of moral or physical truths with the poetic or religious images said to embody or represent those truths. Augustine makes it pointedly clear that we would be much better off without the fables.

There is one further, important area of discussion, however, in which Augustine implicitly endorses the utility of fiction and fables. That discussion is about the nature of truth and falsity in Book II of the *Soliloquies.* A personified Reason basically teaches Augustine in this interior dialogue that the false exists as some kind of imitation or similitude of the true.[23] The tree in a painting or the face in a mirror is a false tree or a false face, but both are likenesses of a true tree or face. Mimes, comedies, and poems lie but only intend to delight, not to deceive (II. ix. 16), and so are relatively innocuous. The false in paintings and other similar resemblances (*simulacra*) strive to be what they represent and tend to be what they are not (II. ix. 17). Comic poetry, for example, neither has any will to be false nor does it have an inherent appetite to be false (making it dangerous). Rather there is simply the necessity of falsehood imposed on it by the will of the author and the limitation of its own conventions (II. x. 18). The unmistakable

---

23. See especially II. x–xii and the end of II. xxx. The phrases are *similitudo veri* and *imitatio veri.* I have used the translation of the *Soliloquies* in Oates, I, and the Latin text in *PL,* XXXII.

implications are that the various art forms which involve representation demand a harmless form of falsehood in the creative processes of the artist and that consequently, although poets lie, they do not deceive.

Furthermore, these artistic representations have their own true existence. Thus the celebrated actor Roscius in a stage performance can be at the same time a true tragic actor but a false Priam. A true painting of a horse is by definition a false horse. And so Reason makes the important point that it is useful for "some things that they be somewhat false in order that they may be somewhat true." The fable of Daedalus will be a true fable when it represents Daedalus flying (an inherent falsehood), and this fable could not be true unless it were false that Daedalus flew (II. xi. 20).

Augustine has been unwillingly led in this path of reasoning, and he objects that there is no truth or basis for truth in the poetic assertion that Medea flew away in a chariot pulled by winged dragons (II. xi. 19). He quotes the line (from Pacuvius) quoted in Cicero's *De Inventione:* "Gigantic winged snakes, yoked together . . ."[24] There is a hidden sting to Augustine's allusion, at least as far as his argument with Reason is concerned, because Cicero's exemplary quotation illustrates what a fable is, as opposed to history or fiction; and Cicero's definition of the fable is that narrative which records events neither true nor like the truth (*nec verisimiles*). Undaunted by the authority of Cicero, Reason responds that the thought or meaning (*sententia*) contained in the verse is an imitation of truth because false thoughts imitate true ones. It is therefore a *falsa sententia* to say that a stone is silver. To say that a stone is false silver is absurd. But to say that tin is false silver is true. The distinction is between *res* and *verba,* things and words, and Augustine notes that he now sees a great deal of difference between what we say about a subject and the subject itself. Pacuvius's expression, his thought, is therefore false because it imitates a true expression.

In the *Soliloquies,* then, there is an implicit endorsement of the methods of artistic invention and representation. This representation even includes the imitation of true statements in false ones. Augustine concedes that fables, although lying, are intended to be useful in addition to being delightful (II. xi. 19). No mention, however, is made of figurative or allegorical purposes, and this endorsement of the methods of representational art is nonetheless not contradicted by the criticism elsewhere of Homer for portraying bad moral examples. This

24. I have used the Loeb *De Inventione,* trans. H. M. Hubbell (Cambridge, Mass.: Harvard University Press, 1949). The translation here of Cicero's quote (I. xix. 27), however, is mine.

endorsement also agrees with the standard of literalism Augustine regularly applies to pagan fable and fiction, insisting as it does, quite in the attitude of Plutarch, that fiction is openly exemplary, or in the cases of fabulous stories, rationally explicable according to realistic phenomenology (e.g., demons posing as beasts for Circe, while the bodies of the men supposedly transformed lie off somewhere actually asleep or in a trance). It must be remembered, though, that in conjunction with the use of I Corinthians 10:1–11 to illustrate allegory in the Bible, Augustine indicates that the Exodus of the Israelites from Egypt has what appears to be in part exemplary implications for Christians. Paul uses the term *figura* here and Augustine *allegoria*. The figure in this case might be the shape of the example and the allegory of it its other meaning. It is precisely here, where the exemplary and literal merge with the figurative and allegorical, that the problems of literary interpretation become very difficult.

The *figmenta* and *fabulae* of the pagan religions and poets are empty and vain, and the biblical references to *fabula* are unvaryingly negative. Poets may lie, even for useful purposes, being "somewhat false in order to be somewhat true," but the Lord never lies. Nevertheless, *allegoria, parabola, aenigma,* and *paroemia (proverbium)* do overlap and function significantly and importantly in both pagan and Christian interpretation. And even the *fabulae* and *figmenta* of the pagans meet Christian *allegoria* and *figura* in that their methods of functioning are essentially identical, based on *similitudo.* The rule of all allegory is that it is construed *per similitudo,* a cardinal tenet of Augustine's theory of biblical interpretation. The description of God's use of likeness or similarity in *Christian Doctrine* II. vi, where the saints are pleasantly understood from the Song of Solomon as the Church's teeth, cutting away error, would seem to be quite close to Reason's description and definition of *fabula* and *figmentum* in the *Soliloquies,* except that Solomon was not lying when he wrote "Your teeth are like flocks of sheep . . ." (4:2). Somehow all the historical, poetic, prefigurative, prophetic, allegorical, and parabolic teachings of the Bible convey truth by likeness or resemblance, but unlike poetic fables and fictions, which represent or imitate truth in a similar way, they do not lie.

Augustine attacks this problem directly in his two treatises on lying, *De Mendacio* and *Contra Mendacium.*[25] A lie has two fundamental

---

25. I have used the English translations of these two essays in vol. 16 of *The Fathers of the Church* (New York, 1952). *Lying* (pp. 53–110) is translated by Sister Mary Sarah Muldowny and *To Consentius Against Lying* (pp. 125–179) by Harold B. Jaffee. I have referred to the Latin text on which these translations are based in vol. 41 of *Corpus Scriptorum Ecclesiasticorum Latinorum* (Prague, Vienna, and Leipzig, 1900).

characteristics: its desire or intention of deceiving and its false meaning or signification (*significatio*).[26] Augustine is at pains to defend the notion that there are no lies in the Bible. However, there are many apparent examples of lying in the Old Testament, which suggest by force of example that lying is justifiable and possibly recommended in certain situations. In the earlier essay Augustine asserts that no deed or speech which is figurative in meaning is a lie (*Lying* V. 7 and 9). He then proceeds to argue that almost every (*fere omnia*) speech and action in the Old Testament is figurative (XV. 26). Consequently, even though the words and events recorded in the Old Testament did in fact happen, they have no exemplary force at all. Augustine refers here to the Galatians 4:24 and I Corinthians 10 passages for apostolic support in construing historical people and events figuratively rather than in an exemplary way. Exemplary words and deeds, he says, are to be found in the New Testament, especially in the Epistles and Acts of the Apostles (XV. 26 and XXI. 42). Augustine elaborates this point in *Against Lying* (XII. 26), observing that everything in the Epistles and Acts of the Apostles is open, because by that time the mysteries veiled in prophetic figures of the Old Testament had been fulfilled or revealed in Christ and the Church. He adds triumphantly that there are no examples of lying or suggestions to lie in apostolic teaching or deeds.

This distinction is radical and profound, denying an exemplary force to even historically accurate deeds and words when those deeds and words are to be construed figuratively. Augustine fully discusses the example of Jacob's deception of Isaac (*Against Lying* X. 24). Jacob did in fact cover himself with goatskins so that he would feel like Esau to blind Isaac, and he did tell Isaac directly that he was Esau. The "proximate" or immediate cause for this deed was indeed the intention of deceiving his father, and his words to Isaac would "seem" to be a lie. But in fact the deed was done and the words were spoken for another reason, to convey a different meaning or signification which is true. Jacob donning the goatskins is Christ bearing the sins of others, and the verbal appropriation by Jacob of his older brother's identity (and birthright) refers to the Church. Not only was the account of these deeds and words written down to convey this true signification (and hence the text does not lie), but the deed itself was done and the words themselves spoken in order to convey this true signification (and so even the deeds and words are only apparent deceptions). No lie is really intended, then, and Jacob is no example of lying because his deception

---

26. See *Lying* III and *Against Lying* XII. 26. In the latter Augustine defines a lie as "a false signification told with desire to deceive" (Jaffee)—*mendacium est quippe falsa significatio cum uoluntate fallendi.*

and apparent lie convey true signification about Christ and the Church. The text of the Bible here and elsewhere has no intention of lying and only means to convey truth.

In *Against Lying* Augustine also elaborates on the precise status of fable, fiction, parable, and riddle (X. 24 and XII. 26 through XIII. 27). Figurative expressions (*tropicae locutiones*), explicitly including parables, metaphors, and even antiphrasis, do not lie or involve lying (X. 24). Augustine cites two of the standard examples of antiphrasis (*lucus* and *Parcae*; see Diomedes) here, but also gives two biblical examples. In the second passage (XII. 26–XIII. 28) he expands his view to include explicitly secular letters. He defines Jesus' parables with the rhetorical definition of fiction (events "told as if they had been done, although they have not been"; Jaffee), but he does not seem to hold to the traditional distinction separating fiction from fable. To fictitious parables he adds the fables of Aesop, Horace's fables of the mice and the fox and weasel, and the fable of the trees choosing a king in Judges 9:8–15. All these are invented narratives (*ficta narrationes*) which have true meanings (*veraces significationes*) and, like lies of the *Soliloquies,* bear a likeness or resemblance (*similitudo*) to the things signified. The invention leads to and is intended for a true signification and conveys a true meaning. Neither fiction nor fable nor parable nor riddle nor metaphor nor any other figure or figurative expression lies insofar as its purpose is to convey a true meaning and it does convey such a meaning.

In the earlier treatise Augustine does reject the lying fabrications of the conversational storyteller who embellishes his narratives with falsehoods for the purpose of pleasing alone (*Lying* XI. 18). Such lies are harmless to the hearer but harmful to the teller, and such fictionalization is lying, because unlike Jesus' parables or Horace's fables its purpose is not to convey truth but only to delight, and it does not contain true signification. It is easy to see here an echo of Horace's *dulce et utile* and Macrobius's distinction of the fable which only pleases and contains or implies no philosophic truth. Like Plutarch, however, and unlike Macrobius, Augustine insists elsewhere that Homer's fictions are to be read for their exemplary and not allegorical or figurative signification. Judging from the passages in *Against Lying*, from his characteristically literal view of pagan myth and fiction, and from his strongly figurative/allegorical expectation for the Old Testament, Augustine would seem to be accepting Aesop but rejecting Homer, possibly Virgil, and definitely Plautus.

All the same, it would seem that Augustine's view of the Bible is fundamentally the same as Macrobius's view of the Homeric and

Virgilian texts. The respective methods of uncovering truths assumed to be concealed in these texts are also basically similar. Macrobius explains away the behavior of the Olympian deities so offensive to Plutarch and others by reading figuratively and symbolically. Augustine similarly explains away the apparent bad example of Jacob deceiving Isaac as being no example at all but an allegory of Christ and the Church. What is really unusual in Augustine's theory is his insistence on the historical accuracy of the Old Testament accounts. But his insistence on the primacy of the text of the Bible no matter what meanings it literally seems to or does convey is precisely Macrobius's view of Homer and Virgil. For Augustine, though, as is clear from his elaboration of Jacob's deception, it is not only the text of the Bible which is inerrant and totally under divine control (for the purpose of conveying Christian truth and so edifying believers in every syllable) but history itself is under that same providential control. Not only is the account of Hagar and Ishmael and Sarah and Isaac recorded for believers as an allegory of the two covenants and so too the record of Jacob's deception, but according to Augustine, the very events themselves are figuratively motivated. It is unquestionable, I think, that in *Against Lying* Augustine is insisting that not only did Moses write down the story of Jacob's deception as an allegory of Christ and the Church but that Jacob's putting on the goatskins and directly lying to Isaac were divinely and figuratively motivated in the very deed and words themselves. Here, of course, God's sovereign control and man's exercise of his free will paradoxically meet. Somehow Jacob was free to deceive and lie with the intention of deceiving and lying (as Augustine admits), and at the same time God was providentially ordering his deception and lie as an edifying prefiguration of Christ and the Church.

We mistake Augustine's thinking when we try to understand his interpretive methods and subsequent Christian exegesis in terms of the distinction between typology and allegory, between Hebraic fulfillment and Hellenic casting aside of the letter. That distinction is too simplistic and does not accord with his thinking, because historical events in the Old Testament are clearly in these terms both typological and allegorical. Augustine has managed this feat by in effect taking over a pagan method applied to Homeric fiction, and especially Homeric and other myth and fable, and applying it to history in the Old Testament. The remarkable effect here is that, as with Homeric and other pagan fabrications, history itself is stripped of exemplary implication. History becomes divine allegory, and so Old Testament history corresponds directly to rituals under the Old, Mosaic Law which prefigure Christ. Just as each ritual prescription, each ac-

coutrement of the tabernacle, each particular of every festival in the
calendar symbolically relate to, prefigure, and are fulfilled in Christ
and His Church, so the events and words of Old Testament history
function in the same way, a way in which they lose their exemplary
force. David had many wives, but the Christian is not to copy his
example or really consider it an example at all, any more than he is to
continue the sacrificial duties of the Old Law. Israelites had to be
circumcised, but Christians do not, because circumcision had a symbolic significance. The underlying attitude has an overwhelming,
explicit New Testament basis and has, of course, become a commonplace of Christian thought.

What is true for sacred, pre-Christian history is probably not true for
other historical accounts, although Augustine does not see any point in
the recording of historical data simply for the sake of having a record
of events. He assumes that there must be some other, greater purpose.
In fact, it might correctly be said that he thinks the only legitimate
narrative of events and words, historical or fictional, is narrative told
for the purpose of conveying some true significance. This assumption
would seem to exclude the legitimacy of any purely narrative, storytel-
ling motive based on the desire to provide pleasure or delight in the
listener. Clearly, for Augustine, although such fictitious creation is
generally harmless, it is strictly speaking lying and of some harm to the
teller. The intention of conveying a true significance and actually
conveying such significance in biblical history, fable, riddles, and
parables remove them from the category of lies. As for pagan letters,
the beast-fables, satires, parables, and other such unmistakably didactic
stories would also seem to be true and acceptable (as opposed to
mythical stories of gods), leaving the fiction of epic, romance, tragedy,
and comedy in that slippery ground indicated in the *Soliloquies* of lying
somewhat in order to convey somewhat of the truth: "being somewhat
false in order to be somewhat true."

[Before and After Augustine]

St. Augustine's view of pagan myth, religion, and literature is by no
means the only early Christian view. One strikingly different approach
is associated with Christian Gnosticism (2nd cent. A.D.). Rather than
reject pagan allegoresis, this approach accepted pagan *rationes* of the
gods as accurate and legitimate, and the Gnostics seem only to claim for
Christianity a superior system of arriving at true knowledge which, it is
conceded, is also concealed in the images and symbols of ancient,
pagan religions. This elitist understanding, subordinating pagan phi-

losophy and religion to Christianity by a process of patronizing accommodation, is clearly illustrated in *The Stromata or Miscellanies* attributed to Clement of Alexandria (late 2nd century A.D.).[27] Clement deliberately syncretizes the myths, rituals, religion, and philosophy of the ancient Egyptians, Greeks, Hebrews, and modern Christians. The riddles, symbols, and allegories found in the Old Testament are identical in nature with those to be found in Plato, Orpheus, and Euripides. Even the New Testament does not fully reveal the truth, which is completely comprehensible only to the Gnostics. The Bible is relegated to a position, along with other texts secular and religious, artistic and philosophic, of subjection to the necessary revelation of Christian gnosis. If not heretical, this position was definitely, as Jaroslav Pelikan, the historian of Christian doctrine puts it, "outside the mainstream" of the development of Christian doctrine.[28] Speaking from a position somewhat outside what was to become solid Christian orthodoxy, Clement writes:

> All then, in a word, who have spoken of divine things, both Barbarians and Greeks, have veiled the first principles of things and delivered the truth in enigmas, and symbols, and allegories, and metaphors, and such like tropes. (V. iv, p. 449, col. 2).

The aspect of concealment is very strong here; the images resist interpretation except under the elitist attack of the Gnostic.

Clement includes here an interesting theoretical discussion based on three kinds of Egyptian symbolic writing. Literal writing or transcription is imitative—drawing a circle, for example, to represent the sun. A second kind involves the transpositional representation of figurative or symbolic language. Finally, enigmatic or allegorical representation is the most difficult because the concealed truth is farthest removed from the means of representing it. Clement's example is the Egyptian representation of the sun as a beetle, making a ball from ox dung and rolling it in front of him, living half the year underground and half above, and procreating himself by inseminating the ball without benefit of female. The enigma here is a clever physical myth.

---

27. For Clement and other ante-Nicene writers I have used *The Ante-Nicene Fathers: Translations of the Writings of the Fathers down to A.D. 325*, ed. Alexander Roberts and James Donaldson, rev. A. Cleveland Coxe, 8 vols. (New York: Scribners, 1899). The *Stromata* appear in vol. 2. The discussion of these related allegories appears in V. iii–xiv.

28. "Outside the Mainstream" is the title of chapter 2 in Jaroslav Pelikan, *The Emergence of the Catholic Tradition*, vol. 1 in *The Christian Tradition: A History of the Development of Doctrine* (Chicago and London: University of Chicago Press, 1971). Pelikan discusses Christian Gnosticism and Clement, pp. 81–97.

More typical of the Latin West (and possibly the Greek church) are the attacks of Clement of Rome (1st cent. A.D.) and Arnobius (3rd cent. A.D.) against pagan allegoresis. The *Recognitions*, associated (probably incorrectly) with Clement, is known through the Latin translation of Augustine's contemporary, Rufinus (4th–5th cents. A.D.).[29] The viewpoint is consistently euhemeristic in the *Recognitions*. In a discourse with St. Peter, Clement explains the pagan religions (beginning X. xvii). He construes Jupiter and the rest of the pagan gods in a literal/exemplary way, insisting that most of them were wicked magicians whose shrines are not shrines at all but their tombs (X. xxiii–xxv). Like the pagan Cotta in Cicero's *De Natura Deorum* and St. Augustine in *The City of God* Clement attacks the inconsistencies of the interpretations of the myths (X. xxvii). After Peter explains to an incredulous Clement how the pagans could have been so stupid as to worship evil men (euhemeristically transformed into deities), Niceta, another interlocutor, explains pagan allegoresis very fully. Etymology is the principal method and physical *rationes* are the principal results (X. xxix–xxxiv and xl–xli). Still another speaker, Aquila, insists on the myths' literal, moral/exemplary force and rejects physical interpretations as arbitrary afterthoughts. Instead of it being, as the pagans declare, that appropriate truths are concealed under base fables, the case really is that the pagan interpreters have veiled the base and unseemly things of the fable with seemly rationalizations (xxxvi).

The Clementine *Homilies* articulate the same view.[30] In *Homily VI* Clement demonstrates his knowledge of pagan allegoresis to Appion (primarily using etymology, as in xiv). He attacks the perverse idea of veiling truth under evil stories (xvii) and asserts that these enigmas and myths are not only not necessary to the expression of the alleged truths but are in fact positive hindrances, because the myths deceive most men with their literal stories and imitatively encourage immorality (xvii). Wicked men must have invented such wicked stories, and so the interpreters, trying to put a better light on them, are doing a more honorable thing (xviii). However, the "poetical allegories" are still inconsistent (xix).

Book III of Arnobius's *Against the Heathens* launches a learned and devastating attack against pagan *rationes*.[31] The images are idolatrous

---

29. *The Pseudo-Clementine Literature* is contained in vol. 8 of *The Ante-Nicene Fathers*. I have used the Latin text, *S. Clementis Romani Recognitiones*, ed. E. G. Gersdorf (Leipzig, 1838).

30. I have used the English translation in *The Ante-Nicene Fathers*, VIII, and the Greek text, with parallel Latin, ed. Albert Dressell (Göttingen, 1853).

31. Arnobius appears in vol. 6 of *The Ante-Nicene Fathers*. I have used the Latin text, *Arnobii Adversus Nationes Libri VII*, ed. Augustus Reifferscheid, in *Corpus Scriptorum Ecclesiasticorum*, IV (Vienna, 1875; rpt. New York: Johnson, 1968).

(III. iii). Both theologians and poets have formulated vile stories (xi). The accounts are inconsistent (xxix). If the so-called gods are physical/cosmological parts of the universe, then they are no gods at all (xxix–xxxiv). The myths are contradictory anyway (xxxvii). Moreover the personifications of Piety, Concord, Honor, and the like are absurd (IV. i–iv). Augustine's literal, euhemeristic reading of pagan myth, then, seems to be a rather solid Christian position by the fourth century A.D. It denies veiled meanings to pagan fables and insists that they must be evaluated in a literal/exemplary way.

The most interesting of these pre-Augustinian positions in the Latin West is that of Lactantius (3rd–4th cents. A.D.), whose discussion of pagan religion and poetry in *The Divine Institutes* is unusually comprehensive, particularly in its attention to theoretical matters, and, I believe, extremely influential on subsequent thought about poetic fiction and allegory.[32] Lactantius attacks the inconsistencies of pagan fables (I. xi), and his view is overwhelmingly euhemeristic. He explains his euhemerism in detail, however, and the result is something which twentieth-century critics would probably call historical allegory. Like Arnobius he does not use the term allegory for the processes of meaning in pagan myth, but the terms he does use and the way he uses them are significant.

In Book I, "On False Religion," Lactantius first posits (in accordance with Romans 1:19–23) that even the pagans knew there was one God who governed all things. In granting that some of the pagan poets express the truth, Lactantius insists on literal/discursive reference much in the manner of Plutarch. Refusing to allegorize, he denies that either Homer or Hesiod expressed divine truth. Homer wrote about human affairs only, and Hesiod shrank from expressing the obvious (I. v)! In the lengthy discussion which follows (I. vii–xviii) the pagan gods are euhemeristically represented as being really men, and their exploits are to be judged in a literal/exemplary way. But these exploits are concealed under the fictional cover of the details of the poet's fables, which transform humans and human deeds into gods and divine actions. Parts of the fables therefore are accurate, but the rest is invented by the poet-storytellers. This poetic process involves feigning, fictionalizing, coloring, pretending, oblique fashioning, figuring, and obscure imaging. The poetic feigning resides in pretending that men were gods and writing about them as if they were divine. This coloring or obscuring is the very basis of poetic creation for Lactantius and involves a figurative misrepresentation or half-lie:

---

32. *The Divine Institutes* is in vol. 7 of *The Ante-Nicene Fathers*. For the Latin I have used the two-volume edition of J. L. Bünemann, *Opera Omnia* (Leipzig, 1739).

> It is the business of the poet with some gracefulness to change and
> transfer actual occurrences into other representations by oblique trans-
> formations (officium poetae in eo sit, ut ea, quae vere gesta sunt, in
> aliquas species obliquis figurationibus cum decore aliquo conversa
> traducat [I. xi. 24]). Nothing, therefore is wholly invented by the poets;
> something perhaps is transferred and obscured by oblique fashioning,
> under which the truth was enwrapped and concealed (Non igitur a poetis
> totum fictum est, aliquid fortasse traductum, et obliqua figuratione
> obscuratum, quo veritas inuoluta tegeretur [I. xi. 30]).
> Thus they so veiled the truth under a fiction, that the truth itself
> detracted nothing from the public persuasion (I. xi. 31–32).

Lactantius describes explicitly how this half-lying coloring works; the
surface details of the fable allude to and hint at the true human story
behind and covered by the fable. Lactantius gives many examples:
Ganymede, fabled to have been carried off by an eagle, was in actuality
stolen away by a legion with an eagle for its standard or on a boat with
the effigy of an eagle at its prow; Jupiter did not really turn into a bull,
because he was actually a man. He snatched Europa away on a ship with
the image of a bull on the prow.

In summarizing the *Institutes* in his *Epitome* Lactantius makes the
same point about poetic fiction in a comprehensive, clear way:

> This is not the usage of the poets to feign in such a manner that you
> fabricate the whole, but so that you cover the actions themselves with a
> figure, and, as it were, with a variegated veil. Poetic license has this limit,
> not that it may invent the whole, which is the part of one who is false and
> senseless, but that it may change something consistently with reason.
> (Non est hoc poeticum sic fingere, vt totum mentiare, sed vt ea, quae
> gesta sunt, figura et quasi velamine aliquo versicolore praetexas. Hunc
> habet poetica licentia modum, non vt totum fingat, quod est mendacis et
> inepti, sed vt aliquid cum ratione commutet [XI].)

Poetry itself, then, becomes associated with euhemeristic transforma-
tion of actual human events into something else, combining the true
and actual with false coloring, which it is the business of the poet to
invent. Trimpi remarks on this poetic coloring and the roughly
synonymous terms *figure, figment, figuration,* being associated with the
literal text as far as Christian interpretation of Scripture is concerned,
allegory being reserved for the Bible and truly hidden meanings.[33]

This Lactantian definition of the "business of the poet" is picked up
by probably the most influential post-Augustinian discussion of myth

---

33. "The Quality of Fiction," pp. 73–75.

and fiction, that by Isidore (7th cent. A.D.) in his *Etymologies.* Via Isidore
it also appears in the subsequent encyclopedic compendia by Rabanus
(*De Universo,* 9th cent. A.D.) and Vincent (*Speculum Quadruplex,* 13th
cent. A.D.).[34] Isidore's discussion "Of the Poets" takes up a long and
important chapter (vii) in Book VIII ("On the Church and the Sects")
and follows a discussion of the pagan philosophers. Poetry originated
in the praise of gods. Tragic poets subsequently excelled in inventing
plots for the image of the truth ("tragici . . . excellentes in argumentis
fabularum ad veritatis imaginem fictis" [vii. 5]). After mentioning
writers of comedy and satire Isidore refers to the theological poets, so
called because they wrote about the gods, and inserts the Lactantian
definition of the "business of the poet" almost verbatim:

> Officium autem poetae in eo est ut ea, quae vere gesta sunt, in alias
> species obliquis figurationibus cum decore aliquo conversa transducant
> (vii. 10).

Isidore immediately concludes that Lucan was a historian and not a
poet ("Vnde et Lucanus ideo in numero poetarum non ponitur, quia
videtur historias conposuisse, non poema"). Commenting on this appropriation from Lactantius and the non-Lactantian reference to
Lucan, Curtius says:

> Isidore, as we see, took this doctrine of Lactantius' over word for word,
> but at the same time combined it with the antique criticism of Lucan, and
> thus gave it a meaning which it did not have in the context of Lactantius'
> rationalistic mythological interpretation.[35]

Curtius is probably mistaken here, because Lactantius is referring to
the essence of writing poetry and not merely a special kind of rationalizing interpretation of myth.[36] Lucan's *Civil War* discards the Olympian deities in Homer and Virgil. Although Lucan's style is persistently
hyperbolic and although he emphasizes unusual, grotesque, and
highly improbable details in his narrative, he has none of the super-
natural background found in Homer and Virgil. The historical facts of
Pompey, Caesar, and the Senate are narrated in a flamboyant way but

---

34. See *De Universo* XV. ii, *PL* CXI, 419–20, and *Speculum Doctrinale* III. cx in *Speculum
Quadruplex sive Speculum Maius* (Douai, 1624; facs. rpt. Graz, 1965), II, 288.

35. Ernst Robert Curtius, *European Literature and the Latin Middle Ages,* trans. Willard R.
Trask (1953; rpt. New York: Harper, 1963), p. 454.

36. I made the same mistake some years ago, criticizing D. W. Robertson, Jr., for giving
a broad significance to this comment rather than the narrower one relating to Lucan,
"Some Kinds of Meaning in Old English Poetry," *Annuale Mediaevale,* 11 (1970), 8 (note
10). I think now that Robertson was basically right.

they are not, in terms of Lactantius's euhemeristic definition, transformed by poetic coloring or figuring combining the false and invented with the true in an obscure veiling of the historically true. Hence Isidore's remark about Lucan and the argument over whether his epic is poetry or mere versified history is eminently appropriate in conjunction with Lactantius's definition of poetry as the result of invented coloring of the true with the false.

Isidore's discussion a few chapters later of the pagan gods (VIII. xi) is thoroughly euhemeristic in orientation. The myths are invented (*fingo, ficta*) and are *fabulae,* but never allegory. Isidore notes that the pagans "try to transfer some of the names of their gentile gods by means of empty fables to physical meanings [*rationes physicas*], and these are interpreted as if they had been composed for the sake of the elements" (xi. 29). With that caveat Isidore demonstrates that he knows many such attempts. Beginning with Saturn as Chronos, time devouring his children, he records a number of physical explanations which, contrary to Augustine, he blames totally on the pagan poets (xi. 29). Interspersed, too, are frequent euhemeristic readings.

Although these physical explanations are based on empty fables, they are clearly not a threat to Christian doctrine in the ways that earlier generations of Christian apologists viewed them. Tragic fables have an image of the truth (VIII. vii. 5), and so do fables of the Aesopian variety, which represent an image of human life (I. xl. 1). In his grammatical discussion of the fable (I. xl) Isidore simply admits that some fables express "the nature of things" (xl. 4). His first example is a commonplace physical interpretation of pagan myth, lame Vulcan as fire (4). Earlier in his grammar (based on Diomedes, Donatus, and others) Isidore cites Vulcan/fire (from *Aeneid* IX. 76) as an example of metonymy (xxxvii. 9).[37] In addition to natural truths some fables express moral truths about living (*ad mores*). Horace's fables of the mice and of the weasel and the fox, Aesop's fables, and the fable of the trees desiring a king in Judges 9 (precisely the group in Augustine) are all examples and all express a "true signification" (*verax significatio*), as in Augustine, through their "fictitious narrative" (*narratio ficta*), xl. 6–15. Also conforming to St. Augustine is the position that the dramatic fables of Plautus and Terence were composed merely for pleasure and have no significant implications for moral or natural philosophy (xl.

---

37. See Coulter, *The Literary Microcosm,* for the origin of this particular symbolic/allegorical interpretation in Homeric criticism (pp. 66–67).

3).[38] Even when these implications do exist in fables, they are not identified in this context as figurative or allegorical.

As with other Christian writers, allegory is primarily in the Bible. Isidore's popular and influential little summary of some of the chief allegories in the Bible (*Allegoriae Quaedam Sacrae Scripturae*) is particularly interesting for its treatment of the basic meanings in the New Testament.[39] All the usual Old Testament interpretations are there with the usual terms. Adam is a *figura* of Christ (3). Eve designates the Church *per mysterium* (4). Enoch, the son of Cain, signifies (*significat*) the impious (7). Seth, whose name is interpreted resurrection (using etymology), shows (*demonstrat*) Christ (8). Noah, meaning rest, is primarily a *similitudo* of the Lord in whom the Church rests (12). Nimrod expresses a type of the Devil (17), and *type* and *figure* are the favorite terms. In the section on the New Testament not only are the chief parables interpreted mainly in terms of the Church (the wise man who builds his house upon the rock signifies the faithful teacher who grounds his teaching solidly in Christ, and the foolish man who builds his house on sand is the heretic who is established in false doctrine, 148–49), but even the historical characters and events are allegorized. The Virgin Mary and Martha both signify the Church (139 and 207). The Magi figure the gentiles (142), and so does Zacchaeus (226). Lazarus signifies the world (241). Barabbas signifies Antichrist (244), and the women who announced the resurrection of Jesus to the Apostles are understood to be the law and the prophets (*lex et prophetia intelliguntur*, 249).

Isidore explains in *Etymologies* VI. i ("On the Old and New Testament") that both Testaments have *historia, mores,* and *allegoria* (11). Although biblical history, including New Testament history, is regularly allegorized and moralized very much in accordance with Augustine's idea that no historical events are worth recording unless there are some greater implications to be found in them or in the record of them, secular history is apparently not to be allegorized and is to be read in a literal/exemplary way (*Etymologies* I. xli–xliv). Furthermore, historical events are significant in themselves (xli. 2 and xliii), and the record of

---

38. In Book XVIII Isidore surveys all sorts of theatrical and dramatic productions. Comic writers are said to treat the private lives of ordinary men and to depict "the debauchery of virgins and the loves of prostitutes" ("Comoedi sunt qui privatorum hominum acta dictis aut gestu cantabant, atque stupra virginum et amores meretricum in suis fabulis exprimebant," xlv). Obviously there is not much edification here in contrast to the fables of Aesop and Horace.

39. *PL,* LXXXIII, 99–130.

past deeds is useful for the exemplary instruction of the present
generation (xliii).

Isidore's discussion of tropes in his grammar includes the standard
discussion of allegory which he found in Diomedes and Donatus (I.
xxxvii). His first example of the trope allegory, the three deer/Punic
Wars, based on *Aeneid* I. 184, has already been discussed. He also
quotes "I have sent ten golden apples" (*Eclogues* III. 71) as an example,
in which the speaker, Menalcas/Virgil, is supposed to be referring to
ten eclogues sent to Augustus.[40] In distinguishing the species enigma
from general allegory Isidore notes that a riddle has only one meaning
which is simply concealed by obscure images, but allegory has two
meanings, a twofold thrust, *vis gemina*, conveying one satisfactiory
(open) meaning and another concealed meaning. Here Isidore's elaboration of Diomedes and Donatus seems to reflect Christian, Augustinian allegorical explication of the Bible with its twofold position
(consistently expressed in Isidore's *Allegoriae Quaedam*) of the validity
of historical fact *and* other meaning. Lazarus is Lazarus, a real man,
who lived and breathed and died and was raised from the dead by
Christ. Without denying the historical validity of these events Lazarus
is also the world.

As in Diomedes, *paroemia* for Isidore "is the adaptation of a proverb
to events and times" (28). Understanding the implication intended in
this species of allegory clearly involves recognition by the interpreter of
the application intended by the speaker or writer. This question of the
open-endedness of possibly analogical applications as opposed to the
closed nature of specifically focused applications arises in Isidore's
discussion of homoeosis or *similitudo* (I. xxxvii. 31–35), which is also
heavily dependent on Diomedes and Donatus. Basically *similitudo* is a
technique of emphasis and illustration by analogy. Something less
known is vividly delineated or demonstrated by its resemblance or
relationship to something better known. One species, *icon* or *imago*,
compares similar things, e.g., Aeneas to Mercury (an example in
Diomedes and Isidore). Parabolic comparisons on the other hand join
basically dissimilar things. Paradigm or *exemplum*, like *paroemia*, is the
application of something said or done to the subject at hand and so is
analogically controlled and closed (Diomedes does not explicitly indicate this control as Isidore does).

---

40. Servius knows this allegorical interpretation and rejects it in his note to this line.
Well he might, since Menalcas says he has sent ten apples to his boyfriend today and is
going to send ten more tomorrow (11. 70–71). It probably occurred to the sensible
Servius that Augustus would not be flattered by being represented as the poet's sweet
little boyfriend.

Later in the *Etymologies,* surveying the books of the Bible, Isidore returns to this question of analogies in conjunction with the three books by Solomon, Proverbs, Ecclesiastes, and Song of Solomon. Obviously influenced by the Septuagint and Jerome's Vulgate, Isidore asserts that the equivalent Greek term for the Hebrew is *parabola* and the Latin *proverbium,* "because in it [the book of Proverbs] under a comparative similitude he [Solomon] made known figures of words and images of truth" (VI. ii. 18). Isidore further notes that although the teachings in the book of Proverbs are directed particularly at individual questions, the speech in Ecclesiastes is directed generally to universal conditions of life:

> Ecclesiastes dicitur, Latine Contionator, eo quod sermo eius non specialiter ad unum, sicut in Proverbiis, sed ad universos generaliter dirigatur, docens omnia, quae in mundo cernimus, caduca esse et brevia, et ob hoc minime adpetenda (ii. 19).

Indeed the Proverbs of Solomon are usually rather narrow in scope and directed to specific kinds of attitudes, people, and events.

A little later in Book VI, discussing parts of books and kinds of discourse in them and about them, Isidore returns to *parabolae* in conjunction with *problemata* (VI. viii. 13). The names of these, he says, indicate that they must be examined carefully, although he admits that in a parable the analogous similitude is open and obvious ("Parabola quippe alicuius rei similitudinem prae se gerit"). Problems, or propositions in Latin, are questions to be solved in disputation. The significant point here, though, is that Isidore consistently sees parables and proverbs as having two parts, statement and application. The application of a proverb (*paroemia*) will presumably be appropriate, and the analogy implied or stated in the telling of a parable will be a more or less effectively "vivid illustration."

Less than a century after Isidore's death Bede (7th–8th cents. A.D.) wrote a work on metrics and figurative language after the models of Diomedes, Donatus, and Book I of the *Etymologies.* In Book II, *On Schemes and Tropes,* instead of Isidore's mainly classical/pagan/poetic examples along with an occasional one drawn from the Bible, Bede relies exclusively on the Bible for examples.[41] Consequently *On Schemes*

---

41. The Latin, ed. C. B. Kendall, appears in Bede's *Opera Didascalica,* in *Corpus Christianorum* (Turnhout: Brepols, 1975), CXXIIIa, 142–171. With this excellent text is printed a commentary by Remigius of Auxerre on Bede's *De Arte Metrica* and *De Schematibus et Tropis* ed. M. H. King. I have used the well-known English translation by Gussie Hecht Tannenhaus, reprinted from the *Quarterly Journal of Speech* in *Readings in*

and Tropes provides not only another rather influential Christian version of classical grammar but also a total incorporation of classical grammatical/rhetorical commonplaces about allegory and related figures into an explicitly Christian context of the Bible. The gloss on it by Remigius of Auxerre (9th cent. A.D.) is also illuminating. "Allegory," Bede writes, according to the standard formula, "is the trope by which something is signified other than what is said" (II ["De Tropis"]. xii). His general example is from John 4:35, where Jesus tells his disciples, "Lift up your eyes, and look on the fields; for they are white already to harvest" (KJV), meaning, as Bede explains, for the disciples to look around them at the people who are ready to be converted and harvested, as it were, for the kingdom of God. Here, as in the classical definitions, is the same question of implied application of the statement. The scene in John is at a well outside a city in Samaria. The woman Jesus talked to at the well has already returned and told her fellow citizens about Jesus, and as Jesus makes the remark to his disciples, apparently the entire population is streaming out to see and hear him. The disciples had meanwhile just suggested that Jesus have something to eat, as they pause at the well (4:31). Their suggestion apparently prompts this and several similar allegorical remarks by Jesus, but the understanding of the particular statement Bede cites depends on making the application of a field of grain ready for harvest to the oncoming crowd of Samaritans (John does not indicate whether the disciples understood or not).

As an example of irony Bede cites Elijah's mocking of the priests of Baal, who in the famous contest with Elijah frantically call on Baal, without success, miraculously to set on fire a sacrificial altar. In the passage Bede quotes (I Kings 18:27) Elijah urges the priests to call even louder, since Baal, who is (ironically) a god, must be talking to someone else, relieving himself in private, or be off on a journey. For irony of expression (antiphrasis) Bede cites Jesus' welcome of Judas, coming to betray Him, with the word "friend" (Matthew 26:50).

Bede's definition of enigma is close to Isidore's. Enigma, he says, "is the expression of an obscure meaning by means of a hidden similitude of things" ("Enigma est obscura sententia per occultam similitudinem rerum," as compared to Isidore's "aenigma vero sensus tantum obscurus est, et per quasdam imagines adumbratus"). His example is

---

Medieval Rhetoric, ed. Joseph M. Miller, Michael H. Prosser, and Thomas W. Benson (Bloomington: Indiana University Press, 1973), pp. 96–122. However, unless specifically indicated, the translations here are my own, because Tannenhaus's English is usually not close enough to the precise sense of Bede's Latin diction and syntax for my purposes.

the phrase "the wings of a dove covered with silver, and her feathers with yellow gold" (KJV) from Psalm 68:13, for which Bede suggests two possible interpretations. One of these had already been developed by Augustine in a rather long discussion of the whole verse (but not identifying the phrase as an enigma),[42] but neither of Bede's suggestions seems to relate to the poetic context of the psalm. The phrase is indeed obscure, though, and Remigius significantly notes that the meaning is said to be hidden because the divine *sensus* lies underneath—thus making enigma indistinguishable from any other biblical allegory (p. 162).

Like the grammarians Bede defines *paroemia* as the application of a *proverbium* to times and events. He quotes two exemplary passages from the Bible and then describes how they are to be applied. The proverbial dog returning to his own vomit (II Peter 2:22) is applied to a person backsliding into sin after he has already done penance for it. This pattern explicitly determines the way Peter applies the proverb (*proverbium* in the Vulgate translating the Greek *paroimia*) in 2:20–22. The application of an Old Testament adage is similarly illustrated. Bede further notes that the Latins call Solomon's book Parables (*parabolas*) "after the Hebrew," while the Greeks keep the "name Paroemiae, that is Proverbs" (*nomen Paroemiarum, hoc est, Prouerbiorum*). Neither Bede nor Isidore, however, comes close to discussing the full complexity of the connections and distinctions between *parabola* and *paroemia* in the Vulgate.

Bede does go on to discuss homoeosis and its three species, icon, parable, and example. Before he does, however, he adds something more and entirely new in this grammatical context about the trope allegory. "It doubtless ought to be noted," he writes, "that allegory occurs sometimes only with deeds, at others only with words" ("Notandum sane quod allegoria aliquando factis, aliquando uerbis tantummodo fit," p. 164). In the lengthy exposition which follows (pp. 164–69), Bede at least once substitutes "work" (*opus*) for *factum* (p. 166). His first example of "factual allegory" (Tannenhaus) is Galatians 4:22, the two sons of Abraham and the two covenants. Verbal allegory is in Isaiah's reference to the branch out of the root of Jesse (i.e., Christ). The next examples pointedly contrast texts with the same allegorical meaning. Bede quotes the historical record of Joseph's being sold to the Ishmaelites for twenty pieces of silver and then quotes as verbal allegory the poetic remark in the prophet Zechariah, "they weighed for my price thirty pieces of silver" (11:12). Bede does not even explain the

42. *Enarrationes in Psalmos, Corpus Christianorum*, XXXIX, 879–81.

obvious allegorical references in both the factual and verbal passages to Christ being sold, although Remigius does in his commentary. So far Bede's meaning is perfectly obvious: sometimes actual events and sometimes words in the Bible have allegorical implications.

Bede significantly continues, though, to distinguish the allegory of historical, typical, moral, and anagogical senses. Two of these distinctions are important; one associates types with allegory and the other separates history from the literal sense. "Also," he writes, "allegory of word or work figuratively declares sometimes a historical meaning, sometimes typical, sometimes tropological, that is, a moral concern, sometimes anagogical, that is, the sense leading to things above" ("Item allegoria uerbi siue operis aliquando historicam rem, aliquando typicam, aliquando tropologicam, id est, moralem rationem, aliquando anagogen, hoc est, sensum ad superiora ducentem figurate denuntiat.")[43] Bede proceeds to give examples of verbal and factual allegory for each of these four categories. Jacob's coat of many colors is factual and morally signifies the virtues God bestows on man. Living the righteous, moral life is verbally indicated by the Lord's remark, "Let your loins be girded about, and your lights burning" (KJV, Luke 12:35). The fact that Enoch, the seventh descendant from Adam, was translated out of this world anagogically means that there will be a Sabbath of bliss and rest for believers at the end of time after the six ages of their good works. Jesus refers verbally to the same gathering of the saints at the end of time when He says, "For wheresoever the carcase is, there will be eagles be gathered together" (KJV, Matthew 24:28).

These moral and anagogical senses are straightforward. The typical is more difficult, and the historical is the most interesting and significant. Remigius glosses the typical as meaning figurative (*TYPICAM id est figuratam*), but Bede himself uses the adjective *spiritalis*, spiritual, and gives only a verbal example. When Jacob blessed Judah, he said, "Judah is a lion's whelp: from the prey, my son, thou art gone up" (KJV, Genesis 49:9). Spiritually, Bede says, this can be construed as referring to the passion and resurrection of Jesus. After the individual examples of each of the four categories Bede calls this the mystical sense, which refers to Christ or the Church: "myticus de Cristo siue ecclesia sensus" (p. 168).

The historical sense is itself allegorical: "For example, history is figured through history [i.e., fact], when the creation of the first six or seven days is compared with the same number of ages of it [i.e., of the

43. Tannenhaus's translation is not trustworthy here.

history of the world]" (p. 166). Jacob's verbal reference to Judah as a lion's whelp going up with his prey refers through historical allegory to the triumphs of David. Historical allegory, then, is still allegory. When Bede continues to discuss the occurrence of all four senses (*sensus*) in one and the same event (*res*) or word, the historical sense is still conveyed allegorically and is not itself the literal sense. "Sometimes," Bede writes, "in one and the same event or word are figuratively indicated history together with the mystical sense about Christ or the Church and tropology and anagogy" (p. 168).[44] "The temple of the Lord," he continues, illustrating with an example, "according to history is the house which Solomon built." According to allegory it is the body of Christ or the Church. According to tropology it is the body of a believing Christian, and according to anagogy it signifies the life of believers with God in heaven. Summarizing his example Bede broadens the historical allegory to refer to "the citizens of the earthly Jerusalem" (p. 169), thereby emphasizing the disconnection between historical and literal senses.

But another tradition does the opposite, associating history and literalness. It is evident in Remigius's gloss, which does explicitly connect history and the letter (pp. 166, 1. 236, and 167, 1. 252), and is outlined in the familiar description of medieval allegoresis in Emile Mâle's *Gothic Image*. Mâle uses the similar example of Jerusalem to illustrate how the medieval mind went about allegorizing.[45] Here a connection is implied between the literal sense and history, a connection emphasized in Mâle's note on the same page (139), which quotes the little distich attributed to Nicholas of Lyre (13th–14th cents. A.D.):

> Littera gesta docet, quid credas allegoria,
> Moralis quid agas, quo tendas anagogia.

Mâle may have gotten this distich from the three prologues to the *Glossa Ordinaria* (12th–13th cents. A.D.) attributed to Nicholas of Lyre in Migne.[46] The first and third quote these lines, and the first two explicitly identify the literal with the historical sense (cols. 28C, also using Jerusalem as an example, and 31D); the long, later "Additiones" make the same explicit connection and quote the two lines again (col. 38B).

Although the letter is also distinguished from history in these four

---

44. Tannenhaus has simply mistranslated this sentence (*Readings*, p. 120).
45. *The Gothic Image: Religious Art in France in the Thirteenth Century*, trans. Dora Nussey from the 3rd French ed. (1913; rpt. New York: Harper, 1958), p. 139.
46. *PL*, CXIII, 25–36.

prefatory pieces, the third rule of interpretation in the second essay posits that under one and the same letter there is both a historical sense and a mystical or spiritual sense (col. 31D). But the relevant passage in the first prologue explains the necessity of the connection between history and the literal sense. It claims for Scripture, as the early Christian apologists did, the unique capacity for containing more than one sense in one literal statement because of God's authorship (28C), and it connects the letter with history and the other three senses with the spiritual. The explanation is unusually clear and is an excellent statement of the theory of later medieval biblical exegesis.

> Nevertheless this book [the Bible] is unique, because one literal passage contains many senses. The reason is that God Himself is the principal author of this book. He has the power not only to use words [*voces*] to signify something (since human beings, too, can and do do this), but He also uses the things [*res*] signified by the words to signify other things. Therefore it is common to all books to signify something with words, but this book is unique in that the things signified by the words [in it] signify something else. According to the first signification, then, which comes from the words, the literal or historical sense is to be understood. But according to the other signification, which occurs by means of the things themselves, the mystical or spiritual sense is understood, which is usually threefold — because, if the thing signified by the words is referred to the signification of the things which should be believed in the new law, then the allegorical sense is to be understood; but if they are referred to those things which ought to be done by us, then this is the moral or tropological sense; and if they are referred to the signification of those things which are to be hoped for in the blessed future, then that is the anagogical sense (this is so-called from *anagō,* which means, "I raise up") — whence the verses:
>
> > The letter teaches deeds, allegory what you should believe,
> > The moral what you should do, anagogy where you are going.[47]

This explanation is basically repeated at the beginning of the third prologue (33C–D), which goes on to discuss the position of parables. If the mystical or spiritual senses of Scripture are unique and involve a double signification which separates the Bible from all other writing,

---

47. "Habet tamen iste liber hoc speciale quod una littera continet plures sensus. Cujus ratio est quia principalis hujus libri auctor est ipse Deus: in cujus potestate est non solum uti vocibus ad aliquid significandum (quod etiam homines facere possunt et faciunt), sed etiam rebus significatis per voces utitur ad significandum alias res: et ideo commune est omnibus libris, quod voces aliquid significent, sed speciale est huic libro quod res significatae per voces aliud significent. Secundum igitur primam significationem, quae est per voces, accipitur sensus litteralis seu historicus: secundum vero aliam sig-

what about parables, since they are common to other writings? Nicholas gets into this discussion by noting that in some places there is only a literal sense, as in the command in Deuteronomy: " 'Listen, Israel, the Lord your God is one Lord. Love the Lord your God with your whole heart' " (33D–34B). This and all similar passages do not require a mystical sense. Nicholas then refers to the parable of the trees choosing a king in Judges 9 and to Jesus' remark that if your right hand offends, cut it off (Matthew 5:30). Such passages are not to be construed literally, because if they were, the Bible would lie, since trees cannot really appoint a king nor did Jesus mean one should literally cut off his hand. By the trees are understood the citizens of Shechem, who made Abimelech king over them, as is explained in Judges 9, and Jesus meant by hand the friend who tries to lead us into an immoral life and whom we should cut off from communiction. Consequently, in parabolic passages the Bible has only a mystical sense and no literal sense at all—"but in these there is only the mystical sense, which is understood by means of the things signified" (34C). Nicholas adds, however, that "some doctors say the parabolic sense is literal."

> This is understood broadly speaking, because where there is no sense signified by the words, the parabolic is first; and therefore broadly speaking it is called literal in that the literal is first when there is no other: and to this signification they themselves [some doctors] say the parabolic is contained under the literal; I, too, speaking this way, have called the parabolic sense literal in many places when writing on the books of Holy Scripture. (34C–D)

With this quibble Nicholas claims parabolic meanings for the domain of uniquely spiritual meanings available only in the Bible. Bede simply discusses parable, icon, and paradigm in the standard grammatical way as three species of homoeosis (xiii), using, of course, obvious biblical examples, but in precisely the way Diomedes, Donatus, and Isidore use pagan examples.

---

nificationem, quae est per ipsas res, accipitur sensus mysticus seu spiritualis, qui est triplex in generali; quia si res significatae per voces referantur ad significandum ea quae sunt in nova lege credenda, sic accipitur sensus allegoricus; si autem referantur ad significandum ea quae per nos sunt agenda, sic est sensus moralis vel tropologicus; si autem referantur ad significandum ea quae sunt speranda in beatitudine futura, sic est sensus anagogicus. Et dicitur ab ἀνάγω quod est sursum tollo. Unde versus:

> Littera gesta docet, quid credas allegoria,
> Moralis quid agas, quo tendas anagogia." (col. 28C–D)

See the article by Anthony Nemetz on double signification, "Literalness and the *Sensus Litteralis*," *Speculum*, 34 (1959), 76–89.

Between the eighth-century Bede and the fourteenth-century Nicholas, Hugh of St. Victor's influential twelfth-century *Didascalicon* distinguishes the letter and history but explains the heuristic value of identifying the literal sense of any narrative as its historical sense [48] (a connection already made in the ninth-century commentary by Remigius on Bede). Hugh distinguishes only three kinds of meaning in Scripture, history, allegory, and tropology. He recommends the study of history first, and in reiterating the commonplace that the New Testament reveals what the Old Testament figuratively conceals, he makes the obvious but very important point that until the truths and fulfillments of prophecy actually occurred in historical time and were recorded in the New Testament the figurative mysteries of the Old Testament could not have been understood (VI. vi., p. 146). Hugh also gives an answer different from Nicholas to the problem of parables, fables, and other literal impossiblities in the text of the Bible. He distinguishes three discrete aspects of meaning; the letter (i.e., the words); sense or literal meaning (*sensus*); and *sententia* (Taylor translates "deeper meaning"), VI. viii–xi. Every text has at least two and sometimes three of these aspects operative—always the second and/or third in conjunction with the indispensable first. When the obvious or literal sense (*sensus*) is inadequate, seems absurd, or has no obviously clear meaning, then the deeper meaning is to be searched for. The *sententia* is never absurd, false, or inadequate. And so for those texts in the Bible where the obvious meaning is a problem, there is in effect no *sensus* at all, only a hidden *sententia* (p. 149).

[Conclusions]

Christianity obviously continued and modified classical, pagan ideas about allegory and various kinds of nonliteral other meanings. One important modification is the more emphatic separation of allegory into two kinds. In one kind there are two meanings, a satisfactory literal or historical sense to which is added some other meaning. The second kind in effect has only one meaning. In the first kind the second, added sense frequently involves historical sequence—Abel as prefiguration of Christ or the three Virgilian deer as symbolic foreshadowings of the

---

48. *The Didascalicon of Hugh of St. Victor,* trans. Jerome Taylor (New York: Columbia University Press, 1961). V. ii distinguishes three kinds of meaning in Scripture, history, allegory, and tropology (pp. 120–21). As in Bede, history here is not equivalent to the letter. However in VI. iii Hugh discusses the convenient, broad use of the term *history* to refer to the literal sense or obvious meaning of words (pp. 137–38).

three Punic Wars — but sequence does not appear to be a necessary trait (e.g., Lazarus as the world). These two senses may involve history or fiction. Historical fact and literally satisfactory fictional event may have allegorical other-meaning. The second kind of one-meaning allegory is more a category of emphasis than a philosophical description. It can be seen in Isidore's definition of enigma, contrary to that of Diomedes where the riddle has only one meaning. And for Augustine, Hugh, and Nicholas parabolic, fabulous, and proverbial locutions in the Bible do not lie, because in effect they have only one meaning — the truth spiritually, mystically, figuratively, or allegorically implied.

The Christian distinction of allegory of words and allegory of facts, deeds, or things is closely related to but does not perfectly reflect these two kinds of allegory. Riddles, fables, and poetic images are verbal and relate to one-meaning allegory, but parabolic fiction, in order to avoid the charge of lying, is also one-meaning. The most complex parabolic or fabulous story, then, may be one-meaning. Even biblical history, when it is unedifying, has only one meaning, although the historical facts do somehow remain historical facts (Jacob's lie). The status of fabulous, parabolic, fictional events remains cloudy in Christian theory, but these probably belong to *verba* and not *res*. Whether *res* or *verba*, the real problem is with their significance, exemplary in one case, literally exemplary and with an added allegorical significance in another, and not exemplary at all but with figurative one-meaning in still another. The same can be said of history, though, where the events, if not always the record of them, are *res*; they may be one-meaning, looking through the events to the real significance, or two-meaning, with literal/exemplary implications and an allegorical significance.

There is in Augustine, Bede, Hugh (V. iii), and Nicholas a clear preference for allegory of things or deeds. This is the allegory of a sovereign God, manipulating and controlling history in prophetically symbolic ways for the edification of later, Christian generations. God not only inspired the writing down of Old Testament history, but He orchestrated the events themselves. Mere words and verbal allegory could be employed by mortals, but only God can order the events of history so as to convey symbolic meaning. In this sense the *res* of biblical allegory could never relate to the deeds and events in secular fiction, which are by contrast human and verbal, and so the writer's intention comes very much into question.

Although the allegory of words and things does not bear very pointedly on the question of concealment, the categories of one-meaning and two-meaning allegorical discourse do. Clearly the obscurity or concealment of a riddle, a basic quality of its surface meaning, directs the hearer or reader toward the one meaning intended. Similarly the intended purpose of making a point in a fable gives direction for the reader through the surface story to that point or moral. The same can be said for a parabolic analogy. It is this kind of fictional creation which Augustine endorses as being useful, even in secular letters. But the concealment of fiction without such obviously purposeful direction is very much in question. To the contrary the Bible unfailingly has certain overriding traits: divinely purposeful inspiration of events and record, of words and meaning; a definite sequence of before and after, of Old and New Covenant, of foreshadowing and fulfillment; and an established domain of doctrinal truth. All of these are usually lacking in secular fiction with the exception of sequential pattern (Virgil's three deer and the Punic Wars).

The concealment of a statement interspersed in a context to which it does not apparently belong is related to the obvious concealment of a riddle. This concealment expects the reader or listener to recognize, for example, that Virgil is not literally talking about unhitching steaming horses at the end of *Georgics* II. The key here and in many similar cases is simple proximity and an apparent shift of reference out of context. This kind of concealment also relates to the "suggestive incompleteness"[49] of Neoplatonic interpretation, a principle which is brought over into biblical interpretation. The apparent falsity or inadequacy of the obvious meaning in a biblical passage hints at the presence of a deeper meaning in that passage. This deeper meaning will conform to orthodox Christian doctrine and will relate, if not necessarily more than superficially, to some details of the literal context. This kind of hinting inadequacy depends, of course, on the expectation about content which the reader brings to the text. If you expect the Homeric texts to embody moral, philosophic, and scientific truths you will, like the Stoics and Neoplatonists, be able to find sufficient "suggestive incompleteness" to hint at the presence of these deeper, allegorical meanings. On the other hand if, like Plutarch or St. Augustine, you approach Homer with the idea that the text must be judged by its apparently literal/exemplary implications, you will probably find it completely unsuggestive of other meanings and will judge him as good or bad, dull or interesting, on those grounds. The same can be said for any other text, including the Bible.

Concealment, then, and hints at the presence of concealed, allegorical meaning could be entirely a question of interpretive expectation. Judging from the medieval predilection for fables and parables with

49. See Chapter 1, p. 9, and note 9.

obviously directed meanings, Christian readers may well have preferred rather obvious, heavy-handed lessons in contemporary letters, and have been accustomed to reserve their interpretive ingeniousness for certain established texts of the past, mainly the Bible but possibly including Virgil and other classical texts, where the assumed concealment could be sophisticated and the hints frequently anything but obvious. The concealment of partial reference or allusion, though, definitely rests on a common area of knowledge shared by writer and reader, and in classical tradition, pagan and Christian, allusion is one kind of allegorical concealment, involving implied meaning.

The difficult aspect of allusion is the allusiveness or potential allusiveness of images which can be shown to have accrued traditional meanings and associations. Is every tree or every mast of a ship in medieval literature a cross, regardless of the literal context? The answer to this for the medieval reader is probably "yes," if you want to interpret whatever work you are reading that way. In the very same manner the modern psychological critic might be asked whether every pencil or necktie is a phallus regardless of the apparent literal context of the work being construed. His answer might well be "yes," if you want to view the work from a Freudian perspective. The point is that neither medieval nor modern interpreters can be made to hold consistently to one or several rules of interpretation, no matter how reasonable and logical, nor can they be restrained from pursuing interpretive practices which appear to be illogical and inconsistent. From a creative perspective, however, medieval writers probably found themselves under the same conditions as modern writers in conveying meaning. They probably could not count on their readers coming to their works with the kind of special expectations which they brought to the Bible and possibly certain other texts of the past. It is clear, though, that medieval and Renaissance poets do allude to traditional associations and contexts of images in order to enhance meaning. Each individual poem and passage must, of course, be examined and construed on its own merits according to the immediate literary context, the images involved, and their traditional uses or implications.

Basic to two-meaning and even one-meaning allegorical implication is similitude, analogous parallelism, relating one image or series of images or thoughts to a different series. This analogous parallelism includes the intended application, general or specific, vague or precise, of a proverb or parable (or any form of homoeosis). With proverbial/parabolic application of meaning and with the moral of a fable it is obvious that allegory is not always concealed in any difficult way. This is manifest from classical theory, the practice of the Bible, and Christian writers. Augustine says it pointedly, for example, when he refers to enigma as "obscure allegory," and we must remember that much medieval allegory involves rather obvious similitudes, analogies, and implied or stated applications.

In solving the problem of parables, proverbs, and riddles in the Bible by asserting that those whose intention is to convey a true meaning do not lie, Augustine not only legitimized portions of the Bible but also legitimized these devices as well as fables and fiction generally, when so directed toward truth. There is at the same time in Augustine and other early and late Christian writers a strong tendency to claim for biblical allegory (including, of course, far more than parabolic, riddling, and proverbial meanings) a special status and to deny to secular letters any such or almost all such capabilities. Allegory is Christian, while physical and moral rationalizing interpretations are pagan. The Christians themselves, however, as D. C. Allen, Seznec, and many others have shown,[50] and as every medievalist knows, soon imitated the ancient pagan apologists, adopting the very interpretations which Augustine, Arnobius, Lactantius, and even Cicero's Cotta had so contemptuously treated, and frequently adding to them another set of similar Christian *rationes.*

With this theoretical and interpretive background the Christian potential for creative, original literary allegory was great. Enigmatic, proverbial, parabolic, fabulous, and fictional allegory were all legitimate as long as their aim was to convey truth. Add to these the narrative of abstractions, beginning with Prudentius (4th cent. A.D.) and Capella (5th cent. A.D.), the other-world parts of romance narratives, and the other-world dream narratives, which are frequently peopled with Prudentian abstractions, and one has a rather complete view of medieval letters. The narrative of abstractions is, of course, the perfect working out of the Macrobian idea of fabulous narrative as the concrete visualization and embodiment of the true world of ideas. There is an obviously close association here between the interpretation of myth as narrative of ideas and the creation of fables as illustrations, demonstrations, or embodiments of concepts or truths. Looking at fables creatively, Priscian remarks that they "should pertain to the utility of life." Looking at them interpretively, Isidore says that they were

---

50. Jean Seznec's *Survival of the Pagan Gods,* trans. Barbara Sessions (1953; rpt. New York: Harper, 1961) is a standard introduction to the subject. D. C. Allen's *Mysteriously Meant* (Baltimore: Johns Hopkins Press, 1970) is a comprehensive study of the European tradition of pagan allegoresis. Then there are the iconographic studies of Praz, Panofsky, Wind, and others.

created by poets in the past to be construed as commenting on the nature of things or mores.

All of this would seem to confirm one of Robertson's major hypotheses, that all worthwhile creative writing in the Middle Ages should be or was thought to be devoted to the presentation or representation of some truth. In the Latin West no truth would probably have been thought to exist outside some Christian boundary, but that probability creates only a minor problem for the twentieth-century critic, for whom much (or even all) truth may exist outside such a domain. However, whether this truth should be narrowly limited to the boundaries, even at their broadest, of Augustinian *caritas,* as Robertson suggests, is extremely dubious. The focus of a riddle clearly could be directed only at a physical tree, a book, or any object whatever— Aldhelm's (7th cent. A.D.) lengthy, final riddle is about that very subject[51]—without any further symbolic implication. The same is true of the allegory of history, biblical as in Bede or secular in Lactantius's euhemerism. And not just in Bede and Lactantius but also in Isidore's example of three deer from Virgil, narrative or narrative fiction may allegorically refer to historical fact. For medieval and Renaissance poets, in fact, Lactantius's understanding of the obscure representation of historical fact is just as significant as the grammatical and philosophic tradition of moral and physical allegory. The concept of fictional concealment of real, historical people and events under the coloring of the marvelous and the impossible certainly bears on some of Spenser's works and also on those of Chaucer and others.

Certainly many of the various fables, fictions, parables, riddles, and gnomes of medieval letters testify by their manifest meaning that they have such a remote relationship to *caritas* that it is basically useless to think of that or any other particular delimitation of truth as a prerequisite in approaching medieval literature. Not only the facts of numerous literary creations but critical theory, pagan and Christian, prove that. In this context there remains, however, the question of irony and ironic concealment of meaning behind the obvious and manifest, of the allegory of statement which conveys a meaning directly opposite of what is said. There is no problem with a character identified as Libido attacking another identified as Pudicitia (*Psychomachia,,* 11.40

---

51. See Glorie's edition and translation of Merovingian enigmas, *Corpus Christianorum,* CXXXIII, 143–540. Aldhelm's 83-line 100th riddle appears on pp. 529–39. One of Tatwine's riddles in this collection (no. 3) is coincidentally about the four senses of biblical interpretation. It stresses the dual aspects of allegorical concealment: discouraging the unworthy but encouraging true believers to search for meaning (p. 170).

ff.). It is not so obvious whether we should, as Robertson seems to suggest, read every medieval narrative which satisfies our modern taste for story-interest as if it were naturally intended to conceal some other meaning. Robertson has certainly alerted modern readers of medieval stories to this possibility. But is Andreas the Chaplain (12th cent. A.D.) bound to be arguing ironically, simply because his argument controverts some basic Christian precepts about sexual attraction and its uses?[52] It is true that Augustine allows a Messianic interpretation of Virgil's *Fourth Eclogue* in contradiction to its acknowledged, intentional reference to another person. Generally speaking, however, medieval theory seems to shy away from irony. Only when pressed, as in the case of Jacob's lie, does the medieval theorist call on something like an ironic, figurative meaning, although of course Bede readily identifies the narrative example of Elijah's ironic remark to the prophets of Baal. This survey of classical and early medieval theory suggests perhaps that such a piece of sustained irony as Swift's *Modest Proposal* would have been at least as susceptible to misinterpretation in the tenth century as it was in the eighteenth—and possibly more susceptible and hence less likely to have been written.

52. Robertson argues this point extensively and persuasively in *A Preface to Chaucer* (Princeton: Princeton University Press, 1963), pp. 391–448.

APPENDIX I

Diomedes on Tropes

Diomedes. Diomedes was a late fourth-century (A.D.) grammarian. His lengthy *Ars Grammatica* contains the most extensive systematic discussion of literary genres in ancient Latin. His treatment of figures of speech is full and representative of Latin grammars. "Concerning Tropes" is translated in toto below from the text in Heinrich Keil, ed., *Grammatici Latini* (1857–70; rpt. Hildesheim: Olms, 1961), I, 456–64. For convenience of reference Diomedes' quotations from standard classical authors are identified in parentheses. Important Latin words from Diomedes' text are occasionally bracketed after the word or phrase which translates them.

[Concerning Tropes]

A trope, as Scaurus says, is a mode of embellished speech and a saying changed from its proper signification to one not its own for the sake of beauty, necessity, polish, or emphasis.[1] Quintilian defines it thus: "A trope is discourse changed from its natural and primary signification to another signification for the sake of adorning speech" (IX. i. 4). The tropes are metaphor, catachresis, metalepsis, metonymy, antonomasia, synecdoche, onomatopoeia, periphrasis, hyperbaton, hyperbole, allegory, and homoeosis. Metaphor is the universal for all these. All the rest seem to be species of it.

Concerning metaphor. Metaphor is the transferring [*translatio*] of things and words from their proper signification to an improper similitude for the sake of beauty, necessity, polish, or emphasis. It occurs in four ways. From animate being to animate being, as in,

---

1. Q. Terentius Scaurus, a famous grammarian of the second century A.D. His works are now lost, but they are frequently cited by later grammarians of antiquity.

they made Tiphys charioteer of the swift ship.[2]
This changed him from a charioteer to a pilot. Also,

cropping the plain far and wide, with snowy lustre.[3] (*Aeneid* III. 538)

From animate to inanimate, thus,

But far off, marvelling from the lofty head of a mountain.[4] (*Aeneid* V. 35)

In place of peak [*cacumen*] he said head [*vertex*] here, which only refers to animate beings. Also,

The unruly mountain is borne abruptly with a mighty rush.[5] (*Aeneid* XII. 687)

From inanimate to animate, as,

if in your heart you nourish so much oak, (*Aeneid* XI. 368–69)

transferred from wood to man. Also,

both of them in the flower of age. (Virgil, *Eclogues* VII. 4)

From inanimate to inanimate, as in,

the rafts reached the sea. (*Aeneid* V. 8).

In place of ships he said rafts. Also,

a steep mountain of water comes next in a mass. (*Aeneid* I. 105)

Some metaphors are common. From the Greek they are called *acoluthoe*, as in,

they made Tiphys charioteer of the swift ship.[6]

Just as we can have a charioteer of a ship, in like manner we can have a pilot of a chariot, as in,

At any time the pilot turns the horses with great force.

Here pilot has been put in place of charioteer. Other metaphors are not common. From the Greek they are called *anacoluthoe*. An example is "head of a mountain." Of course, we cannot alternatively have the peak of a man, as we had the head of a mountain. Now we ought to know that some metaphors are reciprocal, and others have only one direction.

Concerning catachresis. Catachresis is a necessary misuse of related significations in place of the proper ones and the usurpation of another denotation, i.e., a speaking lacking proper signification and usurping another denotation as if it were its own. It differs from metaphor in

---

2. A quote from a now unknown ancient source. The grammarian, Charisius, whose work Diomedes knew and used, has the same quote in a similar passage (Keil, I, 272). Tiphys was the pilot of the Argonaut. Some of the quotations and references for which Diomedes is the only source are simply passed over without comment.

3. The reference is to four horses, omens, seen by Aeneas.

4. The reference is to Acestes getting a glimpse of Aeneas's ships at sea.

5. Part of an epic simile comparing Turnus to a gigantic mass of rock sweeping down a mountainside.

6. See note 2.

that a metaphor conveys the designation it has, while the other utilizes a different designation, because there is no proper designation. For example, he who kills a brother or a sister is called a parricide, although properly only he who kills his father may be a parricide.[7]

Concerning metalepsis. Metalepsis is the shifting [*dilatio*] of the proper signification of words through transumption. It is a saying descending by homonymy to the proper signification, as in,

hid them in black caves.[8] (*Aeneid* I. 60).

From black, dark caves are understood; from dark caves, caves having darkness, and through this to the point, vast caves.

Concerning metonymy. Metonymy is called *transnominatio*. Now it is a saying changed from one proper signification to another. Now it can occur in six ways. (1) By means of that which is contained for that which contains; thus,

They set up the great bowls and crown the wine. (*Aeneid* VII. 147)

Of course, they do not crown the wine but the bowls. (2) By means of that which contains for that which is contained; thus,

river, most beloved of heaven. (*Aeneid* VIII. 64)

Here, heaven, which contains the gods, is used for them. (3) By means of the author or ruler for what is authored or the subject, as this,

without Ceres and Liber, Venus grows cold. (Terence, *Eunuch*, 1.732)

Of course, bread is to be understood for Ceres, wine for Liber, and copulation for Venus. (4) By means of what is authored or the subject for the author or ruler, as in,

We pray the wine, for here the god is propitiously present.[9]

(5) By means of what does something for what it does; thus, "better oared."[10] Of course, the oars do not make it better, but the speed which comes from the oars. (6) By that which is done for that which does it, as "numb cold."[11] Also,

and gloomy fear,[12] (*Aeneid* I. 202)

which is what makes them gloomy or sad.

---

7. *Fratricida* is rare but classical. Diomedes is correct, however, about the uses of *parricida*.

8. Homonymy (from ὁμωνῦμία) means verbal identity or the use of equivalent words.

9. This quotation is attributed to Plautus in Servius's *Commentary on The Aeneid*, under I. 724.

10. The phrase occurs in *Aeneid* V. 153 and refers to the ship, Scylla, winner (V. 245) of a race.

11. A verbal allusion to but not exact quotation of a phrase in *Georgics* IV. 259.

12. Fear, of course, precedes and produces the gloom.

Concerning antonomasia. Antonomasia is the substitution of another word in place of the proper one. It replaces a noun with its signification, and a designation functions in place of the noun. Now antonomasia is developed in three ways, either from the mind, from the body, or externally. From the mind, as,

and the noble son of Anchises,[13] (*Aeneid* V. 407)

i.e., Aeneas. From the body, as

therefore with these words to the winged one,[14] (*Aeneid* I. 663)

i.e., Cupid. Also, "the lofty one himself" (*Aeneid* III. 619).[15]

Also concerning antonomasia. Antonomasia is a designation functioning in place of a noun, as occurs in "of arms and the man" (*Aeneid* I. 1), where Aeneas is understood. Also Neptune is understood to be referred to by the "conqueror of the sea" (*Aeneid* V. 799). Like this is "the lofty one himself." Epithet is a species of antonomasia. Now epithet is a saying placed before a proper noun for the sake of building up, for tearing down, or for identification. Epithets build up this way: "divine Camilla" (*Aeneid* XI. 657). They tear down, thus,

and the contriver of crimes, Ulysses. (*Aeneid* II. 164)

They identify thus,

Larissean Achilles. (*Aeneid* II. 197)

Now epithets are applied in three ways, from the mind, from the body, and externally. From the mind are "the noble son of Anchises" (*Aeneid* V. 407)[16] and "the disdainer of the gods, Mezentius" (*Aeneid* VIII. 7). From the body, as,

speaks these words to winged Love, (*Aeneid* I. 663)

and "handsome Iulus."[17] External epithets are divided into several species, for they derive from place, function, or condition [*eventus*]. From place occurs when Ulysses is called *Ithacus* or *Pelasgus;* from function when Caieta is called "nurse of Aeneas" (*Aeneid* VII. 1); and from condition when Tenedos is called "rich island of plenty" (*Aeneid* II. 22).

Concerning synecdoche. Synecdoche is a saying more or less declaring more than it signifies. Now sometimes a part is understood from a reference to the whole. At others, the whole is understood by the naming of a part. A part from the whole occurs in,

---

13. The English phrase here, "son of Anchises," is one word in Latin, *Anchisiades*.

14. Diomedes simply leaves out *Amor* in his citation of this line in order to create an antonomasia. Actually "winged" is an epithet, and Diomedes subsequently quotes the same line (including *Amor*) as an example of epithet.

15. Referring to Polyphemus, the Cyclops.

16. See note 13.

17. A frequent phrase in the *Aeneid,* e.g., V. 570.

a mighty sea from above, (*Aeneid* I. 114)
for he does not mean that the whole sea struck the ship but part of it,
i.e., a wave. Also,

were bringing both a fountain and fire.[18] (*Aeneid* XII. 119)
The whole from a part, as in,

just as your sterns and your pubes. (*Aeneid* I. 399)
By stern a ship is signified, by pubes, whole men.

Concerning onomatopoeia. Onomatopoeia is a saying fashioned so
as to imitate the signification of a non-verbal [*confusa*] sound, as,

and raise a tinkling and shake the cymbals round about for the
Mother; and the clang of trumpets.[19]

And also when we say doors creak [*stridere*], sheep bleat [*balare*], bronze
tinkles [*tinnire*], and others similar to these.

Concerning periphrasis. Periphrasis is a very extended [*numerosior*]
saying, an amassing of comments on the general significance of a
subject, a circumlocution describing a subject with polish in a very long
circuit of words. Its purpose is to embellish a subject which is beautiful
or to avoid a subject which is unseemly. It embellishes in order to
extend shortness with brilliance. It avoids in order to talk around
foulness. To extend shortness with brilliance, thus,

And now early Aurora, leaving the saffron bed of Tithonus,
sprinkles the earth with light. (*Aeneid* IV. 584-85)
Of course, he could have said, "Now it became daylight" or "Day
began." To talk around foulness, thus,

and spreading over his spouse's bosom, sought peaceful sleep in
his members. (*Aeneid* VIII. 405-06)
This, of course, by a circumlocution, which properly avoids indecency,
describes sexual union. Also,

lest by too much excess the use of the fruitful soil be dulled and
the inactive furrows covered with mud.[20] (*Georgics* III. 135-36)

Concerning hyperbaton. Hyperbaton is a very long delaying of
speech in the same sense[21] and a transposition of words which disturbs
their order. But that is the general trope; for it has five species:
anastrophe; diacope, or as some call it, tmesis; dialysis or parenthesis;
synchysis; and hysterologia. Anastrophe is the inversion of words
[*dictiones*] contrary to the proper order of syntax [*oratio*] and an
arbitrary order of two words in reverse with no other word interposed,
as,

18. Some water, not a whole fountain, is being brought for a sacrifice.
19. From *Georgics* IV. 64 and *Aeneid* II. 313 and XI. 192.
20. A reference to equine conception.
21. I.e, there is no transfer of sense of a word as occurs in other tropes.

transtra per et remos, (Aeneid V. 663)

where, of course, the order is *per transtra.* Similarly, "*lupi ceu*" (*Aeneid* II.
355). A diacope or tmesis is the arbitrary separation of a compound
word with another word interposed, as,

septem subiecta trioni, (Georgics III. 381)

since, joined together, it ought to be *septemtrioni.* Dialysis or parenthesis
is the interposition of a separately reasoned expression, as,

> Then he begins—for he was concealed by the whole band of
> leaders thronging about—to encourage his rejoicing cohorts,
> (*Aeneid* XI. 12–13)

where the order should be: then he encourages his rejoicing cohorts,
for he was concealed by them thronging about. Also.

> Aeneas—for a father's love would not allow his mind to be at
> ease—sends Achates hurrying ahead to the ships, (*Aeneid* I.
> 643–44)

ought to be ordered like this: Aeneas sends Achates hurrying ahead to
the ships. Synchysis is a hidden hyperbaton that is completely mixed
together, as,

> *vina bonus quae deinde cadis onerarat Acestes*
> *litore Trinacrio dederatque abeuntibus heros*
> *dividit, (Aeneid* I. 195–97)

since the order should be: *deinde heros dividit vina quae bonus Acestes
onerarat cadis et de Trinacrio litore abeuntibus dederat.* Also,

> *tris notus abreptas in saxa latentia torquet . . .*[22]

and so on, where the proper arrangement is the following: *tres notus
abreptas in saxa torquet, saxa mediis fluctibus latentia, quae Itali aras vocant,
dorsum immane mari summo.* Hysterologia or hysteron proteron occurs
when that which ought to be first is put in the second place. The order
of the sense is inverted after it is recited, as,

> Then Dawn illuminated the earth with Apollonian light and
> dispersed the dampening shadow from the sky. (*Aeneid* IV. 6–7)

Of course, the shadow of night ought to go away first and then the sun
rise. Also,

> and they set about parching it in the flames and crushing it
> under the stone. (*Aeneid* I. 179)

Concerning hyperbole. Hyperbole is a saying or remark [*sententia*]
which exceeds the credibility of what is actually true, for the sake of
increasing or diminishing. For increasing, as in whiter than snow or
swifter than the East Wind. For diminishing, as in these: slower than a
tortoise and lighter than leaves. Also, as in,

---

22. *Aeneid* I. 108, referring to I. 108–10, which is rearranged by Diomedes.

He has no more room to stand in his garden than where the bucket drawn out of the well rests.[23]

Also, as this in Virgil,

She could have flown over the topmost blades of untouched corn without hitting the tender ears in her course or made her way over the midst of the sea poised on the swelling wave without touching her feet on the flood.[24] (*Aeneid* VII. 808–11)

Concerning allegory. Allegory is a speaking [*oratio*], saying one thing and signifying something else by means of similitude [*similitudo*] or antithesis [*contrarium*], as in Virgil,

and now it is time to unloose the necks of our steaming horses. (*Georgics* II. 542)

This means that the poem [*carmen*] is to be ended. Also,

Maecenas, and spread your sails, flying over an open sea. (*Georgics* II. 41).

Of course, the author does not mean what he says, a voyage, to be understood, but the support of Maecenas for the completion of his poems [*carmina*]. There are seven species of this trope: irony, antiphrasis, aenigma, charientismos, paroemia, sarcasm, and astismos. Irony is a saying rendering a meaning contrary to the sense of the words by harshness of its articulation, as,

Indeed you reap outstanding praise and great spoils.[25] (*Aeneid* IV. 93)

The import here, unless it were harshly articulated, would not be one of censuring but of praising. Also,

Did I lead the Trojan adulterer to ravage Sparta?[26] (*Aeneid* X. 92)

Unless this were supported by harsh articulation, it would appear to confirm what it intends to deny. Antiphrasis is a saying, conveying meaning by antithesis, as in the designation for war [*bellum*], which is not at all good [*bonum*], or for a grove [*lucus*], which does not shine [*luceat*] at all, or the Fates [*Parcae*], who are not at all sparing [*parcant*].[27] It differs from irony in that irony alters signification in the articulation of it and by mental effect, whereas antiphrasis names the contradiction. Aenigma is an obscure [*obscura*] meaning conveyed by means of a hidden similitude of details. It is a saying not intelligible by the

---

23. Charisius has the same example (Keil, I, 275). The author is unknown. Whoever is referred to has a very small garden.

24. An exaggerated reference to Camilla.

25. Juno makes this remark to Venus, meaning to censure her.

26. Juno is speaking in a council of the gods. She, of course, did not lead Paris to Helen.

27. The only etymological antithesis here which is not obvious is *bellum-bonum*. The adjective *bonus* is related to *bellus* (pretty): *bellus* < *benulus* < *benus* = *bonus*.

obscurity of allegory, for it reveals one thing openly but conceals something else by means of an obscure contradiction,[28] as in,

The same mother who bore me is soon born of me.

This signifies that ice is frozen water and thaws back into water again. Also this example: "The sea was congealed in clay on a wooden plain, where human flesh was playing with bones." The meaning intended here is that salt was in an earthen saltcellar on a table where a hand tossed dice about. Charientismos is a trope by which disagreeable things are expressed in a more pleasant way. It is a saying conveying a different meaning by things which are more pleasing to the ear. For example, when we ask whether anyone has been looking for us and the reply comes, "Best wishes" or "Good luck," it is understood that no one has been looking for us.[29] Paroemia is the application of a common proverb to events and times, when something is meant other than what is said, as in,

to kick against the pricks, (Terence, *Phormio,* 1. 78)

and as in, "We will pay out digested organs,"[30] where the meaning is that we will know from the result. Sarcasm is completely hateful and hostile mockery expressed by means of a figure, as is this,

Indeed, Trojan, lying there, measure out the fields and that Hesperia you sought in war.[31] (*Aeneid* XII. 359-60)

Astismos is a trope of many facets and numerous capabilities, for astismos is understood to include whatever is free from rustic simplicity and is polished with a measure of genteel refinement [*urbanitas*]. It is the many-faceted species of allegory with refinement, as is this in Virgil,

Let him who does not hate Bavius love your poems, Maevius, and let him also harness foxes and milk he-goats. (*Eclogues* III. 90-91)

Also as this: "When Philip wanted to bring Persia under his sway and had dispatched his army against it, he wrote that he had dispatched his

---

28. Diomedes also defines aenigma under improprieties of speech. "Aenigma is a meaning [*sententia*] confused by incredibilities," Keil, I, 450.

29. An example also in Donatus (Keil, IV, 402), explained by Pompeius (Keil, V, 311). Pompeius gives the source as the comic poet Afranius.

> Now we have in Afranius a young man asking the slave, "has anyone been looking for me?" And the slave replies, "good luck," i.e., no one has—as if he spoke to soften a painful reply.

Clearly the young man was anxiously expecting someone to have been inquiring about him and was quite disappointed that such had not been the case. The Greek sense seems to differ. Charientismos is gracious but witty ridicule. See Herodianus and Cocondrius under irony in Matsen's Appendix II.

30. Alluding to reading omens by examining the organs of sacrificial animals.

31. Turnus is addressing the corpse of an enemy he has just slain in battle.

soldiers, since he understood they were wracked by insurrection, and that it was the part of good men to help in such a time."[32]

Concerning homoeosis. Homoeosis is the vivid delineaton [*demonstratio*] of something less known by its similitude to something which is better known and the representation [*descriptio*] of something unknown by its similitude to what is better known. It has three species: icon or characterization, parable, and paradigm. Icon is a representation portraying some figure or a mutual comparison [*comparatio*] of characters or of those things which happen to characters, as:

> like a god in face and shoulders,[33] (*Aeneid* I. 589)

and,

> in everything like Mercury.[34] (*Aeneid* IV. 558)

Also,

> Such, tamed by the reins of Pollux of Amyclae, was Cyllarus. (*Georgics* III. 89–90)

Here, of course, a horse is compared with a horse. Parable is a comparison of things or managements different in kind. Now it occurs in eight ways. By means of condition, as in,

> Even as Diana supervises her choruses on the banks of the Eurotas or along the heights of Cynthus,[35] (*Aeneid* I. 498–99)

and so on. By means of size, as in,

> just as when two cloud-born Centaurs descend from the high top of a mountain.[36] (*Aeneid* VII. 674–75)

By means of color, as in,

> just as one dyes Indian ivory with bloody purple.[37] (*Aeneid* XII. 67–68)

By means of voice, as in,

> while he raises horrible cries to heaven, like a stricken bull, bellowing and fleeing the altar.[38] (*Aeneid* II. 222–24)

By means of similitude, as in,

> Like the bees busy at work in the flowery countryside under a spring sun.[39] (*Aeneid* I. 430–31)

---

32. An example from Demosthenes, *Third Philippic* 12. Diomedes almost certainly took this example from the grammarian Charisius (Keil, I, 277), who presumably translated Demosthenes' Greek into Latin. The anecdote is about Philip of Macedon's conquest of the people of Oreus—not, as Diomedes has it, of Persia—on the ostensibly benevolent (but actually hypocritical) excuse of helping them out in a time of trouble.
33. Aeneas is being described.
34. A vision appearing to Aeneas is being described.
35. Dido is being described and compared to Diana.
36. Catillus and Coras are being described here, leading out their contingents in Aeneas's army.
37. Lavinia is blushing.
38. Laocoon is being described in the coils of the serpents.
39. The building of Carthage is underway.

By means of energy, as in,

> just as when fire whips across a cornfield with southerly winds raging.[40] (*Aeneid* II. 304–05)

By means of height, as in,

> as lofty, near the flowing rivers, whether on the banks of the Po . . .[41] (*Aeneid* IX. 679–80)

By means of emotion, as in,

> Thus families are silently thunderstruck at the first impact of death, while the bodies are not yet laid out and mourned.[42] (Lucan, *Pharsalia* II. 21–23)

There is also the comparison by means of dissimilitude. It has the force of emphasizing [*praeferendi*], as in,

> Not thus, when a frothing river streams over broken embankments,[43] (*Aeneid* II. 496–97)

and as in,

> Not so precipitously do they seize the plain in the two-horse race.[44] (*Aeneid* V. 144–45)

In these, of course, those things are put forth which are compared by dissimilitude. Paradigm is the detailed exposition of an example or the report of a past event, indicating persuasion or dissuasion. Persuasion, as in, "Antenor was able to escape from the midst of the Greeks" and so forth.[45] Also, "Was not Athena able to burn up the Greek fleet?"[46] And dissuasion in,

> Or was it not thus that the Phrygian shepherd entered Sparta?"[47] (*Aeneid* VII. 363–64)

Dissuasion,

> Or have they not seen the walls of Troy, built by the hand of Neptune, sink down in flames?[48] (*Aeneid* IX. 144–45)

40. The reference is to Aeneas's sudden awareness of the destruction of Troy going on around him.

41. The reference is to two tall warriors, Pandarus and Bitias, who are like two mighty oak trees.

42. Romans, struck dumb by portents of evil, are compared to members of a household learning of a sudden death in the family.

43. The Greek forces are being described breaking in to sack Troy.

44. Chariots seizing the plain. The beginning of a race among ships at sea is being described.

45. *Aeneid* I. 242 and continuing through 249. Venus is putting up the example of Antenor to Jupiter in contrast to the treatment of Aeneas.

46. *Aeneid* I. 39. Juno meditates on the achievements allowed Athena in contrast to the thwarting of Juno's own desires.

47. These words are spoken by Amata, mother of Lavinia, objecting to Lavinia's betrothal to Aeneas, whom she compares here to Paris, "the Phrygian shepherd."

48. Turnus suggests here that the bad omens received by him and the Rutulians really apply to the Trojans who, in the example he cites, have already suffered great misfortune.

APPENDIX II

From
Spengel, *Rhetores Graeci*

by

Patricia Matsen

CONTENTS

Prolegomenon

In contributing this appendix to Philip Rollinson's *Classical Theories of Allegory* I hope to place the student who does not read Greek in a better position to follow the whole sequence of known classical definitions of allegorical terms. In the three volumes of Spengel's *Rhetores Graeci* (Leipzig, 1853–56; reprinted Frankfurt, 1966) there are thirty-six Greek texts which range in date of composition from the fourth century B.C. (Aristotle) to the early Christian and perhaps Byzantine eras. When ancient Greek learning again became widely available to the Latin West after the fall of Constantinople (A.D. 1453), these writings of Greek rhetoricians had a deep impact on Renaissance critical theory. It is difficult, however, for the modern student who does not read Greek to realize the extent to which this is true. A case in point is Hermogenes (second century A.D.): "During later antiquity, Byzantine times, and the Renaissance Hermogenes was probably the most read and most influential Greek rhetorician."[1] Yet of the five works which survive under the name of Hermogenes only the *Progymnasmata* (Spengel, ii, 1–8), a fragmentary work, is available in English translation. *On Staseis* (Spengel, ii, 131–74), *On Invention* (Spengel, ii, 175–262), *On Forms* (Spengel, ii, 263–425), his major treatises, and an essay, *On the Method of Deinotēs* (Spengel, ii, 426–56) remain untranslated.

I have assembled my translations of certain texts concerned with the definition and theory of types of "other-speaking" and "other-meaning." These are (1) Allegory, (2) Antiphrasis, (3) Irony, (4)

---

1. George Kennedy, *The Art of Rhetoric in the Roman World 300 B.C.–A.D. 300* (Princeton: Princeton University Press, 1972), p. 619. The reader may also find helpful George Kennedy, *The Art of Persuasion in Greece* (Princeton: Princeton University Press, 1963) and L. D. Reynolds and N. G. Wilson, *Scribes and Scholars: A Guide to the Transmission of Greek and Latin Literature,* 2nd ed. rev. and enl. (Oxford: Oxford University Press, 1974).

Enigma, (5) Metaphor, (6) Fable, (7) Parabole and Paradeigma, (8) Paroimiai, (9) Eidolopoiia, Ethopoiia, Prosopopoiia. I have not included in my selections translations of works that are available in the Loeb Classical Library or in any other current English translation.

In order that my reader may be better able to place in their context those rhetorical works from which I have made my selections, I shall here attempt a broad outline of the general historical development of Greek rhetoric in antiquity. Ancient Greek rhetorical works fall into three categories: (1) the comprehensive treatise on the art of rhetoric; (2) the textbook on the rules and methods of rhetorical composition (e.g., "Progymnasmata"); (3) the dictionary of rhetorical terms (e.g., "On Figures," "On Tropes"). To a great extent this classification reflects the directions in which the study of rhetoric developed in antiquity.

Rhetoric, the technique of persuasion in the courts and assemblies, was introduced at Athens by teachers from Sicily in the last half of the fifth century B.C., and it developed as part of the sophistic movement, the most important representative of which was Gorgias of Leontini (c. 483–376 B.C.). But the father of the comprehensive treatise on the art of rhetoric was Aristotle (384–322 B.C.), who regarded rhetoric as a branch of the art of reasoning and thus laid the foundations of philosophical rhetoric. For Aristotle, the function of rhetoric was "not so much to persuade, as to find out in each case the existing means of persuasion" (*Rhetoric*, I. i. 14, Loeb translation).

Greek rhetoric took a new direction in the middle of the third century B.C. Political conditions made great public oratory unnecessary, and as Greek culture spread over the Mediterranean world, rhetoric became a discipline taught in the schools. Characteristic of this period was the cultivation of the so-called Asianist style (florid and emotional). Textbook oratory—declamatory exercises according to fixed rules and methods—developed, and by the first century B.C. there appeared many schoolbooks of the type called "Progymnasmata." (These I have described in my introduction to Fable). Our earliest extant Progymnasmata, however, is that of Theon (first century A.D.).

While rhetoric was flourishing in the third century B.C., it was also being attacked by the philosophical schools on the ground that as general education it had no subject matter and no definite aims. The attack came mainly from the Stoics and the Epicureans. Epicurus had said that rhetoric was of no use either to the philosopher or to the statesman. The Stoics did make some contribution to the study of rhetoric, for they were interested in definitions and correct diction, but like the Epicureans, they said that it was of no real value.

Rhetoric, however, found a champion in Hermagoras of Temnos (c. 150 B.C.), who in the six books of his *Technai rhētorikai* revived rhetorical theory which had been neglected by the Asianists. In reply to the criticisms of the philosophers he maintained that rhetoric did have a subject matter and that it was the purpose of rhetoric to deal with all problems, both particular (*hupothesis*) and general (*thesis*), that were not of a technical nature. Hermagoras developed four "stances" (*staseis*), questions, which he held were adequate for attacking all problems.

Hermagoras, however, did not deal with matters of style. About a century after Hermagoras (c. 50 B.C.) the so-called Atticist movement came into being reacting against the Asianists and standing for a return to the standards of the great classical Attic writers (Xenophon, Plato, Lysias, Demosthenes). The imitation (*mimēsis*) of classical models and the fitting of rhetorical rules to classical standards made technical instruction of lesser importance than aesthetic considerations. Thus literary criticism was born, as may be seen in the writings of Dionysius of Halicarnassus, a Greek rhetorician who taught at Rome (30–8 B.C.). Dionysius's contemporary, Caecilius of Calacte, a Greek-speaking Jew who also taught rhetoric at Rome under Augustus, developed a theory of figures (*schēmata*) and thus fathered the later schematographic corpus. Caecilius's work on figures is not extant, but Phoebammon (sixth century A.D.?) does quote Caecilius's definition of a figure: "A figure [*schēma*] is a turning [*tropē*] to an unnatural form of thought and diction [*eis to mē kata phusin to tēs dianoias kai lexeōs*]" (*On Rhetorical Figures*, Spengel, iii, 44, 8–9).

The last phase of ancient Greek rhetoric, the so-called Second Sophistic period, began in the second century A.D. with the rejuvenescence of the Greek spirit in the Asian centers of Greek culture. It is characteristic of this period that epideictic ("display") oratory was popular and was the main concern of such writers as Herodes Atticus (A.D. 101–177) and Aelius Aristeides (A.D. 117–189). In the schools first-century doctrines were put aside and an ornate manner of expression was cultivated. The most important rhetorician of this period was Hermogenes (born c. A.D. 150), who, in addition to adapting the stasis method of Hermagoras to his system, also tried to develop definitive laws of style. Other influential rhetoricians of the Second Sophistic were Minucianus, Alexander, Rufus, Longinus and Apsines.

Above I listed the nine allegorical terms for which I have selected and translated definitions from the Spengel *Rhetores Graeci*. My work is divided into nine chapters, one for each allegorical term. At the beginning of each chapter an introduction describes for the reader what the term meant to the ancient rhetoricians who studied and defined it. After my introduction I give the definitions (texts), usually presented in their Spengel sequence. Immediately following the translations I list the texts that I have omitted by their author's name, date, title of work, and Spengel pagination.

In the introduction to each chapter I also give my reasons for selecting the definitions included as well as my reasons for those which I have excluded, since I have not for every allegorical term considered it useful to translate all the texts that belong to it. If a text has already been translated into English, I mention and summarize it in the introduction and list it under Texts Omitted. I have done the same for texts which, in my opinion, are merely repetitive. For the definition of each term I have chosen only those texts which seem to me to be archetypal, or atypical, or of particular interest in some other respect. It may seem to the reader that, especially in the chapters Irony, Metaphor, Parabole and Paradeigma, I have often included texts which are rather repetitious. An observant reader will discover that these texts do vary significantly in verbal expression and choice of examples so as not to say exactly the same thing. The texts in question belong to the schemato- and tropographic corpus.

Now works that classify and define terms (dictionaries) are by nature repetitive. Works of this sort compiled by ancient rhetoricians or grammarians are entitled *peri schēmatōn* ("On Figures") or *peri tropōn* ("On Tropes"). It is characteristic of the *peri tropōn* not to be didactic but simply to record and classify rhetorical facts. The writer normally begins with a preface on the concept of a trope, followed by an index of tropes. The body of the work consists of an explanation of each trope in the order given in the index. Each entry consists of a verbal definition followed by one or more examples from literature. Usually there is no syntactical connection between the entries. The works *peri schēmatōn* not only follow this format but also frequently contain material similar to that of the works *peri tropōn*. For example, both Polybius Sardianus and Trypho list *parabolē* and *paradeigma* as forms of *homoiōsis*.

Yet there are extant in the tropographic corpus five works which so closely resemble one another that textual critics have concluded that they ultimately all derive from one source. The texts in question are:

Trypho, *peri tropōn,* Spengel, iii, 191–206;
Gregorius Corinthius, *peri tropōn,* Spengel, iii, 215–26;
XXXI Anonymous, *peri tropōn,* Spengel, iii, 227–29;
Cocondrius, *peri tropōn,* Spengel, iii, 230–43;
Georgius Choeroboscus, *peri tropōn poiētikōn,* Spengel,
    iii, 244–56.

These ascriptions may reflect the Byzantine practice of attaching the name of a famous grammarian to a Byzantine summary text, as Gregorius Corinthius and Georgius Choeroboscus could not have composed the texts ascribed to them. Trypho was a grammarian of the Augustan Age and may have written a *peri tropōn,* of which this text is a descendant. Nothing is known about Cocondrius. The text ascribed to Gregorius Corinthius by Spengel, who was following Walz (although the manuscript ascription is to Trypho), also appears in a fourth-century papyrus, some six or seven centuries earlier than Gregorius Corinthius. The date for Georgius Choeroboscus is the fifth or sixth century, but there seems to be a reference in the text to Symeon Metaphrastes, whose date is the tenth century. Moreover, the style and the use of Christian examples are not characteristic of Choeroboscus's other writings. M. L. West has examined these five texts with respect to their contents and, on the basis of the "distribution of the ancient examples between them, and . . . the choice and arrangement of the tropes," has concluded that Trypho and Gregorius Corinthius "seem to represent two branches, already separate in antiquity, of a single tradition." West also concludes that Choeroboscus represents a version of Gregorius Corinthius in which many of the examples from classical poetry have been either replaced or supplemented by biblical ones; that Cocondrius and XXXI Anonymous not only represent even more remote versions of Gregorius Corinthius but also (like Trypho and Gregorius Corinthius) closely resemble each other.[2]

    Although there are indeed many similarities in these texts, I find that there are significant differences as well. For illustration, let us compare Trypho and Gregorius Corinthius on metaphor with respect to definition, arrangement of material, and examples cited. Trypho: "Metaphor is expression transferred from the proper to the improper for the sake of emphasis or resemblance." Gregorius Corinthius: "Metaphor is a part of speech transferred for the sake of either emphasis or resemblance." Trypho follows his definition with one

2. M. L. West, "Tryphon *De Tropis*," *Classical Quarterly,* n.s. 15 (1965), 230–48.

example of transference from an animate being (A) to an inanimate being (I). This is followed by another A to I for resemblance. Trypho then says that metaphor happens "in fourfold manner" [*tetrachōs*]: A to A, I to I, A to I, I to A, and he gives one example for each manner of transference. Gregorius Corinthius, on the other hand, follows his definition with the statement: "And there are five species [*eidē*] of metaphors." He says that these are A to I, I to A, A to A, I to I, and "from action to action" [*apo praxeōs epi praxin*]; he then gives an example for each species. With respect to the first four species he says that A to I and I to A are for emphasis, but that A to A and I to I are for resemblance. For "from action to action" he cites the improper transference of weaving from webs to plans (*Od.* 4, 739). Gregorius Corinthius then closes his entry with the statement: "But some metaphors are indicative of emphases and do not preserve the resemblance; others preserve both the resemblance and the emphasis." Trypho, however, ends his entry abruptly with his last example cited without comment. Gregorius Corinthius's entry is approximately 223 words long; Trypho's approximately 113. Gregorius Corinthius cites five examples; Trypho eight. Three of Gregorius Corinthius's examples are the same as Trypho's. In both entries all of the examples are taken from Homer, the majority from the *Iliad*. Thus I think that my reader will find significant and useful variation in the definitions of other allegorical terms that have been selected from these and other texts of the tropo- and schematographic corpus.

Because I have made my translations literal, the reader may find their style awkward. My excuse is that my sole aim has been to provide the reader who does not read Greek with as accurate a translation as I could produce. In my translations I have identified quotations from standard classical (and biblical) authors in parentheses if they did not require further annotation. Sometimes, however, I have been unable to identify the author. I have annotated my translations only at places in which I think some obscurity in the text may interfere with the reader's understanding of the author's intent. In each translation important Greek words have been transliterated into English characters, with a macron to indicate eta and omega. Those words which are transliterated are placed in square brackets after the word or phrase which translates them. I have listed the texts with the names of the authors as given by Spengel, even when the attribution is doubtful. The anonymous texts are identified by Roman numeral (the Spengel author number) in front, for example, XXIX Anonymous.

Patricia P. Matsen
University of South Carolina
May 1979

I. ALLEGORY

Introduction

In this section I shall give all seven of the texts which define and illustrate allegory [*allēgoria*] because I think that there is significant difference in the accompanying material even in texts in which the initial verbal definitions are quite similar. Longinus, who is talking about style, treats allegory simply as "other-speaking." Tiberius calls Demosthenes' use of prolonged metaphor allegory. Trypho's definition of allegory as the technique of saying one thing while implying another is similar to those found in modern handbooks of rhetoric. The remaining four texts are spin-offs from Trypho. But XXIX Anonymous gives an example from the Bible. Gregorius Corinthius tells us that allegory is used whenever circumstances prevent writers from using plain speech and takes his example from Callimachus's *Iambi*. Cocondrius is important because he not only gives examples of both prolonged (Alcaeus) and single (Homer) allegory but also tells us that there are two species of allegory, irony and enigma. Finally, Choeroboscus, who has much in common with Gregory of Corinth and XXIX Anonymous, adds an example of physical allegory excerpted from Homer.

TEXTS

1. Longinus (3rd cent. A.D.), *Art of Rhetoric*. Spengel, i, 307, 8–29.

[On Style]

But, on the other hand, *allēgoria* adorns speech by changing expression and signifying the same thing through a fresher expression of a different kind. For that which is commonplace, threadbare and endlessly repeated leads to satiety, exactly as the common and usual of foods and of as many things as pertain to vision or the rest of sense-perception are despised and do not attract the attention of the organ of perception and the spirit answering to the organ of perception. And it is necessary that from his sense of hearing the judge be enticed and induced by appetizing and pleasant dressings and allurements, just as by rich and fine cookery, and this ought to be done by means of attentive and flattering expressions. For these are means of persuasion, weapons of delights and of art which is trained for persuasion. For it is not the same, not even to a small degree, to call unpleasant [aēdes] 'sour' [agleukes], 'joyless' [aterpes], and 'not for one's gratification' [ouk en chariti]; and to call beautiful [kalon] 'very beautiful' [perikalles]; and excessively [lian] 'very effectively' [mala anutikōs] and sometimes 'exactly' [komidē]; and in place of well [kalōs] 'excellently' [hupereuge]; and for strange [atopon] 'overgrown' [huperphues]; for terrible [deinon] 'headstrong' [schetlion]; for hopou 'hina' and 'hei' (as, "where [hei] we cross to the sanctuary of the Huntress");[1] for to ask as a favor of [paraitēsasthai] 'to obtain the leave of' [paresthai]; for to beg from [deēthēnai] 'to entreat' [antibolēsai]; for simply [haplōs] 'in a few words' [en brachei]; and for moderately [metriōs] 'somehow or other' [hamēgepe].

2. Tiberius (date unknown), On the Figures in Demosthenes. Spengel, iii, 70, 3–11.

It is allēgoria, then, whenever someone expresses any of important matters in metaphors which are able to signify the important. But the figure is greatest and clearest in him in reference to Meidias: "For the fact that his wickedness is dependent upon his power and wealth is a rampart against any attack, since indeed if stripped of his property he is worth nothing; but now, I think, this is his protection."[2] For here grasp all the images of the rampart.

3. Trypho (1st cent. B.C.), On Tropes. Spengel, iii, 193, 8–12.

On Allēgoria. Allēgoria is speech [logos] which makes precisely clear some one thing but which presents the conception of another according to likeness to the greatest extent. For example,

> The straw of which the bronze spreads on the ground
> in greatest numbers.[3]

---

1. hopou, hina, and hēi each mean 'where.' hopou is an indefinite adverb of place; hina is an adverb of place; hēi is the feminine dative singular of the relative pronoun used as a dative of place.

2. This quotation does not give the full text of the passage (see Against Meidias, 138–39, 1). Here Tiberius simply gives the gist of the metaphor, and probably expects his readers to recall the passage in its entirety.

3. Il. 19, 222: phulopis, "battle-cry" in line 221 is the antecedent of "of which." In this metaphor the slaughter in war is compared to the work of the sickle in harvest time; "the bronze" [chalkos] thus has double meaning.

4. XXIX Anonymous (date unknown), *On Poetic Tropes.* Spengel, iii, 207, 18–23.

Allēgoria. Allēgoria, then, is speech [*lexis*] which says one thing but which presents a conception of another, as that which is said to the serpent: "Thou art accursed above every beast of the field" (*Genesis* 3: 14, KJV, abridged). It being understood allegorically in reference to the mental serpent, the Devil.

5. Gregorius Corinthius (12th cent. A.D.), *On Tropes.* Spengel, iii, 215, 21–216, 8.

Allēgoria. Allēgoria is speech [*phrasis*] making clear some one thing but presenting a conception of another. And then suitably do they apply *allēgoria* whenever either on account of caution or on account of awe they cannot explain openly, as in the iambic verses of Callimachus:

> The very fire which you kindled has advanced
> with great flame; but restrain the raging
> horse's running.[4]

For these things are not spoken in the proper sense since the discourse is neither concerning fire nor concerning a horse-race, but fearing, as it were, to show it plainly, he corrected his excess of over-boldness.

6. Cocondrius (date unknown), *On Tropes.* Spengel, iii, 234, 27–235, 18.

Allēgoria. Allēgoria is speech [*phrasis*] which makes one thing precisely clear but which presents another notion, as in Alcaeus:

> I am aware of the lie of the winds.
> For one wave rolls from this side,
> and another from that, but we are always
> carried in the middle, struggling greatly
> with a dark storm.[5]

For through these successive verses offhand a storm at sea is understood, but in truth a certain disturbance of political affairs is brought to light. But already even in Homer are single allegories:

> . . . Otherwise
> you had worn a tunic of stone for as many
> wrongs as you did us.–(*Il.* 3, 56–7)

---

4. Callimachus (fragment 195, 23–29) "attacks in iambics a schoolteacher . . . for shamefully abusing his own pupils, bidding him in the guise of a well-wisher not to do this, lest he be caught." (C. A. Trypanis's translation from the ancient *Diegesis* of this iambus; Loeb ed., p. 126).

5. I have translated the text as given by Cocondrius; for another text, see Denys Page, *Sappho and Alcaeus* (Oxford, 1959), pp. 185–86.

And the line:

> And indeed there is a surfeit of battle-
> cry for men.–(*Il.* 19, 221)

And:

> And indeed the bronze spreads on the ground.–(*Il.* 19, 222)

And:

> The harvest is least, whenever Zeus turns
> the scale, who administers war for men.–(*Il.* 19, 223–4)

But the species of *allēgoria* are two: irony [*eirōneia*] and enigma.

7. Georgius Choeroboscus (4th–5th cents. A.D.), *On Poetic Tropes.* Spengel, iii, 244, 13–245, 13.

Allēgoria. Allēgoria is speech [*lexis*] saying some one thing and presenting another notion, as that which is said in Holy Writ, where God says to the serpent: "Thou art cursed above all cattle" (*Genesis* 3: 14, KJV, abridged). For the speech is to the serpent, but we take it analogously in reference to the Devil, that is to say, allegorically. And this is employed both on account of solemnity and on account of caution. On account of solemnity, as in the case of matters concerning Hera in the verses in which Zeus says to her:

> Or do you not remember when you were hanging
>   from on high;
> and from your two feet I let down two anvils;
> and around your hands I threw a golden chain.–(*Il.* 15, 18–20)

The notion of which is this: joined together by the boundary of air are both earth and water which he calls also "anvils" on the ground that they are heavier than the rest of the elements, and a "golden chain" he calls the bright light from the sun which has been poured around the air, to which the air has been united.[6] But on account of caution, as "he undid her maiden girdle" (*Od.* 11, 245), instead of 'he seduced.' And, as in Callimachus:

> But you have kindled the fire until it has
> gone forward with a great flame . . .

And again:

6. The defense that the Homeric gods were to be understood allegorically originated with Theagenes of Rhegium (fl. c. 525 B.C.) and found its way into the Stoic school of philosophy through Stesimbrotus of Thasos (fl. late 5th cent. B.C.). As in this example, it was mostly natural phenomena that were to be understood in the gods. The most important surviving work of such Stoic allegory is the *Homeric Allegories* of Heraclitus (1st cent. A.D.). See Albin Lesky, *A History of Greek Literature* (Apollo edition), pp. 209, 329, 675.

But restrain from running your raging horses,
do not take a second turn around the post,
lest they drive the chariot beside the turning-
    post
and you be pitched head foremost.[4]

This is not spoken in the proper sense since to him the speech is neither concerning fire nor chariot-racing, but, being afraid, as it were, to say what he wished, he made use of *allēgoria.*

II. Antiphrasis

Introduction

Antiphrasis means "opposite-" or "contrary-expression." Six texts in Spengel deal with this trope. That of Tiberius is atypical in that he does not use the term *antiphrasis*, but calls it *to antikeimenon*, "that which is set over against," for example, "Iphicrates was not in the habit of doing such and such," meaning that Meidias was. This is prolonged irony.

The other texts define antiphrasis as we know it, and of these, that of Trypho presents the most lucid and complete discussion. From Trypho we learn that antiphrasis occurs when the opposite of what is meant is expressed by means of negation or antithesis, as when Homer calls Achilles "not the most feeble of the Achaeans." Or it is a brief, euphemistic irony of one or two words, as when we refer to the Erinyes (Furies) as the Eumenides ("the Well-Disposed"). Trypho calls this manner of expression "adding" [*parakeimenon*], and says that because of the inherent irony it "does not depend on delivery" [*chōris hupokriseōs*].

Although XXIX Anonymous, Gregorius Corinthius, Cocondrius and Choeroboscus seem to have copied their definitions of antiphrasis from Trypho, it is curious that, with the exception of *Il.* 1, 330 (Trypho, Gregorius Corinthius, Cocondrius), they give examples which differ from Trypho and from one another. XXIX Anonymous and Choeroboscus give brief, one-sentence definitions ("speech signifying the opposite by the opposite"), and do not mention "euphemistic" antiphrasis, whereas the longer texts of Gregorius Corinthius and Cocondrius do.

TEXTS

1. Tiberius (date unknown), *On the Figures in Demosthenes*. Spengel, iii, 66, 6–20.

Concerning Expression by the Opposite [*peri antikeimenou*]. Expression by the opposite occurs whenever he says something not about the matter in hand but the opposite in reference to another person, signifying this through that person, and this somewhat resembles emphasis. For again, wishing to say what things Meidias was doing, he mentioned them by the opposite for Iphicrates: "He was not in the habit of going by night to the houses of the goldsmiths, nor was he in the habit of rending the garments which had been prepared for the festival, nor was he in the habit of corrupting a trainer, nor yet was he in the habit of preventing a chorus from learning" (*Against Meidias*, 63). For by the opposite he is saying these things against Meidias. And again: "I do not go around beaming with joy at the success of others and rejoicing publicly" (*On the Gown*, 323). For he says this, I suppose, because the opponents do such things.

2. Trypho (1st cent. B.C.), *On Tropes.* Spengel, iii, 204, 3–18.

Concerning *Antiphrasis*. *Antiphrasis* is speech [*lexis*] presenting the opposite by the opposite or by adding independently of delivery, and it is added independently of delivery on account of the irony. By the opposite the opposite is expressed by negation [*antiphrazetai*] thus:

Since not the most feeble of Achaeans hit him–(*Il.* 15, 11)

–but the best, clearly. And:

Nor therefore when he saw those two did Achilles
  laugh–(*Il.* 1, 330)

–but he was confused and pained. Sometimes also the opposite itself is presented, for example, 'not the worst, but the best.' But by adding, things that are said euphemistically and dress up badness [*tēn kakian*], as whenever we call anger 'pleasant,' and the Erinyes 'Eumenides,' (i.e., "the Well-Disposed") and the producer of pain 'disagreeable,' and the ugly ape 'very handsome,' and the left hand 'of good name' [*euōnumon*], and salts 'seasonings.'

3. XXIX Anonymous (date unknown), *On Poetic Tropes.* Spengel, iii, 212, 6–8.

Antiphrasis. Antiphrasis is speech [*logos*] signifying the opposite by the opposite, as whenever someone calls the blind man, 'seer' [*bleponta*].

4. Gregorius Corinthius (12th cent. A.D.), *On Tropes.* Spengel, iii, 222, 19–29.

Antiphrasis. Antiphrasis is speech [*phrasis*] clothing as far as is in its power badness [*tēn kakian*] by means of things better than that which is being presented, for example, whenever we call a beggar 'wealthy,' anger 'sweet.' Or antiphrasis is speech [*lexis*] signifying independently of delivery the opposite by the opposite. And it is stated either by euphemism or by opposition. By euphemism, whenever we call the thorn upon which it is not possible to walk 'bramble' and anger 'sweet.' But by opposition:

> Nor therefore when he saw those two did Achilles
>   laugh–(*Il.* 1, 330),

instead of 'he was hurt.'

5. Cocondrius (date unknown), *On Tropes*. Spengel, iii, 233, 10–20.

Antiphrasis. Antiphrasis is speech [*lexis*] introducing the opposite by opposites or by additions. And by opposites:

> Nor therefore when he saw those two did Achilles
>   laugh–(*Il.* 1, 330),

instead of 'he was pained.' And:

> But the two flew not unwillingly–(*Il.* 5, 366),

instead of 'willingly.' And by additions, just as we are accustomed also to call the Erinyes 'reverend goddesses' [*semnas theas*], and Persephone 'Honied-one' [*Melitōnēn*], and the ape 'handsome,' and such-like.

6. Georgius Choeroboscus (4th–5th cents. A.D.), *On Poetic Tropes*. Spengel, iii, 251, 4–7.

Antiphrasis. Antiphrasis is speech [*lexis*] signifying the opposite by opposites, as when one might call the blind man 'far seeing,' or vinegar 'sweetmeat,' or say that white is "like an Aethiopian.'

III. IRONY

Introduction

Irony is expression which pretends the opposite of what it says and which may be directed either at ourselves or at our neighbors. Of the twelve texts in Spengel which define irony [*eirōneia*], I have chosen seven which seem to me to make significant contributions to the history and theory of this trope.

I have omitted the earliest discussion of irony, that of the fourth-century-B.C. rhetorician Anaximenes of Lampsacus (= [Aristotle], *Rhetorica ad Alexandrum*), because this work has been translated into English many times. Anaximenes (*Art of Rhetoric*, chapter 21) defines irony as "saying something while pretending not to say it, or it is to call things by opposite names." He finds the technique of "saying something while pretending not to say it" very useful for reminding the audience of something at the end of both the divisions and the final conclusions of speeches.

I have also omitted the discussion by the second-century-A.D. rhetorician Alexander, whose brief definition ("Irony is speech pretending to say the opposite") is followed by one example each from Euripides and Demosthenes. He then lists, without definitions, discussions, or examples four species of irony: mock-modesty [*asteismos*], sneering [*muktērismos*], sarcasm [*sarkasmos*], scoffing [*chleuasmos*].

The third text that I have omitted is the discussion by Tiberius, who simply defines irony as "that which signifies the opposite by the opposite," and follows this with two examples from Demosthenes' third *Olynthiac* (24, 27). Tiberius, however, does seem to me to make one important observation when he says that in the *Against Meidias*, Demosthenes "has employed irony in a new way in reference to himself: 'But I am he who—whether someone wishes to consider it madness (for

119

it is madness perhaps to do something beyond one's capability) or ambition—consented to be choregus' (69)."

I have also omitted the very brief text on irony by Zonaeus because he simply defines irony as "speech pretending the opposite of what it says," and quotes Euripides, *Medea*, 509–13.

Finally, I have omitted the discussion of irony by Choeroboscus, because it is verbally similar to XXIX Anonymous, and therefore adds nothing of substance that is not said in that text.

I have printed Phoebammon's discussion because he says that irony is a figure of thought, a species of enallage.

From the treatise *On Figures* by Aelius Herodianus I have excerpted the section from the chapter "Concerning Figures of Thought" in which he talks about irony as a kind of emphasis [*epitasis*], and then lists and defines six "rather refined" species of irony: sarcasm [*sarkasmos*], ridicule [*diasurmos*], taunt [*epikertomēsis*], derision [*katagelōs*], conjecturing [*eikasmos*], wit [*charientismos*]. Each of these is directed at some other person, not at oneself.

Because of the richness of the examples therein, I have printed XXIV Anonymous, which defines irony as "emphasis of badness through fair-sounding words."

I have included Trypho's "Concerning Irony" in which he informs us that irony is spoken "with a certain moral delivery" [*meta tinos ēthikēs hupokriseōs*], and also points out that irony is meant partly for our neighbors and partly for ourselves.

I have printed the discussion of irony in XXIX Anonymous because of the vivid descriptions of scoffing, sneering, and sarcasm. But I have bracketed the last paragraph of this text, because the description of *asteismos* is more appropriate to sneering than to mock-modesty.

Gregorius Corinthius lists *eirōneia, sarkasmos*, and *asteismos* as separate lexical entries. I print all three of these. He points out that delivery accompanies irony, combines scoffing with sarcasm, and gives a lucid definition of mock-modesty [*asteismos*].

The last text printed in this section is that of Cocondrius, who considers irony to be a species of *allēgoria* (see Allegory 6). He mentions two species of irony, *antimetathesis* and *enantiōsis*, which are not found in any of the other discussions. Altogether, he names eight species of irony, and in defining these he makes many subtle distinctions.

TEXTS

1. Phoebammon (5th–6th cents. A.D.), *Notes on Rhetorical Figures*. Spengel, iii, 53, 21–29.

Concerning Forms of *Enallagē*. In relation to *enallagē* are four figures of thought: irony, doubting [*diaporēsis*], ridicule [*diasurmos*], apostrophe. Of these, irony is speech [*logos*] opposite to those things which we are arguing, signifying them by emphasis, so that when I charge someone with meddlesomeness and profitmaking, I say: 'So-and-so who always keeps quiet and never interferes with another person's business,' pointing out by my demeanor that I hold the opposite opinion concerning him.

2. Aelius Herodianus (date unknown), *On Figures.* Spengel, iii, 91, 16–93, 1.

[Concerning Figures of Thought]

Of the figures of thought two names are uppermost, emphasis [*epitasis*] and weakening [*eklusis*]. Of these, to emphasis is assigned irony [*eirōneia*], and to weakening is assigned detraction [*katabolē*].

Irony is speech [*logos*] signifying the subject matter through opposites by emphasis, as in Euripides, when Medea, proclaiming all the benefits that she had initiated for her husband, adds very emotionally:

> So then, in return for this you have made
> me happy among many throughout Hellas, and I,
> wretched, have you for my wonderful and faith-
> ful husband, if cast out from my land, I shall
> wander in exile, bereft of home, alone with
> only my children.–(*Medea*, 509–13)

Weakening [*eklusis*] occurs when the intensity of great matters is abated in the minds of the listeners by triviality of expression, as when Aeschines says: "Do you not remember his odious and incredible words? How you once, men of iron, listened patiently when he came forward and said, 'Certain men are stripping the city; the twigs of the people have been cast under; we are being stitched like a mat'" (*Against Ctesiphon*, 166). For these words are out of proportion to the subject matter at that time.

But of irony there are established the following rather refined species: sarcasm [*sarkasmos*], ridicule [*diasurmos*], taunt [*epikertomēsis*], derision [*katagelōs*], conjecturing [*eikasmos*], wit [*charientismos*]. Now sarcasm is moral speech [*logos ēthikos*], spoken with the face grinning, for example:

> In truth much work has been accomplished without me;
> indeed he built a wall, and drove a ditch on it,
> wide, great, and on it he attached stakes.–(*Il.* 9, 348–50)

Ridicule is ironic speech [*logos eirōnikos*], spoken for the disparagement of one's neighbors, for example:

> But then one other stood up to prophesy.–(*Od.* 20, 380)

Taunt is provocative speech [*logos erethistikos*], composed for the purpose of paining one's enemies, for example:

> Now sit you here keeping off dogs and pigs,
> and be you not lord of strangers and beg-
>   gars.–(*Od.* 18, 105–6)

And derision is whenever we mock at some action of those who are unsuitably emboldened, for example:

> Othryoneus, I praise you beyond all mortals,
> if truly indeed you shall accomplish all those
>   things
> that you undertook for Dardanian Priam.–(*Il.* 13, 374–6)

And conjecturing is whenever we put down our neighbors with the aid of a simile, for example:

> Ah me! how the greedy fellow runs on at the
>   mouth
> like an old furnace-woman.–(*Od.* 18, 27–8)

And wit is moral speech [*logos ēthikos*], presenting with grace the speaker's ridicule for someone, for example:

> See now! how very nimble the man is, who
>   lightly somersaults.[1]

3. XXIV Anonymous (date unknown), *On the Figures of Speech*. Spengel, iii, 140, 26–142, 8.

Concerning Irony. Irony is emphasis of badness through fair-sounding words, as the poet in the ninth book, when Achilles says to Odysseus concerning Agamemnon:

> In truth he has accomplished much with-
>   out me;
> indeed he has built and driven a wall.–(*Il.* 9, 348–9)

And, pointing out the uselessness of the wall, he says:

> But not even so can it restrain the
>   strength of
> manslaying Hector.–(*Il.* 9, 350–1)

By saying "he has accomplished much without me," he augmented the actions of Agamemnon. For in ironies we augment those things which we despise. Some also call that which is inferred ironic. For example, Achilles, disparaging himself because he was dishonored by Agamemnon, says:

---

1. *Il.* 16, 745. Patroclus mocks Cebriones, Hector's charioteer, as he falls, mortally wounded, from the chariot. In lines 746–47, he goes on to say that if he were in the sea diving for oysters, he would be very good at it.

> But now since I am unwilling–(*Il.* 9, 356),

instead of 'I cannot, in view of the prejudice which Agamemnon holds concerning me.' For, remembering Agamemnon's words:

> Flee then, if your heart urges, nor do I
> beg you to stay, for with me are other
>   men
> who will honor me, etc.–(*Il.* 1, 173 ff.),

Achilles says to Odysseus:

> But, Odysseus, with your help and that of other kings–(*Il.* 9, 346).

And again:

> Tomorrow when I have made sacrifice to Zeus
>   and all the gods,
> and loaded well my ships and am rowing out to
>   sea,
> you will see, if you wish–(*Il.* 357-9),

hinting that he is not at leisure, that these things await him in consequence of the application of the former things. And the orator says in the *On the Halonnese:* "[Philip] has deprived the Pheraeans of their city and has established a garrison in the citadel in order that, forsooth, they might be autonomous (32)." For they received a garrison from him and lost their freedom. Next: "And he made an expedition against Ambracia and the three cities in Cassopia, Pandosia, Boucheta, and Elateia, colonies of the Eleians; and when he had burned the land and had forced his way into the cities, he handed them over to be slaves to Alexander his own brother-in-law (32)." Then, ironically: "He indeed does vehemently wish the Hellenes to be free and autonomous, as his deeds make clear (32)." And in another section: "So insolently has he dealt with you that he says that, if the people of Cardia do not wish to submit to arbitration, he will compel them on the ground that you are powerless and unable to force the Cardians to give you your rights; and indeed, since you cannot, he says that he will compel them to do this (44)." Next, the ironic statement: "Is he not manifestly showing great kindness to you? (44)"[2]

4. Trypho (1st cent. B.C.), *On Tropes.* Spengel, iii, 205, 1-15.

Concerning Irony. Irony is speech [*logos*] making clear the opposite by the opposite with a certain moral delivery, as in Euripides, when Medea says that Jason, who has done her many wrongs, has made her happy; and similarly also Telemachus says to one of the suitors:

2. The author of the *On the Halonnese* is no longer considered to be Demosthenes, but is probably the well-known orator Hegesippus, who also was a consistent opponent of Philip. For an account of the historical events mentioned in the quotations, see N. G. L. Hammond, *A History of Greece to 322 B.C.*, 2nd ed. (Oxford, 1967), pp. 560-62.

> Antinoos, how well you care for me, as a
> father for his son.–(*Od.* 17, 397)

For in fact Antinoos showed no fatherly concern for him. On the contrary,
moreover, he even desired to kill him. And when Orestes says to Tyndareus:

> The father who has begotten the finest
> daughters–(Euripides, *Orestes*, 750),

who has produced the worst. Part of irony is meant for our neighbors, and part
for ourselves. Now the part which refers to our neighbors is called sneering
[*muktērismos*] and scoffing [*chleuasmos*], and that which refers to ourselves,
mock-modesty [*asteismos*].

5. XXIX Anonymous (date unknown), *On Poetic Tropes*. Spengel, iii, 213,
15–214, 12.

Irony. Irony is speech suited for delivery [*logos hupokritikos*], making clear the
opposite from the opposite. And the species of irony are four: scoffing
[*chleuasmos*], sneering [*muktērismos*], sarcasm [*sarkasmos*], and mock-modesty
[*asteismos*].

Scoffing. Now scoffing is speech [*logos*] brought forward with a smile, as
when we laugh at and call the one who throws his shield away in battle a brave
warrior.

Sneering. And sneering is disparaging speech [*logos diasurtikos*] with the
closing of the nostrils, as when we reproach someone who has been caught at a
crime and say, 'You have done a fine deed and one worthy of a prudent man,'
while also blowing a breath through our nostrils.

Sarcasm. And sarcasm is speech [*logos*] emphasizing dishonor by nice words,
as when we say to one who in the acquisition of greater honor has fallen into
evils, 'You have brought yourself to great glory and honor, friend.'

[*Asteismos*. And *asteismos* is a disparaging speech [*logos tis diasurtikos*], har-
moniously organized, as when we say either declaratively or interrogatively to
one who knows nothing, 'For as you are, you are the talk of the erudite,' and all
such things as one ought to examine in the compositions of others and ought
oneself to attempt to compose with fitting harmony and arrangement.]

6. Gregorius Corinthius (12th cent. A.D.), *On Tropes*. Spengel, iii, 222, 4–18.

Irony. Irony is speech [*phrasis*] spoken with delivery contrariwise to the literal
meaning, for example:

> Antinoos, how well you care for me, as a
> father for his son.–(*Od.* 17, 397)

Sarcasm. Sarcasm is speech [*phrasis*] spoken contrariwise to the literal meaning with scoffing, for example:

> Now indeed, Melanthius, you will keep watch
>   all night
> resting on a soft bed.–(*Od.* 22, 195–6)

Mock-modesty [*asteismos*]. Mock-modesty is speech [*phrasis*] which morally emphasizes the better through opposites, for example, if someone who is wealthy should say that he is poor, and the craftsman that he is unskilled, and a nobleman that he is a nobody. But some have defined mock-modesty to be an affectation of the truth.

7. Cocondrius (date unknown), *On Tropes.* Spengel, iii, 235, 19–236, 19.

Irony. Irony is speech [*logos*] making clear the opposite through the opposite with a cetain moral delivery, and part of it is in reference to ourselves and part in reference to our neighbors. That which is in reference to ourselves is called mock-modesty [*asteismos*] and interchange [*antimetathesis*], and that which is in reference to our neighbors scoffing [*chleuasmos*], sneering [*muktērismos*], wit [*charientismos*], taunt [*epikertomēsis*], ridicule [*diasurmos*], opposition [*enantiōsis*]. For these are the species of irony. Now mock-modesty is speech of itself containing prejudice against another, for example:

> Antinoos, how well you care for me, as a
> father for his son.–(*Od.* 17, 397)

But interchange [*antimetathesis*] is irony emphasizing affectation of blame for oneself and of praise for a neighbor, for example, 'For I was not fighting, nor was I advancing, but I was fleeing; he, on the contrary, acted.' Sneering [*muktērismos*] is scoffing [*chleuasmos*] with some movement and drawing together of the nostrils. But sarcasm is also scoffing to the point of grinning and displaying the teeth along with it. But wit [*charientismos*] with pretended friendliness becomes irony for evil and harm. And taunt [*epikertomēsis*] is irony which brings out the pleasure of the speaker, as is:

> See now! how very nimble the man is, who
>   lightly somersaults;
> if indeed he should also be in the fishy
>   sea,
> he would satisfy the hunger of many men.[1]

And ridicule [*diasurmos*] is irony which disparages vocal expression [*to epos*], as:

> Although you are a fluent orator, Thersites,
>   your words are confused.–(*Il.* 2, 246)

And opposition [*enantiōsis*] is expression [*lexis*] which signifies the opposite by the opposite, as, 'Indeed Odysseus was not fleeing, nor was he feigning madness.' And unseparated jest [*skōmma ou diakechōrismenon*] accompanies all these. But likeness [*eikasma*] is jest by resemblance, as is the line in Eupolis:

But they liken us to a bulb, a ripe
fig.–(Fragment 345, Kock)

And some not very elegantly place both proverbs and fables under allegories.

Texts Omitted

8. Anaximenes of Lampsacus (4th cent. B.C.), *Art of Rhetoric (Rhetorica ad Alexandrum)*. Spengel, i, 208, 14–30. Translated by E. S. Forster in *The Works of Aristotle Translated into English*, XI (Oxford, 1946).

9. Alexander (2nd cent. A.D.), *On Figures of Thought and Speech*. Spengel, iii, 22, 29–23, 9.

10. Tiberius (date unknown), *On the Figures in Demosthenes*. Spengel, iii, 60, 6–19.

11. Zonaeus (date unknown), *On Figures According to Thought*. Spengel, iii, 164, 12–20.

12. Georgius Choeroboscus (4th–5th cents. A.D.), *On Poetic Tropes*. Spengel, iii, 254, 23–255, 8.

IV. Enigma

Introduction

The word *ainigma* — "enigma," "dark saying," "riddle" — appears first in extant Greek literature in Pindar (Fragment 164 Bowra).[1] Five texts in Spengel describe this trope. I print two of these, Trypho and XXIX Anonymous. Trypho's treatment of enigma is the more comprehensive and the more profusely illustrated. First, he defines enigma as "speech mischievously [*kakoscholōs*] contrived for obscurity, concealing that which is to be apprehended, presenting something either impossible or inexplicable." After he explains how enigma differs from allegory ("allegory becomes obscure in either diction or thought, but enigma in both"), he names and gives examples of six ways of producing enigma.

XXIX Anonymous defines enigma, gives several examples of it which are quite similar to those in Trypho, and then says that "enigma differs from allegory in that the latter occurs for the sake of persuasion or dissuasion or on account of solemnity, but enigma for the sake of contrived obscurity alone."

I have omitted the texts of Gregorius Corinthius, Cocondrius, and Choeroboscus. As printed by Spengel, the Greek text of Gregorius Corinthius is almost impossible to construe beyond the initial definition of enigma as "speech [*phrasis*] which attempts to render thought concealed and complex."[2] The text by Cocondrius is only six lines long, and says that enigma is expression which "conceals that which is to be

---

1. Another name for *ainigma* is *griphos*, from *griphos*, a fishing-net or basket, and so, metaphorically, anything intricate. Athenaeus (*The Deipnosophists*, x, 69–87) gives a generous selection of *griphoi* from comedy and other literary sources. See below, note 5.
2. For some interesting reconstructions and suggestions for this text, see M. L. West, "Hesiodea," *Classical Quarterly*, n.s. 11 (1961), 142–45; and M. L. West, "Tryphon *De Tropis*," *Classical Quarterly*, n.s. 15 (1965), 230–48.

apprehended by removing the contingent attributes." He then says that in the following verse, Chaeremon is talking about a grapevine:

> In spring, the bride; later, with summer, a
> child;
> but in winter she goes rejoicing with the
> wind.

The twenty-four line discussion by Choeroboscus begins with this definition and biblical example of enigma: "Enigma is speech [*logos*] keeping dark and concealed within itself that which is to be apprehended, as the question propounded to the Philistines by Sampson, in which he says, 'From the eater came forth meat' (Judges 14:14), signifying the very lion which he had killed, and the discovery in its mouth of the honeycomb." The rest reads like abbreviated Trypho, with the exception that his explanation of how enigma differs from allegory is verbally similar to that of XXIX Anonymous.

TEXTS

1. Trypho (1st cent. B.C.), *On Tropes.* Spengel, iii, 193, 13–195, 8.

Concerning Enigma.[3] Enigma [*ainigma*] is speech [*phrasis*] mischievously contrived for obscurity, concealing that which is to be apprehended, presenting something either impossible or inexplicable. And it differs from allegory in that allegory becomes obscure in either diction or thought, but enigma in both, for example: "The weaker [*hēssōn*] suffered [*algēsas*] and brought up the son of Thetis." For 'the inferior' [*cheirōn*] is 'weaker' [*hēssōn*]; 'suffered' [*algēsas*] is 'toiled' [*ponēsas*]; the meaning is that Cheiron the Centaur reared Achilles. And again:

> Earth, son of Binder, died when deprived of
> containers,

instead of Aias, son of Telamon, died when he failed to gain the arms. For *gēs* is Aias; <*kata*> *desmou* is 'of Telamon;' containers [*angeiōn*] are the arms.[4] And:

---

3. See above, note 1.

4. The Greek is: *gēs ethane katadesmou hot' angeiōn aphamarten.* The nominative singular *Aias* (Ajax) resembles *aias* the genitive singular of *aia*, epic form for *gaia*, another form of *gē* (earth), the genitive singular of which is *gēs. Katadesmou* is genitive singular of *katadesmos* (band), which is equivalent to *telamōn* (i.e., Telamon), a band for supporting something (e.g., a shield or sword). Arms (armor) may be construed as "containers" for the body.

> There are two sisters, one of whom gives
>   birth to
> the other, and she herself in turn becomes
>   her daughter.[5]

For he is speaking of day and night. And enigma occurs in six ways: by similarity, by oppositeness, by contingent attribute, by information, by homonym, by riddle-word. By similarity, for example, Androcydes, the Pythagorean, used to say: "Don't step over a yoke [*zugon*]," instead of Don't offend against Right; "Don't nourish those with crooked talons," instead of Avoid robbers; "Don't eat black-tail," instead of Don't utter a false word (for the false turns black and becomes dim in its extremities); "Don't sit on a choenix," that is, Don't come to rest in a day's wage, but pay in advance; "Don't stir a fire with a knife," that is, Don't provoke the angry man with words. And the Hesiodic saying:

> Do not take and eat from undedicated caul-
>   drons –(*Works and Days*, 748–9),

that is, Don't be immoderate and greedy. And in life also some events occur enigmatically in a similar manner, for example, during weddings the omen-takers pound sesame or barley since they are many-seeded. And by oppositeness, for example: "A man and not a man, seeing and not seeing, hits and does not hit with a stone and not a stone a bird and not a bird sitting and not sitting upon a tree and not a tree." This has been said in reference to an eunuch who has hit a bat with a pumice-stone and missed because of not seeing accurately. The eunuch is "a man and not a man." The bat is "a bird and not a bird," for it is not feathered but flying. And "seeing and not seeing" is not seeing well, for he was dim-sighted. "Sitting and not sitting" because the bat is hanging upside-down. The fennel-stalk is "a tree and not a tree." The pumice-stone is "a stone and not a stone." "Hits and does not hit" because that which is cast misses its mark. And by contingent attribute [*kata sumbebēkos*], as:

> I have two brothers, two only.
> Now as long as they live, they do
>   not look upon the sun;
> but when they die and come to the
>   hands of men,
> they see the sun, and fight each
>   other.

He is talking about knucklebones, I think. And by information [*kata historian*], for example, "Trito-born."[6] By homonym, as is the oracle given to

---

5. Athenaeus (x, 75) attributes these lines to the *Oedipus* of Theodectes of Phasilis (c. 375–334 B.C.), who was a student of Aristotle, a writer on rhetorical subjects, a composer of popular riddles in verse, and a tragic poet.
6. An epithet of Athena, the meaning of which is unknown, but various explanations were given for it in antiquity.

Alexander Molossus: "Beware of the WAXY ONE."[7] For he thought it was the river in Italy, but it was another one. In fact, when a waxed tablet had been given to him, he read this, and was slain by treachery. And by riddle-word [*kata glōttan*], whenever one calls the sea "wide-belly," Athena "sparkling-eyes," and the mouse "long-tail."

2. XXIX Anonymous (date unknown), *On Poetic Tropes.* Spengel, iii, 209, 12–23.

Enigma. Enigma is speech [*phrasis*] contrived for obscurity, so as to disguise that which is to be apprehended. For example: "Don't step over the yoke," that is to say, Don't destroy or offend against Right. And, furthermore, "Don't nourish those with crooked talons," that is to say, Don't feed robbers. And, "You will not taste of black-tails," that is to say, You will not publish falsehood (for this becomes dim in the end and impairs also the liar); "Don't stir a fire with a knife," that is to say, Don't provoke further an angry man. And enigma differs from allegory in that the latter occurs for the sake of persuasion or dissuasion or on account of solemnity, but enigma for the sake of contrived obscurity alone.

Texts Omitted

3. Gregorius Corinthius (12th cent. A.D.), *On Tropes.* Spengel, iii, 224, 27–225, 6.

4. Cocondrius (date unknown), *On Tropes.* Spengel, iii, 236, 20–26.

5. Georgius Choeroboscus (4th–5th cents. A.D.), *On Poetic Tropes.* Spengel, iii, 253, 7–31.

7. Alexander Molossus (died 330 B.C.) was king of Epirus, brother of Olympias, and so uncle of Alexander the Great. He went to Italy to aid the Tarentines against the Romans. According to Justin (xii, 2), he was slain by a Lucanian while crossing the river Acheron in Bruttium.

V. Metaphor

Introduction

Aristotle is the first to speak to us concerning metaphor. In chapter XXI of the *Poetics*, he defines metaphor as four kinds of transference: "Metaphor is the application of an alien name by transference either from genus to species, or from species to genus, or from species to species, or by analogy, that is, by proportion. Thus from genus to species, as: 'There lies my ship'; for lying at anchor is a species of lying. From species to genus, as: 'Verily ten thousand noble deeds hath Odysseus wrought'; for ten thousand is a species of large number, and is here used for a large number generally. From species to species, as: 'With blade of bronze drew away the life,' and 'Cleft the water with the vessel of unyielding bronze.' Here αρυσαι, 'to draw away,' is used for ταμειν, 'to cleave,' and ταμειν again for αρυσαι,—each being a species of taking away. Analogy or proportion is when the second term is to the first as the fourth to the third. We may then use the fourth for the second, or the second for the fourth." (Translation by S. H. Butcher)

In the third book of the *Rhetoric*, Aristotle is concerned with prose style, and says that it should have lucidity and propriety. The language, moreover, should have a "foreign" [*xenikos*] quality, that is, distinctive, away from the common. Nevertheless, the appearance of naturalness should always be maintained. In contrast to the poet, the stylistic resources of the orator are few: "Proper and appropriate words and metaphors are alone to be employed in the style of prose; this is shown by the fact that no one employs anything but these. For all use metaphors in conversation, as well as proper and appropriate words; wherefore it is clear that, if a speaker manages well, there will be something 'foreign' about his speech, while possibly the art may not be detected, and his meaning will be clear. And this, as we have said, is the

chief merit of rhetorical language." (*Rhetoric*, III. ii. 6. Translation by
J. H. Freese)

Since it is such an important element of prose style, Aristotle discusses metaphor at great length (III. ii. 6–xi. 16). "Above all, it is metaphor
that has lucidity [*to saphes*], pleasure [*to hēdu*], and a foreign quality [*to
xenikon*]." (ii. 8. My translation) He goes on to say that metaphors must
be appropriate, and this is brought about by keeping proper proportion. For if metaphors are used to adorn, one must take them from the
better species in the same genus; if to censure, from the worse. (ii. 9–10)
They should be of agreeable sound. (ii. 11) Metaphors must not be too
far-fetched. In general, clever enigmas are a source of good
metaphors. (ii. 12) Metaphors must be derived from things beautiful to
the senses; for example, there is a difference between "rosy-fingered
dawn" and "red-fingered." (ii. 13). In iii. 4, he explains how unsuitable
metaphors (i.e., ridiculous, too dignified, too tragic) contribute to
frigidity of style. In iv, he discusses simile as metaphor. After a chapter
on composition (v), he resumes his discussion of metaphor to say that
metaphors contribute to the dignity of style, but one must avoid the
poetical metaphor (vi. 4). After several chapters in which he takes up
other problems of style (vi. 5–ix), he again takes up metaphor in
chapters x–xi. In chapter x, he says that smartness of style and
argument make easy learning possible, and that smart sayings [*ta asteia*]
and arguments (enthymemes) depend on antithetical statement,
metaphor, and actualization ("putting things before the eyes"). Of the
four kinds of metaphor, the one that meets with the most approval is
the one based on proportion, as in "Thus Pericles said that the youth
which had perished in the war had disappeared from the state as if
someone had removed the spring from the year" (x. 7). In chapter xi.
1–5, he says that "putting things before the eyes" is accomplished by
means of metaphors and similes. These must be taken from things that
are familiar and proper, but not too obvious. Chapter xi. 6–16 is a
discussion of smart sayings [*ta asteia*]. He says that most smart sayings
are derived from metaphors. But they are also derived from adding
deception. He goes on to discuss the means of deceiving one's listener:
apophthegms, well-made riddles, paradoxes, jokes, play upon words,
proverbs, and hyperbole. Proverbs are metaphors from species to
species (xi. 14). Approved hyperboles are also metaphors; for instance,
you could call a man with a black and blue eye a "basket of mulberries"
(xi. 15–16).

Let us leave Aristotle and turn to the discussion of metaphor in the
On the Sublime. In chapter 32, the author takes issue with Caecilius with
regard to the number of metaphors that should be used in the same

passage. Whereas Caecilius said that they should be limited to two, or at most three, our author says that if we take Demosthenes, Xenophon, and Plato as our models, we will find that in passionate and descriptive passages both the number and the boldness of metaphors contribute to great writing.

Since both the *Rhetoric* of Aristotle and the *On the Sublime* are available in English translations, I have excluded them from the texts printed below. There are eight other texts in Spengel which treat metaphor extensively. I have printed all of these below except the "Concerning Metaphor and Parabole," from the treatise *On Style* (chapters 78–90), which was long attributed to Theophrastus's pupil Demetrius of Phaleron. There are three recent English translations of this work. Here I shall give its main points. "Demetrius" says in his opening paragraph: "Now, first, it is necessary to make use of metaphors, for these contribute especially both pleasure and magnitude to speeches. One must not, however, crowd them, since, in that case, we shall compose a dithyramb instead of a speech. And one must not use metaphors which have been transferred from afar, but on the spot; and they must be based on sameness, for example: a general, a steersman, a charioteer are similar to one another, for all these are rulers. Therefore will speak with certainty both he who calls the general 'steersman of the state' and, contrariwise, he who calls the steersman 'ruler of the ship'." The reader will recognize Demetrius's primary source, Aristotle. The main purpose of this whole discussion is to instruct the writer of prose in the proper use of metaphor. For example, Demetrius warns the writer that, whenever metaphor seems dangerous (i.e., ridiculous), it should be altered to simile [*eikasia*]. For simile is expanded metaphor, protected by the words "just as" [*hōsper*] (80). Several chapters later, he says that in making metaphor simile, "one must aim at brevity and in displaying no more than the 'just as'; otherwise, instead of a simile, you will have a poetic comparison [*parabolē poiētikē*]." And he adds that one must not put these extended comparisons [*parabolai*] into prose narratives without the greatest caution (89–90).

The first text printed below is the one from the *On Invention*, attributed to Hermogenes. It is atypical in that it calls metaphor "trope," and is critical of those who talk about metaphor in terms of going "from inanimate beings to animate beings and the reverse" (see nos. 2, 3, 4, 5, 6, below). The main point of Hermogenes' discussion seems to be that, if one employs a metaphor of the category "ridiculous," it is better not to give an immediate explanation of it for the reason that it will go unnoticed by all but the keenest of minds if the explanation is delayed.

Next, the group of texts consisting of Trypho, XXIX Anonymous, Gregorius Corinthius, Cocondrius, and Choeroboscus presents definitions of metaphor that bear a close resemblance to one another. For all say that metaphor is expression transferred from the proper to the improper for the sake of emphasis or resemblance. Indeed they derive their main idea from Aristotle, *Rhetoric*, III. xi. 1–5. There Aristotle explains a type of proportional metaphor that has the function of "setting before the eyes" [*to pro ommatōn poiein*], or contains what he calls "activity" [*energeia*]. He means that words that signify "activity" set things before the eyes. He says that Homer creates the appearance of "activity" when he talks about inanimate things as if they were animate. And Homer attaches the attributes of animate beings to inanimate objects by means of the proportional metaphor. Thus, starting from Aristotle's "from animate to inanimate," it was possible for others to discover three more "species" of metaphor: "from animate to animate," "from inanimate to animate," and "from inanimate to inanimate." To the above, however, Gregorius Corinthius and Choeroboscus add a fifth species, "from action to action."

The last text, XXXI Anonymous, gives the same definition for metaphor as the group above, but the main difference is that it does not talk about the four categories of transference ("from animate to inanimate," and so on), but only two, "from body to body," and "from action to action." Mention is also made of metaphors of the proportional type which have a reciprocal relationship between their parts and those which do not. Finally, there is mention of transference from "genus to genera," but the example given could also be called "from genus to species."

TEXTS

1. Hermogenes (2nd cent. A.D.), *On Invention: part four.* Spengel, ii, 254, 17–255, 21.

Concerning Trope. Trope is making a word significant not by means of subject matter but by means of alien matter, it being possible to be common both to the subject and to that which is exemplified from outside, a thing which is also called metaphor in the grammarians, not, as those say, from inanimate beings to animate beings and the reverse. For, on the whole, rhetoric, making no close investigation of either animate or inanimate beings, uses alien expressions as follows. For example: "The affairs of the city have been drained dry" instead of 'have been abandoned,' and "They tame." For there is exemplified in the former expression the banquet and in the latter the taming of wild beasts, matters not under consideration in the speech. But if someone should take hold of this form and should also complete the expression of the trope in a connected manner so as to put in all the comparison, he would have done a service, but if he should fall short, it is in rather bad taste. For example: "We have trained against ourselves an enemy so old." For when he had taken and spoken an expression from the games, he gave the immediate explanation: "Or let someone point out to me from what other place than ourselves Philip has become strong, etc." It is necessary, however, to know that all those things that are effective in completing the trope will be interpreted immediately, but all those that are rather ridiculous escape notice at a great interval in time and are evident to the expert but are not evident to the unskilled. Now this expression, being dignified, was interpreted immediately, but "The affairs of the city have been drained dry," if it had the explanation immediately at hand, would be rather ridiculous, but, placed at a great interval, goes unnoticed and is not even evident. For somewhere a little below he will say: "Philip is drunk on the magnitude of his accomplishments." Therefore the expression "to be drunk" has been set in motion from the beginning of "has been drained dry," and "to be drunk" seemed to be rather ridiculous immediately adjacent to "has been drained dry." "To dream," however, being dignified, when adjacent to "to be drunk," adorned the speech. For dreaming is common to those who are drunk.[1]

2. Trypho (1st cent. B.C.), *On Tropes.* Spengel, iii, 191, 23–192, 19.

Concerning Metaphor. Metaphor is expression [*lexis*] transferred from the proper to the improper for the sake of emphasis or resemblance. For emphasis, as:

> But the spear rushed through, being eager.–(*Il.* 15, 542)

For the word "being eager" [*maimōōsa*], essentially "being ready" [*prothumoumenē*], being specifically assigned to an animate being, how has been assigned to the spear which is inanimate. And for resemblance:

> But all the feet of many-fountained Ida
> were shaken.–(*Il.* 20, 59)

And:

> On heads of a mountain.–(*Il.* 2, 456)

---

1. Hermogenes takes his illustrations from Demosthenes: "The affairs of the city have been drained dry": third *Olynthiac*, 22; "They tame": third *Olynthiac*, 31; "We have trained against ourselves an enemy so old. Or let someone point out to me from what other place than ourselves Philip has become strong": third *Olynthiac*, 28; "Philip is drunk on the magnitude of his accomplishments" is immediately followed by "and dreams many such things in his mind": first *Philippic*, 49 (in the Demosthenic corpus, the Philippics immediately follow the Olynthiacs).

For "feet" [*podes*] and "heads" [*koruphai*] would be said in reference to human beings, but in reference to a mountain "lower parts" [*hupōreiai*] and "ridges" [*akrōreiai*]. But metaphor occurs in fourfold manner: from animate beings to animate beings, as "shepherd of the people"; for both are animate. From inanimate beings to inanimate beings, as "saving a seed of fire"–(*Od.* 5, 490). From animate beings to inanimate beings, as:

> Fixed in the ground, longing to taste
> flesh–(*Il.* 11, 574; 21, 168),

and:

> The shameless stone was rolled.–(*Od.* 11, 598)

From inanimate beings to animate beings, as:

> But unquenchable laughter arose among
> the blessed gods.–(*Il.* 1, 599)

3. XXIX Anonymous (date unknown), *On Poetic Tropes.* Spengel, iii, 208, 1-19.

Metaphor. Metaphor is a part of speech [*meros logou*] transferred from that which is properly said to another thing for the sake of resemblance or emphasis. And its species are four. From an animate being to an animate being, for example: if we call the king 'shepherd' (metaphorically from the shepherd of the flocks), for the shepherd and the king both are also animate beings. From animate being to inanimate being, for example: if we should call the ridge of the mountain 'head of a mountain,' for head [*koruphē*] is properly employed in reference to a human being, which is animate, but the mountain is inanimate. From inanimate to inanimate, for example: if someone who has hidden coals of fire in ash should say that he is protecting a seed of fire (which is employed in reference to grain and the like—whatever are inanimate beings—and fire is the same); or, if he should say that the flame was poured, for to be poured goes properly with wet things—from which it is employed metaphorically also in reference to fire. And from inanimate to animate, for example: if someone calls the brave and unyielding man 'adamantine', for adamant is an inanimate being, but the man is animate.

4. Gregorius Corinthius (12th cent. A.D.), *On Tropes.* Spengel, iii, 216, 9-217, 8.

Metaphor. Metaphor is a part of speech [*logou meros*] transferred for the sake of either emphasis or resemblance. And there are five species of metaphors. For some of them are from animate beings to inanimate beings; others, contrariwise, from inanimate beings to animate beings; others from animate beings to animate beings; others from inanimate beings to inanimate beings; others from action to action. From animate beings to inanimate beings, whenever the poet says in reference to spears:

> And many in the middle before touching
>   white flesh
> are fixed in the ground, longing to taste
>   flesh.–(*Il.* 11, 574-5)

For 'longing' belongs to animate beings, the very thing which he has conferred on the spear which is inanimate. And this has been said for emphasis. But from inanimate beings to animate beings, as:

> But unquenchable laughter arose.–(*Il.* 1, 599)

For 'unquenchable' was transferred from fire which is inanimate to laughter which is animate, and this too for emphasis. From animate beings to animate beings, as calling the king of the multitudes a 'shepherd' of the people. For, in fact, both are animate beings. For, as flocks are subject to the shepherd, so are multitudes to the king, and the king is a shepherd. But this has been said for resemblance. From inanimate beings to inanimate beings, as in:

> Saving a seed of fire that he might not have
>   to get a light from elsewhere.–(*Od.* 5, 490)

For, in fact, both are inanimate beings. From action to action, as:

> Already somewhere he is weaving some plan in
>   his heart.–(*Od.* 4, 739)

For weaving is properly assigned to webs, but now it has been employed in reference to the preparation of a plot.

But some metaphors are indicative of emphases and do not preserve the resemblance; others preserve both the resemblance and the emphasis.

5. Cocondrius (date unknown), *On Tropes.* Spengel, iii, 232, 14-233, 9.

Metaphor. Metaphor is a part of speech [*meros logou*] transferred from that which is properly spoken to another thing for the sake of resemblance or emphasis:

> And all the earth around laughed–(*Il.* 19, 362),

and,

> But the hordes of foot-soldiers kept
>   on flowing–(*Il.* 11, 724),

and the spears "longing to taste flesh" (*Il.* 11, 574). But metaphor occurs in four ways: either from animate being to inanimate being, or from inanimate being to animate being, or from animate being to animate being, or from inanimate being to inanimate being. Now from animate being to inanimate being: "head of a mountain" (*Od.* 10, 113), "feet of Ida" (*Il.* 20, 59); for 'head' is properly said in reference to living beings as is also 'feet,' but 'ridges' and 'lower parts' in reference to a mountain. And from inanimate being to animate being:

> He is a fence from evil war for the
> Achaeans.–(*Il.* 1, 284)

Metaphorically he has called Achilles "a fence" of the Hellenes for the reason that the very security which walls offer to cities this Achilles offered to the Hellenes. And from an animate being to an animate being:

> But then he went to Atreus' son, Agamemnon,
> shepherd of the people. (cf. *Il.* 2, 18 and 243)

For the herdsman of sheep is properly called a 'shepherd,' but the shepherd is an animate being as is also the king. And from an inanimate being to an inanimate being:

> Saving a seed of fire that he might not have
> to get a light from elsewhere.–(*Od.* 5, 490)

For in fact the seed which is cast into earth is an inanimate being, likewise also the spark of fire.

6. Georgius Choeroboscus (4th–5th cents. A.D.), *On Poetic Tropes.* Spengel, iii, 245, 14–246, 21.

   Metaphor. Metaphor is speech [*lexis*] transferred from one thing to another, or transferred from that which is properly spoken for the sake of resemblance or emphasis; and it has four species. For either it is conveyed from animate beings to animate beings, or from inanimate beings to inanimate beings, or from inanimate beings to animate beings, or from animate beings to inanimate beings. And from animate beings to animate beings, as whenever someone calls the king 'shepherd of the people,' for herding, being of animate beings, has been transferred back to animate beings, since just as sheep are made subject to their shepherds, so also to their kings the persons in their power—for the herdsman of flocks is properly called a shepherd—both, at any rate, are animate, the king and the herdsman of the flocks. And from inanimate beings to inanimate beings, as whenever someone who has hidden a coal of fire in ashes says that he has saved for himself a 'seed of fire.' For the seed, which is properly said in reference to fruits which are sown, now was employed in reference to hot embers. Or, whenever someone says, "A great flame has been poured on the wood"; for 'to be poured' is appropriate to wet things. And from inanimate beings to animate beings, as when Odysseus says to Ajax:

> For you, who were such a tower to them,
> perished.–(*Od.* 11, 556)

For the tower, which is inanimate, has been mentioned in reference to Ajax, who is animate. Also: "The sea saw and fled" (*Psalm* 114: 3); for 'seeing' is properly said in reference to animate beings, but the sea is inanimate.[2] And from animate beings to inanimate beings, as whenever someone calls the ridge [*akrōreian*] of a mountain a 'head' [*koruphēn ē kephalēn*], for *koruphē* and *kephalē* are said in reference to animate beings. And again:

> But the spear rushed through, being
>   eager.–(*Il.* 15, 542)

And again:

> And many in the middle before touching
>   white flesh
> Are fixed in the ground, longing to
>   taste flesh.–(*Il.* 11, 574–5)

For "being eager," "longing," and "to taste," which are animate, have been said in reference to inanimate spears. Likewise also: "on the heads of a mountain" (*Il.* 2, 456) and "feet of many-fountained Ida" (*Il.* 20, 59), it being needful to say 'ridge' and 'lower part'. But there is also a fifth species of metaphor, from action to action, as:

> Already somewhere he was weaving some plan
>   in his heart.–(*Od.* 4, 739)

For "weaving," being spoken in reference to webs, now has been transferred to the preparation of a plan.

7. XXXI Anonymous (date unknown), *On Tropes.* Spengel, iii, 228, 1–229, 7.

These [3] are common to our ordinary language, but they come to the surface in poetic language; for this reason they have also been called "poetic." And some of them were employed for the sake of ornament, as metaphor, but others for the sake of necessity, as catachresis.

Metaphor is speech [*lexis*] transferred from that which is properly named to that which has a different name, for reason of either resemblance or emphasis. For resemblance:

> But all the feet of many-fountained Ida
>   were shaken.–(*Il.* 20, 59)

---

2. Obviously a late addition to the text, this biblical example belongs to the species "from animate beings to inanimate beings" described below (the text there also shows evidence of having been tampered with verbally).

3. "These": tropes. This treatise is but a fragment of sixty lines (Spengel, iii, 227–29). *Tropos* is first defined ("speech or expression invented or turned from the proper to the improper by some reason for a more comely explanation"); then an explanation of the etymology of *tropos* is given; next fifteen "most generic" *tropoi* are named, beginning with metaphor. The remainder of the treatise, however, is concerned with metaphor only.

For this relation which feet have to the body the lower part [*hupōreia*] has to the mountain. And for emphasis:

> . . . but the woman
> they found to be as large as a head
> of a mountain.–(*Od.* 10, 112–13)

For metaphorically he mentioned a mountain's prominence [*exochēn*], wishing to emphasize the magnitude of the woman.

Moreover, some metaphors are transferred from action to action, others from body to body. Now from body to body, as:

> But first Telamonian Ajax, fence of
> the Achaeans.–(*Il.* 6, 5)

And from action to action, as "to weave" is 'to plan.' Furthermore, some metaphors have a reciprocal relationship, others do not. And reciprocal are metaphors such as these:

> But the charioteer of the dark-prowed
> ship spoke aloud,

and "steersman of horses." For they have a certain middle ground with each other, namely, the one directs aright the course of horses, the other that of ships. But metaphors such as the following do not have a reciprocal relationship:

> An island around which a boundless sea
> is wreathed.–(*Od.* 10, 195)

For he has said that the island is "wreathed" instead of 'surrounded by water from all around,' which indeed he could not say in reciprocal manner, that a crown 'flows around our head in a circle'—for such is ridiculous. Moreover, some metaphors are transferred from genus to genera:

> To embark upon speeding ships, which be-
> come horses
> of the sea for men; and they traverse much
> water.

By metaphor he has called ships "horses". For just as we ride on land by means of horses, so on the sea we are lifted up by ships.

Texts Omitted

8. Aristotle (4th cent. B.C.), *Rhetoric.* Spengel, i, 123, 11–145, 17. Translated by J. H. Freese in the Loeb Classical Library (1939).

9. Dionysius or Longinus (3rd cent. A.D. ?), *On the Sublime.* Spengel, i, 280, 1–282, 20. Translated by G. M. A. Grube in The Library of Liberal Arts (1957).

10. Demetrius (3rd cent. B.C. ?), *On Style.* Spengel, iii, 280, 13–283, 9. Translations: W. Rhys Roberts in the Loeb Classical Library (1927); T. A. Moxon (Everyman, 1934); G. M. A. Grube, *A Greek Critic: Demetrius on style* (Toronto, 1961).

VI. Fable

Introduction

The fable [*muthos*] was one of several *progymnasmata*, "preliminary exercises," designed to train very young students of rhetoric in composition. This method used the part as a pattern for the whole. One learned how to compose a whole speech by first becoming expert in its parts. The principal exercises were: Fable [*muthos*], Narrative [*diēgēma*], Moral Anecdote [*chreia*], Maxim [*gnōmē*], Refutation and Confirmation [*anaskeuē* and *kataskeuē*], Commonplace or locus communis [*koinos tropos*], Encomium [*enkōmion*], Comparison [*sunkrisis*], Piece Written in Character [*ēthopoiia*], Description [*ekphrasis*], Abstract Question [*thesis*], Introduction of a Law [*nomou eisphora*]. Each exercise was considered to be especially suitable for practice in one or more of the three types of oratory, forensic, deliberative, and epideictic.

There are extant in Greek five works entitled "Progymnasmata." Four of these are concerned with theory and Spengel prints them. The fifth, a collection of *progymnasmata* by Libanius (4th cent. A.D.), is merely an anthology of exercises. For example, under "Fable" he simply tells three fables without commentary. The "Progymnasmata" of Aelius Theon (probably 1st cent. A.D.), Hermogenes (2nd cent. A.D.), Aphthonius (4th–5th cents. A.D.), and Nicolaus (5th cent. A.D.) are our sources for the definition and theory of composition of the fable. As the "Progymnasmata" of Hermogenes and Aphthonius are available in English translation, I have omitted them. But the discussions of fable by Theon and Nicolaus are the more important for the history of literary criticism for the reason that more in the way of historical information and rhetorical theory is presented than in those of Hermogenes and Aphthonius.

Hermogenes' chapter "Concerning Fable" is only forty lines long in the Greek. Hermogenes says that fables are good for the souls of the young, simple to compose, and ancient in origin. They are false, but "altogether useful for any of the matters in life." Then he tells how to make fables plausible by making the characters suit the subject, for example, let apes imitate humans. Next he shows how to "extend and contract" the same fable by adding or leaving out speeches. Finally, he says that the narrative of the fable should be "free from periods and close to sweetness," that the statement which points out the moral of the fable will sometimes be placed before, but other times after, the fable, and that orators sometimes use fable as a substitute for *paradeigma*.

The "Definition of Fable" by Aphthonius is even more brief, twenty lines of Greek, the last eight of which tell a fable. Aphthonius defines fable as "false discourse copying truth" (see Theon). The purpose of fable is exhortation. The most successful type of fable is that which is called "Aesopian." He divides fable into "rational," "moral," and "mixed." These he defines as follows: "And rational is that in which a human being has been fabricated doing something; moral is that which represents the character of irrational beings; mixed is that which is of both, irrational and rational." (The reader will soon notice that Theon criticizes this method of classifying fables.) Finally, Aphthonius says: "When you prefix the exhortation on account of which the fable has been formed, you call it a *promuthion*, but an *epimuthion* when you have introduced it last." The discussion ends with "The Fable of the Ants and the Grasshoppers Which Exhorts the Young to Labors."

Now I shall let Theon and Nicolaus speak for themselves.

TEXTS

1. Aelius Theon (1st cent. A.D.), *Progymnasmata.* Spengel, ii, 72, 27–78, 13.

[Concerning Fable.]

Fable is false discourse copying truth. But it is necessary to know that at present the examination does not concern every fable, but those for which after the exposition we restate the argument of which it is a copy. Sometimes, however, we state the argument before we introduce the fables. And they are called Aesopian and Libyan, or Sybaritic, Phrygian, Cilician, Carian, Egyptian, and Cyprian. But of all these, there is a single difference in respect of one another, the fact that the distinguishing class is attached to each of them, as: 'Aesop said,' or 'a Libyan man,' or 'a Sybarite,' or 'a Cyprian woman,' and likewise for the rest. But if no qualification signifying the class exists, more commonly do we call such 'Aesopian.' But those who say that the ones composed on brute beasts are of a different kind than the ones composed on men, and that the impossible ones are of a different kind than the ones pertaining to the possible, seem to me to make foolish assumptions, for all the forms are in all the aforesaid. But they are named Aesopian in general, not because Aesop was the first inventor of fables (for Homer, Hesiod, Archilochus and some others who are older than he are manifestly experienced; and in particular Connis the Cilician, Thouros the Sybarite, and Cybissos of Libya are remembered by some as creators of fables), but because Aesop used them more profoundly and more skillfully; just as a certain meter is named Aristophanic or Sapphic or Alcaic, or something else from another poet, not because these poets are the only or the first to have invented the meters, but because they used them to the greatest extent. Some ancient poets prefer to call fables *ainoi*, others *muthoi*. But those who have composed in prose most certainly go beyond bounds in respect of calling them *logoi*, not *muthoi*, whence they call also Aesop *logopoios*. And Plato in the dialogue on the soul in one place names it *muthos* but in another *logos*. And it has been called *muthos*, seeing how it is a *logos*, since the ancients used to call *legein* also *mutheisthai*. But it has been called *ainos* because it encompasses also a certain counsel, for all the subject matter refers to a useful suggestion. Now, however, some call even riddles [*ainigmata*] *ainoi*. And this exercise: for in fact we report the fable and we inflect it and combine it with narrative, we extend it and we contract it, and it is possible also to restate an argument for it; and, again, if an argument has been set down first, it is possible to fashion together a fable suitable to it; and, furthermore, in addition to these activities, we refute and we confirm it. Now what the narrative is we have made clear in the section on moral anecdote [*chreia*],[1] but in fables the style ought to be simpler, naturally suitable, and as much as possible without elaboration and clear. For that reason it is also necessary first to learn by heart as many fables as it is possible to find so narrated in the ancients; but it is also useful, when a complete fable has been told, for the learner to become accustomed to begin fables gracefully, just as Hesiod:

> Thus spoke a hawk to a nightingale with
>   variegated throat.–(*Works and Days*, 203)

For from what followed,

> But foolish whosoever wishes to contend
>   against the stronger–(*Works and Days*, 210),

it is made clear that a nightingale was struggling against a hawk. And then the hawk, because he had become angry and had carried her away, thus spoke those things. But one must inflect fables and moral anecdote into numbers and oblique cases, and especially one must cultivate accusative cases because the ancients also reported the majority of fables in this manner, and very properly,

---

1. Theon's original order of exercises was changed by an ancient editor so as to have the same order as those in Hermogenes and Aphthonius: fable, narrative, moral anecdote, and so on. The original order was *chreia, muthos, diēgēsis*, etc., and Theon says in his introduction that he begins with the *chreia* for the reason that it is "short and easy to remember" (Spengel, ii, 64, 29ff).

as Aristotle says. For they speak not from their own character, but refer to olden times, so that they may justify their seeming to say impossible things. But it is not always necessary for one to follow the agreement of the given case, just as if compelled by law, but one must administer some things and employ a mixed style, so that one case is stated first but has changed into a different one in what follows; for just the variety of this is rather pleasing. There is this sort of fable also in the *Socratic Phaedo*, in the speech of Zopyrus. For he begins with the accusative case: "So then, Socrates, they say that the youngest son of a king gave as a favor to someone a lion's cub." But a little below he changed into the nominative case, thus: "And it seems to me that the lion, being reared with the boy who was now a young man, followed him wherever he walked, and so the Persians said that he was in love with the young man, etc."[2] But we combine in the following manner. When we have set forth the fable, we add a narrative, as is proper, or contrariwise, the narrative first and the fable second. Take, for example, the fiction that a camel who had wished for horns was also deprived of his ears. Having first made this statement, we shall add the narrative in this fashion: 'Croesus the Lydian also seems to me to have suffered something similar to this camel'—and then follows the whole narrative about him. And we extend by lengthening the speeches put into the mouths of characters and by describing a river or some such thing, but by doing the opposite we contract. And we add an epilogue in the following way whenever, after a fable has been told, we attempt to bring to it an appropriate didactic explanation. For example: "A dog was carrying a piece of meat alongside a certain river, and when he saw his own shadow down under the water, having assumed that there was another dog with a bigger piece of meat, he threw away what he had, and, leaping into the river to grab it, went under water."[3] And we shall add the explanation thus: 'You see that often those who reach out for greater things also destroy themselves in addition to their very own possessions.' But for even one fable there might be several epilogues, we taking our material from individual subjects in the fable, and, contrariwise, for one epilogue there might be very many fables represented therein. Now that we have proposed that the function of the epilogue be simple, we shall assign to the young men the fashioning of a fable suitable to the matter which has been put forward. And they will be able to do this readily when they have been filled with many fables: those they have received from ancient writings, those only they themselves have heard, and those they have made up by themselves. But we shall refute and confirm in this manner. Since indeed even the fable-maker himself admits that he composes things both false and impossible, but plausible and helpful,

---

2. In the first statement, the verb *phasi*, "they say," takes the infinitive *charisasthai*, "to give as a favor," which has its subject *huion*, "son," in the accusative case. In the second statement, *leōn*, "lion," nominative case, is the subject of the verb *dokei*, "seems." (I have not been able to discover the source of this quotation. I do not know the work referred to here as the "Socratic Phaedo," but I assume that Zopyrus (a Thracian?) is one of the speakers.)

3. This fable is first found in Aesop; see no. 133 (Perry).

one must refute those who point out that he says implausible and inconvenient things; but one must confirm by means of opposites. For these are the topmost headings into which the particulars fall. Moreover, the introduction [*prooimion*] must be suitable to the fable. And after the introduction one must set forth the fable, and sometimes also apply it, the very thing which one need not always set out in detail in a speech. But next one must move on to the proof and refute each of the things that have been said in turn, beginning from the first things, and, in respect of each part of the fable, attempting to have plenty of words for each topic. And one must choose his proofs from the following commonplaces: from the obscure, from the implausible, from the improper, from the elliptical, from the superfluous, from the unfamiliar, from the contradicting, from the arrangement, from the inconvenient, from the dissimilar, from the false. Now obscurity comes to pass either through one word or even more; through one, whenever someone uses words either contrary to custom or equivocally, and through more, whenever it is possible—there being nothing either added or preventing—to receive in many senses that which has been said. For example:

ego s' ethēka doulon ont' eleutheron.–(Menander?)

For it is not clear whether he has made him free [*eleutheron*] instead of slave [*doulon*] or slave instead of free. But concerning clarity, it will be stated more precisely a little later in the section on narrative [*peri diēgēmatos*]. But the implausible is that which can have taken place or can have been said, but is disbelieved when we say that it is not reasonable for such a person as this to have suffered or to have said this particular thing in this place, or at this time, or in this manner, or for this reason. And the same argument also concerns the improper. But the elliptical is the superfluous whenever one passes over any of the things that can be said, or says something which is nothing, for example, either a character or a subject or a time or a manner or a place or a cause or anything of this sort. And the unfamiliar is that which is contrary to believed information, or that which is said contrary to common notions; for example: if someone should say that men were not fashioned by Prometheus but by another one of the gods, or should say that the ass is a thinking being or that the fox is foolish. But the commonplace 'from the contradicting' is of this sort: whenever we show the fable-writer himself being inconsistent to himself; and we must not make use of this commonplace in the beginning, but whenever we refute one of the middle or final parts; then, we also show it to be opposite to that which has been said before. Our proof 'from the arrangement,' moreover, we shall attempt by means of the accusation that what ought to have been said first in the fable has not been reported at first, and what ought to have been said at the end is set forth elsewhere, and that, on the whole, each thing has not been said in proper order as we should be able to do. In addition, the commonplace 'from the inconvenient' is obvious, and one which we shall use even more for the refutation of the epilogue. But 'from the dissimilar' and 'from the false' only pertain to refutations of the epilogue. Now 'from the dissimilar' is whenever matters in the fable are in no respect or not quite appropriate to the epilogue; and 'from the false' is whenever they do not completely agree, as when the fable-writer says that those who reach out for more things are also deprived of what they have. For this is not always true. But we shall confirm from the opposite commonplaces. But it is necessary to sum up the argument whenever refutations and confirmations are many and strong; then, whenever they are few and weak, one must not pass over the summary. For here we shall employ ridicule, amplification or diminution, digressions, characterizations, and, generally, all the figures of speech. For, just as we have said, this exercise differs little from forensic speech. And the same commonplaces are useful for both the refutation and the confirmation of narratives.

2. Nicolaus (5th cent. A.D. ?), *Progymnasmata.* Spengel, iii, 451, 27–455, 5.

[Definition of Fable.]

Of all the preliminary exercises, they assigned the fable first. Just as when avoiding the hard to manage in complete speeches those who ordained these things discovered the need for preliminary exercises, so also they assigned the fable before the rest of the preliminary exercises, it being not intricate in nature and simpler than the rest as well as possessing a certain kinship with poetry, in changing from which there was no need for the young to encounter the overwhelmingly strange and in no way familiar. But it is well to know this also, that some have named fables Aesopian, others Sybaritic, Phrygian and Lydian, having invented the appellations from certain commonplaces or characters. Some have called Sybaritic those composed of rational animals only, and Aesopian those composed of irrational and rational animals, but Lydian, Phrygian and Libyan those composed of irrational animals only. And some fables are composed of gods (for example, Hera dwells with Zeus), which depend on philosophy alone, for it belongs to it to interpret well the allegories in them. But some also do not even call these fables, but 'mythic narratives' [*muthika diēgēmata*], mixing them up with the stories concerning metamorphoses and things similar to them. But, whichever way it might be, the philosophers will disclose the allegories in them, as has been said before.

On the ground that preliminary exercises are both parts and wholes, one must see that the fable would be only one of the parts. For it does not complete its own speech, but always takes its function from others, a thing which is characteristic of a part. But sometimes it itself also completes its own speech.

Of the species belonging to oratory, we say that fable quite clearly belongs to the deliberative. For either we exhort the listener to something, or we turn him away from something by means of the fable. But now to some it seemed to be useful also for the practice of the three species. For where one says 'we exhort' or 'we deter,' the property characteristic of deliberation is preserved; where we make an attack against wrongdoers and describe false things plausibly, the forensic part is maintained; where we use language that is pure and proceed with plainness at the same time as we are praising, we do not keep far from the panegyric form. Above all, it is customary, they say, in panegyric speeches to admit fables. And those who have thought in this manner for this reason also have assigned the first rank to it, since indeed it gives us practice in the three species, they say. But it is well, obviously, that the fable dispenses the useful to the deliberative. For with attraction it helps those who are being persuaded, deterring them from bad things and exhorting them to seek good things, and, with sweetness, accustoming them to cling to the advantage. And it contributes something also to the parts of the public speech. For, of the five existing parts, it will train us in narrative; in fact, in fabrication itself we learn how one must describe that which happens.

Fable is false discourse copying truth by means of persuasive composition. It is 'false discourse' since indeed it is by common consent composed of false things, and 'copying the truth' since indeed it could not produce its own self, not having any resemblance to the truth. But one must examine how it is composed persuasively and whence this might be. But this is from many sides. From places, around which the subject animals in the fable are accustomed to pass their time. For example, it is necessary when talking about elephants or Libyan ostriches to fashion the fable according to the unique features of the land in which these beings naturally exist, inasmuch as it is dry and sandy, lest the story be made about a fertile and well-watered land. From seasons, in which the subject animals in the fable are accustomed to appear. For example, if we should talk about the song of grasshoppers or nightingales, in spring and summer these, but it is not plausible for them to be presented in winter. From words, which harmonize with the nature of each being, for it is necessary to attach good-hearted words to sheep, savage ones to wolves, and to a fox deceitful and knavish ones; but to apes all things which incline toward human intelligence. And from subjects which do not transgress the quality of each being, so that we may not say that the mouse was making plans concerning the kingdom of the animals, or that the lion was captured by the odor of cheese; and again the eagle is introduced as rapacious for fawns and lambs, but the jackdaw is introduced as having no such thing in mind at all. But if such a thing should ever happen, it is necessary that the one who is fashioning something contrary to nature arrange it beforehand and furnish from the fable the intention for that which is being fashioned. For example, if sheep should converse with wolves in a friendly manner, the friendship must be arranged beforehand, and all other such things. And in this manner you might compose the fable convincingly. And fable [*muthos*] is said to originate from *mutheisthai*, which is *legein*, not that we do not speak also in other discourse, but because by it we first learn to speak publicly. But some called it also *ainos*, from the exhortation [*parainesis*] through it, but others *logos*. And it is necessary that the style of the fable be rather simple and not insidious, and free from every cleverness and periodic description, so that both the intent be clear and the things said appear no greater than the quality of the subject characters, especially whenever the fable is composed of irrational beings. In this way, therefore, it must be simpler, changing little from the practice in ordinary language. And it differs from moral anecdote [*chreia*] and maxim [*gnōmē*] because in them the exhortation is from true things, but here through false; and those we refute, but fable by no means; and there, plausibly and definitely, we confirm moral anecdotes and maxims, praising or attacking the one who has spoken, but here, referring the speech to no one, so we advise with thought that is familiar, imperceptibly bringing assistance to the young.

Texts Omitted

3. Hermogenes (2nd cent. A.D.), *Progymnasmata.* Spengel, ii, 3, 1–4, 17. Translated by C. S. Baldwin, *Medieval Rhetoric and Poetic to 1400* (1928; rpt. Gloucester, Mass.: Peter Smith, 1959), pp. 23–28.

4. Aphthonius (4th–5th cents. A.D.), *Progymnasmata.* Spengel, ii, 21. Translated by Ray Nadeau, *Speech Monographs*, 19 (1952), 264–85.

VII. Parabole and Paradeigma

Introduction

In the authors translated below, *parabolē* and *paradeigma* are treated under two headings, proof and figures or tropes. At the beginning of rhetorical theory they stand as part of logical proof (induction). For, as Aristotle so clearly states in Book II, chapter xx of his *Rhetoric*:

"It remains to speak of the proofs common to all branches of Rhetoric, since the particular proofs have been discussed. These common proofs are of two kinds, example [*paradeigma*] and enthymeme (for the maxim is part of an enthymeme). Let us then first speak of the example; for the example resembles induction, and induction is a beginning.

"There are two kinds of examples; namely, one which consists in relating things that have happened before, and another in inventing them oneself. The latter are subdivided into comparisons [*parabolē*] or fables, such as those of Aesop and the Libyan." (Loeb translation, p. 273)

Thus *paradeigma*, example, is historical fact or action. Fable is pure fiction, but *parabolē*, comparison, illustrates the point in question by comparing and applying cases that are easy to suppose and are of such kind as occur in real life (Aristotle's example of comparison is "the sayings of Socrates" [*ta Sōkratika*]). This distinction between *paradeigma* and *parabolē* is maintained even when they are treated as figures or tropes. Demetrius defines *parabolē* as extended simile, and the reader will observe below that *paradeigma* and *parabolē* are often classified as types of *homoiōsis* (see nos. 5 and 6).

The first text printed below is a concise account of the relationship of enthymeme and paradeigma according to the epitomizer of Longinus. The second text is the beginning of Apsines' chapter, "Concerning Paradeigma." In the rest of the chapter (Spengel, i, 373, 8–375, 12), he explains how to compose a good paradeigma. The paradeigma is to be taken "from similarity," "from opposition," "from increasing," "from diminishing," and so on; and since paradeigmata are by nature flat (they are narratives), one ought to use vigorous figures of speech in them. The third text is from the chapter *peri apodeixeōs,* "Concerning Demonstration," by Rufus, whose text consists of a lexicon of rhetorical terms. Rufus takes his examples of paradeigma and parabole from Demosthenes. The final four texts, those of Herodianus, Polybius Sardianus, Trypho, and Cocondrius, are similar in nature. Each one makes subtle distinctions between the terms defined, and names and illustrates their peculiar functions.

Of the four texts which I have omitted, the most important, that from the *On Proofs* by Minucianus, recently has been translated into English. Minucianus's definitions of paradeigma and parabole are basically Aristotelian. I have also omitted the brief definition of paradeigma in VIII Anonymous (Anonymous Seguerianus), because the contents are repetitive. Since the *Progymnasmata* of Aphthonius is available in English translation, I omit this text which gives parabole and paradeigma as headings under which the truth of a moral anecdote [*chreia*] and a maxim [*gnōmē*] can be demonstrated. Finally, I have omitted the text by Choeroboscus, whose definitions are brief and his illustrations biblical. He says that parabole is "speech [*phrasis*] which brings the meaning into view through similar and familiar things," and his example of parabole is Luke 15:11ff. He defines paradeigma as "discourse [*logos*] having emphasis of comparative proof for some other thing," and his example of paradeigma is Proverbs 6:6.

TEXTS

1. V Anonymous, *On Rhetoric* (epitome of Longinus, *Art of Rhetoric;* date ?). Spengel, i, 321, 23–322, 9.

But the enthymeme tells the speaker's reasoning [*sullogismon*], incomplete, however, and sometimes in need of conclusions and premises; and it is either demonstrative or refutative or didactic or paradeigmatic. But if it has included the paradeigma, it has become a complete proof [*epicheirēma*]. For this is an enthymeme brought to completion, perfected from every side; and the universal parts of constructive reasoning are two, enthymeme and paradeigma. And paradeigma is a particular similar to a similar particular, a well-known particular of an unrecognized particular, but the enthymeme is an abridgement of the paradeigmata. For the things which have been sown in many paradeigmata the speech gathers up and says through enthymemes; wherefore the mention of paradeigmata is an exegesis, as it were, of the enthymemes.

2. Apsines (3rd cent. A.D.), *Art of Rhetoric.* Spengel, i, 372, 28–373, 8).

[Concerning Paradeigma.]

Parabole differs from paradeigma in this way, in that parabole is taken from inanimate or irrational beings. From irrational, as in Homer:

> But as when a stalled horse corn-fed at a
> manger.–(*Il.* 6, 506)

But from inanimate, as in Demosthenes: "For just as of house and boat, I think" (second *Olynthiac*, 10). But paradeigmata are taken from persons who have already existed, as in Demosthenes: "Alcibiades is said to have lived according to that ancient standard of prosperity" (*Against Meidias*, 143). Every paradeigma has its material from those who have lived, but it is taken either from familiar or from strange persons.

3. Rufus (2nd cent. A.D.), *Art of Rhetoric.* Spengel, i, 468, 15–27.

[Concerning Demonstration.]

Now paradeigma is a recollection of past matter in view of resemblance of that which is in question, for example: "Those men, moreover, to whom the speakers did not show favor nor did they love them just as these now love you, for forty-five years ruled the Hellenes with their own consent, and brought up into the Acropolis more than ten thousand talents, etc." (third *Olynthiac*, 24).

But parabole is a recollection of matter existing and taking place in view of resemblance of that which is in question: "For just as of house and boat, I think, and of the rest of such things, the parts below ought to be stronger, so also the beginnings and the presuppositions of actions ought to be true and just" (second *Olynthiac*, 10).

4. Aelius Herodianus (date unknown), *On Figures.* Spengel, iii, 104.

But parabole is a comparison of a similar matter either coming to pass or able to come to pass:

> But as a lion approaching flocks that have no
> shepherd.–(*Il.* 10, 485)

And *homoiōsis* is a comparison of a similar matter, for example:

> As birds.–(*Il.* 3, 2)

But it differs from parabole in that it is spoken for the most part through abridgement and is expressed independently of correspondence with the object of comparison [*chōris antapodoseōs*].

But *antapodosis* is expression [*phrasis*] corresponding with the parabole and unfolding it altogether with those things which are taking place:

> So the son of Tydeus attacked the Thracian
> men.–(*Il.* 10, 487)

And paradeigma is a setting forth of actions in repect of the similarity of the objects for the sake of exhortation or dissuasion or simple explanation, as:

> I remember this deed of old—it is not at
> all new—
> how it was, and I'll tell it among all you
> friends:
> the Kouretes and staunch Aitolians were
> fighting.–(*Il.* 9, 527–29)

For it has been employed for the sake of dissuasion. But for the sake of exhortation, for example:

> Or do you not know what fame brilliant
> Orestes won
> among all men, when he killed the father-
> slayer,
> tricky-minded Aegisthus.–(*Od.* 1, 298–300)

And for simple explanation:

> Like the one which once in wide Knossos
> Daidalos built for lovely-haired Ariadne.–(*Il.* 18, 591–92)

But *eikōn* is delineation of bodies according to part either with comparison or through bare impression. With comparison, for example:

> In eyes and head like Zeus who delights in
> thunder,
> But like Ares in loins, and in chest Posei-
> don.–(*Il.* 2, 478–79)

And through bare impression:

> Bent in shoulders, dark-hued, curly-headed.–(*Od.* 19, 246)

5. Polybius Sardianus (date unknown), *On Figuration.* Spengel, iii, 106, 15–107, 31.

[Concerning the Forms of Constructive Reasoning.]

Homoiōsis is speech by which we liken one thing to another, and there are three forms of it: parabole, paradeigma, eikon. Parabole is matter compared to matter on the basis of some relationship for the sake of amplification or emphasis or clearness. For amplification:

> As when the husband of lovely- haired
> Hera lightens . . .
> so often in his breast Agamemnon groaned
> aloud.–(*Il.* 10, 5, 9)

And for emphasis:

> But he fell on them as when a rushing wave
> falls
> on a swift ship.–(*Il.* 15, 624–25)

And for clearness:

> ". . . but brilliant Odysseus
> overhauled him close, as near as to the
> breast of a woman
> fair-girdled is the rod she pulls in her
> hands carefully
> as she draws the spool out and along the
> warp."–(*Il.* 23, 759–62: trans. by R. Lattimore)

And some *parabolai* mark correspondence with the object of comparison [*antapodotikai*], others are independent. The following sort mark correspondence with the object of comparison:

> And as a lion springs among cattle and breaks
> the neck
> of a calf or cow . . .
> so the son of Tydeus both from their chariot
> harshly forced, although they were unwilling. –(*Il.* 5, 161–64)

And in the parabole there is correspondence with the object of comparison. But those which are spoken apart from any correspondence with the object of comparison are independent, for example:

> For just as young children or widow women
> they make lament with each other for going
> home.–(*Il.* 2, 289–90)

But paradeigma is speech with exhortation or dissuasion or demonstration of certain things through the comparison of similar things. With exhortation:

> Or do you not know what fame brilliant
> Orestes won,

etc. (*Od.* 1, 298). And with dissuasion:

> Since not at all long lived the son of
> Dryas, strong Lycurgus.–(*Il.* 6, 130)

And paradeigma contains demonstration thus:

> You stubborn gods are more jealous than
>   other beings,
> you who begrudge goddesses to sleep with
>   men . . .

Then:

> As when rosy-fingered dawn chose Orion . . .
> As when Demeter of the lovely hair with
>   Iasion . . .
> So now in turn you begrudge a mortal man
>   to be next to me.–(*Od.* 5, 118-19, 21, 25, 29)

So-called induction is closely connected with paradeigma. But induction [*epagōgē*] is whenever by having set forth any of similar matters we lead on into that which we are persuading, for example:

> In skill is the woodcutter far better than
>   in strength.
> And again with skill the pilot on the dark
>   sea,
> directs his swift wind-buffeted ship.–(*Il.* 23, 315-18)

Then he leads on to:

> And with skill charioteer surpasses charioteer.–(*Il.* 23, 319)

6. Trypho (1st cent. B.C.), *On Tropes.* Spengel, iii, 200, 3-201, 2; 201, 12-26.

[Concerning *Homoiōsis.*]

Homoiōsis is speech [*rhēsis*] by which we set one thing beside another, and there are three forms of it: eikon, paradeigma, parabole. Eikon is speech [*logos*] attempting visibly to liken through that which is parallel, in respect of that which is parallel, for example:

> As a great ox stands out from all in the
>   herd.–(*Il.* 2, 480)

And size, figure, color attend eikon. And either wholes are pictured in respect of wholes, for example:

> . . . prudent Penelope
> like to Artemis–(*Od.* 19, 53-4),

or parts in respect of parts, for example:

> Like Ares in loins, and in chest Posei-
>   don.–(*Il.* 2, 479)

And figure in respect of figure, for example:

> As move tribes of swarming bees.–(*Il.* 2, 87)

And color in respect of color, for example:

> But as when some woman stains ivory with
>   purple.–(*Il.* 4, 141)

And size in respect of size, for example:

> For the Cyclops' great club was lying
>   beside the pen . . .
> as a mast of a twenty-oared vessel.–(*Od.* 9, 319, 22)

Paradeigma is insertion of a past event on the basis of a similarity of the subjects for the purpose of advice for the sake of exhortation or dissuasion. For the sake of exhortation, as:

> Or do you not know what fame brilliant
>   Orestes won
> among all men, when he killed the father-
>   slayer,
> tricky-minded Aegisthus, who had slain his
>   father?–(*Od.* 1, 298–300)

And for dissuasion:

> Since not at all long lived the son of Dryas,
>   strong Lycurgus,
> who struggled with the heavenly gods.–(*Il.* 6, 130–31)

But paradeigma differs from parabole in that paradeigma is taken from past events, but parabole from unlimited possibilities.

Parabole is speech [*logos*] presenting the subject with vividness through comparison of similar matter, for example:

> But the assembly was moved, as the big
>   sea-waves of the Icarian deep.–(*Il.* 2, 144)

And *parabolai* come into being in fourfold manner: from emotion to emotion, from disposition to disposition, from nature to nature, from action to action. Now from emotion to emotion:

> As when welcome . . .–(*Od.* 5, 394)

And from disposition to disposition:

> As when a man who has seen a snake steps
>   back . . .
> so he again withdrew into the crowd of
>   proud Trojans.–(*Il.* 3, 33, 36)

And from nature to nature:

> As the generations of leaves, so also
>   those of men.–(*Il.* 6, 146)

And from action to action:

> But they, as reapers face-to face with
> each other.–(*Il.* 11, 67)

7. Cocondrius (date unknown), *On Tropes.*

a. Spengel, iii, 240, 1–27. *Parabolē.*

Parabole is comparison of matter on the basis of some analogous similarities,
for example:

> As a mountain snake at a hole waits for a
> man.–(*Il.* 22, 93)

But it takes place either action to action, or emotion to emotion, or disposition
to disposition, or nature to nature. And when it is action to action:

> But they, as reapers face-to-face with
> each other.–(*Il.* 11, 67)

And when it is emotion to emotion:

> As when a father's life appears welcome
> to his children,
> he who lies in sickness suffering strong
> pains.–(*Od.* 5, 394–95)

Or from disposition to disposition:

> As when a man who has seen a snake steps
> back.–(*Il.* 3, 33)

Or from nature to nature:

> As the generations of leaves, so also
> those of men.–(*Il.* 6, 146)

But there are some *parabolai* which offer amplifications of pleasure, of sorrow,
of suffering, of fear, and of thought. Of pleasure:

> As a lion rejoices which has come upon
> a large carcass.–(*Il.* 3, 23)

And of sorrow:

> As snow melts on high places on mountains.–(*Od.* 19, 205)

And of suffering:

> And as a lion crushes the helpless off-
> spring of a swift deer.–(*Il.* 11, 113)

And of fear:

> As when a man who has seen a snake steps
> back.–(*Il.* 3, 33).

And of thought:

> As when country heifers around cows in
> herds.–(*Od.* 10, 410)

b. Spengel, iii, 241, 19–242, 4. *Paradeigma.*

Paradeigma is representation of someone to someone, categorically, and it comes to pass for the sake of either exhortation or reduction [*apagōgē*]. And for exhortation, as to Telemachus:

> Or do you not know what fame brilliant
>   Orestes won
> among all men, when he killed the father-
>   slayer . . .
> But you, friend—for I see that you are
>   very large and comely—
> be brave in order that one of those born
>   afterwards may speak well of you.–(*Od.* 1, 398–99; 301–2)

But for dissuasion:

> You behold the wretched doom of Actaeon,
> whom the raw-meat-eating bitches, which
>   he had reared,
> tore asunder.–(Euripides, *Bacchae*, 337ff).

And for the sake of reduction:

> In skill is the woodcutter far better than
>   in strength,
> and again with skill the pilot on the dark
>   sea
> directs his swift wind-buffeted ship.–(*Il.* 23, 315–317)

Texts Omitted

8. Minucianus (2nd cent. A.D.), *On Proofs.* Spengel, i, 418, 1–15; 418, 28–419, 11. Translated by Prentice A. Meador, Jr., "Minucian, On *Epicheiremes*: an Introduction and a Translation," *Speech Monographs*, 31, (1964), 54–63.

9. VIII Anonymous (2nd–3rd cents. A.D.), *Art of Rhetoric.* Spengel, i, 447, 3–13.

10. Aphthonius (4th–5th cents. A.D.), *Progymnasmata.* Spengel, ii, 24, 20–30; 27, 3–17. Translated by Ray Nadeau, *Speech Monographs*, 19 (1952), 264–85.

11. Georgius Choeroboscus (4th–5th cents. A.D.), *On Poetic Tropes.* Spengel, iii, 254, 1–6; 17–22.

VIII. Paroimiai

Introduction

Paroimiai, proverbs, need little discussion. It is obvious that they are a kind of "other-speaking." Aristotle says: "Proverbs also are metaphors from species to species. For example, if someone introduces something on the ground that he himself will experience some good from it, and then is harmed, it is as the Carpathian says of the rabbit, for both men have experienced that which has been mentioned" (*Rhetoric*, III, xi, 14).[1] Only one text in Spengel deals specifically with *paroimiai*.

TEXT

1. Trypho (1st cent. B.C.), *On Tropes*. Spengel, iii, 206, 18–22.

[Concerning *Paroimia*.]

Paroimia is speech [*logos*] which has been said in the beginning with reference to another thing, but which is spoken circuitously by us with reference to one of those which have the same character, as in Sappho: "For me, neither honey nor bee."[2]

---

1. Carpathus is a small island. When the original pair of rabbits multiplied, the farmers' crops were ruined. See *Corpus Paroemiographorum Graecorum*, vol. II, ed. Leutsch (1851; rpt. Hildesheim, 1965), p. 176, no. 94, and p. 758, no. 91.

2. Trypho alone ascribes this proverb to Sappho; see *Corpus Paroemiographorum Graecorum*, vol. I, ed. Leutsch and Schneidewin (1839; rpt. Hildesheim, 1965), p. 279, no. 58: "said of those who do not wish to experience anything good along with the deprecated."

IX. Eidolopoiia, Ethopoiia, Prosopopoiia

Introduction

These three terms, with the general meaning of "invention of characters," are derived from: *eidōlon*, "phantom," "image"; *ēthos*, "disposition," "character"; *prosōpon*, "face," "character," "person"; **poiia*, "making." *Eidōlopoiia* and *prosōpopoiia* are sometimes regarded as species of *ēthopoiia*. In the authors considered here, these terms are viewed both as rhetorical exercises and as figures or tropes.

Definitions of *eidōlopoiia* vary. In the *On the Sublime* (chapter fifteen), it is simply the equivalent of *phantasia*, poetic imagination. In Aphthonius and Hermogenes, it is the putting of words into the mouth of a person who is dead. For Polybius Sardianus, it is one of nine figures closely connected with *eikōn*. Only two texts in Spengel deal with *eidōlopoiia* as a heading separate from ethopoiia and prosopopoiia.

In the chapter called "Concerning Epilogue" in his *Art of Rhetoric*, Apsines says that epilogue is tripartite, containing recollection of what was said, pity, and exaggeration; however, he discusses only recollection, and says that ethopoiia and prosopopoiia are two of the means by which recollection is achieved. He defines prosopopoiia: "Now *prosōpopoiia* is the introduction of a person who is not present in the courtroom, a person on a journey or dead, or a fatherland, or a command, or legislation, or another of similar kind to these." And concerning ethopoiia, Apsines says: "Furthermore, there is recollection from that which is called *ēthopoiia*. And *ēthopoiia* is speech [*logos*] conferred upon concealed persons, for example: 'What now will those who will see me being led into the prison say?' "

In the chapter called "Concerning *Ēthopoiia*" in his *Progymnasmata*, Hermogenes says that ethopoiia is "imitation" [*mimēsis*] of the character of a person in question, as for example: "What might Andromache say

160

to Hector?" But whenever we confer person [*prosōpon*] upon a thing,
that, Hermogenes says, is prosopopoiia. In ethopoiia we form words
for a person who exists, in prosopopoiia we form a person which does
not exist. "And they say it is *eidōlopoiia* whenever we form words for the
dead." Hermogenes goes on to describe *ēthopoiiai*. They consist of
definite and indefinite persons. The words must be suited to persons
and occasions. They are "moral," "emotional," or "mixed." The
"moral" are those in which character is predominant. The "emotional"
are those in which passion is predominant. The "mixed" blend character and passion, for example, "What words might Achilles say to
Patroclus? For in fact there is passion on account of the slaying of
Patroclus, and character is in that which he is planning concerning
war."

Aphthonius, in his *Progymnasmata*, distinguishes between the three
terms as follows: "*Ēthopoiia* is imitation of character of a subject person. But its distinctions are three: *eidōlopoiia, prosōpopoiia, ēthopoiia.*
And *ēthopoiia* is that which has a known person, but shapes for itself
only the character, whence it is also named *ēthopoiia*. For example, what
words might Heracles say when Eurystheus was giving him orders?
Here Heracles is known, but we shape for ourselves the character of
the speaker. *Eidōlopoiia* is that which has a person known, but dead and
having ceased from speaking, as Eupolis has fashioned in the *Dēmoi*,
and Aristeides in the *On Behalf of the Four*, whence it is also named
eidōlopoiia. But *prosōpopoiia* is whenever everything is fashioned, both
character and person, just as Menander made Elenchus (for *elenchos* is a
thing, of a truth, not even a person). Whence it is also named *prosōpopoiia*, for the reason that person is formed together with character."
Aphthonius next describes the three categories of ethopoiia, "emotional," "moral," and "mixed."

As an example of ethopoiia as a rhetorical exercise, I give in full
the "Definition of *Ēthopoiia*" from the *Progymnasmata* of Nicolaus. His
account has not been translated into English and it is more extensive
than those of Hermogenes and Aphthonius.

In the *On the Figures of Thought and of Speech* by the second-century-
A.D. rhetorician Alexander there are definitions of ethopoiia and
prosopopoiia, with illustrations taken from Demosthenes and Aeschines. He defines ethopoiia: "But *ēthopoiia* is whenever we create
existing persons and confer upon them certain words in order that
they may seem to be more believable than if we ourselves spoke them."
Of prosopopoiia, he says: "*Prosōpopoiia* is modelling of a person, either
never having existed to begin with, or having existed but no longer
living."

The author of *On the Figures in Demosthenes*, Tiberius, says that ethopoiia is used to avoid "the offensiveness of criticisms." His examples are so interesting that I have printed this text.

I have also printed the discussion "Concerning *Metathesis*" by Phoebammon, who lists prosopopoiia and ethopoiia among the six figures of thought "in which one transposes what he desires to do from himself to another person."

Finally, two brief treatments of ethopoiia remain to be mentioned. Zonaeus defines it as "whenever we provide words for inanimate things." And similar to this is the definition found in XXVII Anonymous, which says that ethopoiia is "the conferring of words upon inanimate or irrational things," and gives as illustrations what a ship shattered upon rocks might say, or "land being broken by the violence of earth tremors."

For prosopopoiia I have printed in full two texts, the "Concerning *Prosōpopoiia*" from the *Progymnasmata* of Theon, and the "Concerning Substitution of Person" by Tiberius, which is closely related to his discussion of ethopoiia.

In addition to those given brief mention above in connection with ethopoiia, four other texts deal with prosopopoiia. Zonaeus calls it the "modelling of a person who either did not exist, or existed but lives no longer," as for example a mother calling a dead child. The XXVII Anonymous gives the same definition as Zonaeus, and also the same example, but adds the comment that the person who has presented this prosopopoiia does it to "induce the hearts of the listeners to pity, the very thing which was otherwise impossible and indecent to do through himself." Finally, the definitions of prosopopoiia in XXIX Anonymous and Choeroboscus are so similar that I shall quote only that of XXIX Anonymous: "*Prosōpopoiia* is the attaching of person to lifeless beings and the fitting of appropriate words to them, for example: 'Let the heavens rejoice' (Psalm 96:11), and 'The sea saw and fled' (Psalm 114:3)."

Texts: Eidolopoiia

1. Polybius Sardianus (date unknown), *On Figuration.* Spengel, iii, 108, 17–22.

Hupotupōsis is rendering of a body peculiarly formed:

> For in fact Prayers are daughters of great
>   Zeus,
> lame, shrivelled, and squint-eyed.–(*Il.* 9, 502–3)

And closely connected with it is *eidōlopoiia,* whenever we invent certain divinities from things, as Homer does the Prayers.

2. Cocondrius (date unknown), *On Tropes.* Spengel, iii, 241, 10–18.

Eidōlopoiia.

Eidōlopoiia is invention of characters [*prosōpon*] either for things or for beings, rational but departed, or irrational but fabled. For things, as whenever we fashion Virtue holding a discussion with Vice. For men who are departed, as whenever we say what kind of words Achilles said when he saw Patroclus in Hades. And for irrational beings, as whenever we say what kind of words the fox said to the wolf.

Texts: Ethopoiia

1. Nicolaus (5th cent. A.D.), *Progymnasmata.* Spengel, iii, 488, 24–491, 13.

Definition of Ēthopoiia.

Having assigned the description [*ekphrasis*] immediately after the comparison [*sunkrisis*] and the *ēthopoiia* after the general question [*thesis*], some have so written. The *ēthopoiia* is well placed after the general question, for in some manner there is a way through this from the general question to the complete cases in point [*hupotheseis*]. For example, there is a certain general question, 'whether one must pursue knowledge'; this is confirmed through workings which we stated in the passages concerning it, but in the *ēthopoiia* we shall say: "A farmer exhorts his son to pursue knowledge." Now, although the farmer's quality has been added, he has not yet made a complete case in point since it still falls short in respect of the circumstances; he did, however, show it more complete than in the general question. And in this manner those have written, but we speak following the prevailing custom and place the *ēthopoiia* immediately after the comparison. *Ēthopoiia* is speech [*logos*] adapting to the subjects, emphasizing character or emotion or the complex of both. Adapting to the subjects, since it is necessary to aim at both the speaker and the person to whom he is speaking. But character or emotion or the complex of both, since one either pays attention to circumstances in general or to that which arises from a state of affairs. For in this respect character differs from emotion; for example, if we should say what kind of words a coward might speak when about to go forth to a battle, we will take thought for the general character present to cowards; but if we should say what kind of words Agamemnon might say perhaps when he had taken Ilium, or Andromache when Hector had fallen, the emotions which are now present will provide the means. Some *ēthopoiiai* are moral, others emotional, others mixed. Moral and emotional are those which we have already made clear, but mixed are those which are from both; for example, if I say what kind of words Achilles might speak when going forth to war after the death of Patroclus. For I shall add elements from his suffering to his character, and I shall produce a mixed *ēthopoiia*. But that which is called *prosōpopoiia*, being nearly the same thing as *ēthopoiia*, some have believed to differ from it in one way, others in another. For some have called it *prosōpopoiia* when it contains both definite persons and definite subject matters, but *ēthopoiia* when it is invented from every side—which they also call *rhēsis*, giving this name to it. But others, most excellent thinkers too, thought *ēthopoiia* to consist of definite persons, but *prosōpopoiia* that in which we both shape persons and confer speeches upon them. But these things they especially attribute to the poets who have the power both to remodel lifeless beings into persons and to procure words for them. And concerning division—the difference being great for those who deal with it—it is necessary to set forth for ourselves the prevailing view that it is divided by the three times, present, past, and future. For those things which some call headings are arguments for the events devised in connection with one of these times. Now we shall begin from the present, and we shall run back to past time, then from there we shall again return to the present. For we shall not go immediately to the future, but we shall briefly make mention of the present, and thus we shall estimate the future. For example, the *ēthopoiia*, What Kind of Words Would Peleus Say, Having Heard of the Death of Achilles? He will not immediately be reminded of his happiness of long ago, but first, after he has lamented his present misfortune, he will compare the good things which happened to him long ago (his marriage with the goddess, the honor from the gods, his many courageous deeds); but then he will weep, giving in addition his present situation (what things surround him as a result of what things) and thus what will be the nature of his prophecy (into what evils it is likely that he will fall on account of the absence of the one who would come to his aid). But it is proper that the style be composed of rather short clauses and of the kind as to be mutually not filled up with periods. For to be concerned with expression is alien to emotion. But to bring in one thing after another concisely and briefly is characteristic of both those who rejoice and those who lament. Now the one who cultivates the beauty connected with expression will not seem to have suffered on such an occasion. But this preliminary exercise is also useful for the three forms of oratory. For in fact in eulogizing and in accusing and in deliberating we are often in need of *ēthopoiiai*. And it seems good to me also for training us in the epistolary style, if really in that too it is necessary to acquire for ourselves foreknowledge of the character of the senders and of those to whom they send. But there is no occasion now for examining the epistolary style itself, whether it is brought up under one of those three forms or under another, especially since for an introduction enough has been said also about them in the statements concerning encomia. But here we shall not need compressed prooemia, where at any rate there is not even need of other such expression, nor yet narratives preserving the sequence. Otherwise, the emotion would be destroyed. Nor will the speech be contentious, but only moving the listener to pleasure or to tears.

2. Tiberius (date unknown), *On the Figures in Demosthenes.* Spengel, iii, 63, 5–64, 4.

[Concerning $\bar{E}$*thopoiia.*]

But it is *ēthopoiia* whenever in avoiding the offensiveness of criticisms we introduce them as produced by other persons; such is the statement in Demosthenes, "Come now, in the name of Zeus, if the Hellenes should demand an account of you of the opportunities which you now have let pass on account of carelessness." And again, "Then, most indifferent of all men" (*On Behalf of Those in the Chersonesus*, 34, 35). For he is bitterly attacking the Athenians through the person of the Hellenes. And those also are the moral figures of *ēthopoiia*: 'It was necessary to say this,' and 'It was necessary to do this,' the very thing which Aeschines has done for Demosthenes by saying, "He ought, although the demos, mad and forgetful of the establishment, wished at such unfitness of times to crown him, to have come forward in the assembly to say: 'Gentlemen of Athens, I accept the crown, but I reject the occasion on which the proclamation is made' " (*Against Ctesiphon*, 211). For although it was possible to speak this thought from his own person, he conferred it upon his adversary. And in Homer, Odysseus, wishing to say to the Achaeans that they do not keep the promises which they made to Agamemnon, turns the argument back to him:

> Son of Atreus, now indeed you, king, the
> Achaeans wish
> to make the greatest reproach to all mor-
> tal men;
> nor for you do they fulfill the promise
> which they made,
> to return when they had destroyed well-
> walled Ilium.–(*Il.* 2, 284–86; 288)

For by doing this he did not in any way give offense to the Achaeans, but he showed that he who had been abandoned by them was piteous, and through his words to him chastised them.

3. Phoebammon (5th-6th cents. A.D.), *Notes on Rhetorical Figures.* Spengel, iii, 52, 5–53, 3.

[Concerning *Metathesis.*]

According to *metathesis* again the figures of thought are six, in which one transposes what he desires to do from himself to another person: and these are *prosōpopoiia, ēthopoiia*, blended [*mikton*], interrogation [*erōtēsis*], inquiry [*peusis*], disclaimer [*apopoiēsis*]. And each of these, perchance *prosōpopoiia, ēthopoiia*, and blended, consists of words which, although willing, we hesitate to say through ourselves, but we transpose them to another person, either existing or not existing, or having existed, but existing no longer. And if not existing, it is *prosōpopoiia*, as in this case: in order that I may charge someone with adultery perchance, I say: 'The occasion itself, during which you were discovered in the place, witnesses against you.' For I personify the occasion and confer upon it the words which I would speak against that man. But when an existing person is presented, it is *ēthopoiia*; for example, so that I may say to him, 'If you had confidence in yourself that you did not do this, you ought to say this and this.'

But blended, so that again I may say to the same man, 'If your father, a good man, were living now, seeing you judged an adulterer, he would say this and this in lament.'

And *ēthopoiia* occurs in two ways, in respect of those present and in respect of those absent. Just as if wishing to refute certain remiss people, so that I may say nothing to them openly, but that which has been spoken to others, so I shall make it public in a narration, for example, that all sinners wait for utter destruction. [Thus, in narrating to them things said to others, I shall make the statement that the divine apostle says, "Do not grumble, as some did and perished"] (First Corinthians 10:10).

Ethopoiia: *Texts Omitted*

4. Apsines (3rd cent. A.D.), *Art of Rhetoric.* Spengel, i, 387, 21–388, 7.

5. Hermogenes (2nd cent. A.D.), *Progymnasmata.* Spengel, ii, 15, 6–16, 9. Translated by C. S. Baldwin, *Medieval Rhetoric and Poetic to 1400* (1928; rpt. Gloucester, Mass.: Peter Smith, 1959), pp. 23–38.

6. Aphthonius (4th–5th cents. A.D.), *Progymnasmata.* Spengel, ii, 44, 20–45, 19. Translated by Ray Nadeau, *Speech Monographs,* 19 (1952), 264–85.

7. Alexander (2nd cent. A.D.), *On the Figures of Thought and of Speech.* Spengel, iii, 21, 23–22, 5.

8. Zonaeus (date unknown), *On Figures According to Thought.* Spengel, iii, 162, 22–24.

9. XXVII Anonymous (date unknown), *On the Figures of Speech.* Spengel, iii, 177, 1–7.

TEXTS: Prosopopoiia

1. Aelius Theon (1st cent. A.D.), *Progymnasmata.* Spengel, ii, 115, 11–118, 5.

[Concerning *Prosōpopoiia.*]

Prosōpopoiia is introduction of a person reciting words indisputably appropriate to himself and to the subject matter. For example, what words a man who is about to make a journey might speak to his wife, or a general to his soldiers in the face of dangers. And in reference to definite persons, for example, what words Cyrus might say while marching against the Massagetae, or what Datis might say when he meets with the king after the battle of Marathon. And under this genus of exercise falls also the species of panegyric, of hortatory, and of epistolary. First of all, however, it is necessary to consider the character of the speaker, what sort it is, and the person to whom the speech is spoken, the present age, the occasion, the place, the fortune, and the subject matter concerning which the future words will be spoken. And next, it is now necessary to say fitting words. For on account of age, some words are suitable to some persons and others to others; the same are not suitable to old and young, but the speech of the younger person will have been blended by us with simplicity and prudence, and that of the older person with understanding and experience. And on account of nature, words of a different kind might apply to a woman and a man; and, on account of fortune, to a slave and a free man; and, on account of habit of life, to a soldier and a farmer; and, according to delivery, to a lover and a man in control of himself; and, on account of race, different are speeches of the Laconian (few and shrill) and speeches of the Attic man (wordy). And we say that Herodotus often speaks like a foreigner, although writing in the Greek language, because he has imitated their words. And words are suitable to both places and occasions, for those spoken in the camp and in the assembly are not the same, nor those in peace and war, nor yet those to the victors and to the vanquished; and the same for as many other matters as are proper to the characters. And besides, individual matters themselves have appropriate style.

But we would be in firm control of this if we speak neither humbly concerning great matters nor proudly concerning small, nor loftily concerning cheap, nor carelessly concerning mighty, nor recklessly concerning disgraceful, nor uncommonly concerning piteous, but we render what is appropriate for each of these matters, at the same time aiming at both that which is harmonious to the person and to the manner and to the time and to the fortune and to each of the aforesaid. Now since the difference of persons and of matters is manifold (for either we ask for something or we exhort or we dissuade or we advise or we ask forgiveness for things which we have done, or some other of such things), it is necessary to speak material appropriate to each of these. When exhorting, therefore, we shall say that that to which we are making our exhortation is possible and easy and fair and proper to occur; that it is advantageous; that it is just; that it is holy (for even this is twofold, either for the gods or for the dead); that it is pleasant; that we do not act alone nor are the first to act; that if we are also the first it is a far better thing to make a beginning of fair deeds; and that when done, it does not produce a change of mind. And one must mention whether some previous service has been rendered by the one who exhorts to the one who is exhorted, and whether, when persuaded at some other time, he was benefited. And there will be the same manner of the attack even if we ask for something for ourselves, but when dissuading we shall attack from the opposites.* And thus we shall make use of speeches, because

*Lacuna

the past is necessary and common to all, and it is involuntary: for those who have understanding are pained least at that which is involuntary. But if it be voluntary, it must be said that he himself is responsible for himself, for those who are unfortunate because of themselves are less pained by self-regard. And it must be stated that even greater than this is evil which many others have suffered and borne calmly. And in addition to these things, that if it is slightly troublesome, well then, it is both fine and notable; then that it is advantageous and that pain is of no advantage for those who have already died. But pity also has great strength for comfort, especially whenever someone makes speeches at a funeral. For the grieved naturally strive against these who think that they have suffered no terrible thing, and, in addition to the pain, it is possible for them to be angry with those who are reassuring, but from those who wail together it is somehow more gracious for the consolations to go forward, as from relatives, for the very reason that after the laments one must introduce didactic speeches. But whenever we ask for forgiveness, we shall find food for the argument from the following. First, that the deed was involuntary, and this because of ignorance or chance or necessity; but if voluntary, it must be stated that it was righteous; that it was customary; that it was advantageous. But one must attempt to prove from topics that are admissible. For not all are suited to all the characterizations which exist under the same species. But this exercise is especially receptive of characters and emotions. Now it is generally sufficient for an introduction, even if lads are trained from so many topics; and for those who are willing to treat characterizations [*prosōpopoiias*] more accurately and more completely, it is possible also to use the materials which will be stated by us a little later in respect of the general questions of proofs.

2. Tiberius (date unknown), *On the Figures in Demosthenes*. Spengel, iii, 64, 5–27.

[Concerning Substitution of Person.]

But it is substitution of person [*prosōpou hupobolē*] whenever, wishing to say something more tolerably, he confers the speech upon another person. For example, in the *Philippics*: "And as I used to hear from one of those who had been in the land itself, a man in no way capable of lying, they are braver than none" (second *Olynthiac*, 23). For the things said are believable on the ground that he had heard them from one who knew. And in many places he blends *ēthopoiia* and substitution of person whenever he attaches speech to a different person. For, wishing to criticize the Athenians for having declined into carelessness, he did not speak from himself, but he conferred the speech upon the Hellenes: "If now the Hellenes shall send to you and say, 'Athenians, you send ambassadors to us who say each time that Philip is plotting against us and all the Hellenes, etc.'" (*On Behalf of Those in the Chersonesus*, 35). And again, in the *Against Leptines*: "But if indeed Leucon sends to us and asks, 'With what charge and finding what fault have you deprived him of his immunity?' what, in the name of the gods, shall we say?" (38). For in this speech he has acted much more strongly as a result of the person of those who speak.

Prosopopoiia: *Texts Omitted*

3. Apsines (3rd cent. A.D.), *Art of Rhetoric,* Spengel, i, 386, 5–387, 3.

4. Alexander (2nd cent. A.D.), *On the Figures of Thought and of Speech.* Spengel, iii, 19, 14–29.

5. Zonaeus (date unknown), *On Figures According to Thought.* Spengel, iii, 162, 25–29.

6. XXVII Anonymous (date unknown), *On the Figures of Speech.* Spengel, iii, 177, 8–19.

7. XXIX Anonymous (date unknown), *On Poetic Tropes.* Spengel, iii, 212, 13–17.

8. Georgius Choeroboscus (4th–5th cents. A.D.), *On Poetic Tropes.* Spengel, iii, 254, 13–16.

SELECT INDEX OF NAMES

SELECT INDEX OF WORDS AND SUBJECTS

in Christian exegesis, 82-83; in Neoplatonic theory, 9

Historia, 81; and allegory, 46-47; with *argumentum* and *fabula*; in Augustine, 46-47, 61-62, 64; in Bede, 76-77; in Isidore, 69, 71; in Nicholas, 77-78; in Remigius, 77

Homoeosis/similitudo; and application, 23; Augustinian rule of Biblical allegory, 60; in Bede, 75; in Bible, 33, 41, 60; in Diomedes, 23, 97-98; in Isidore, 72; in Macrobius, 13; species, 23

Hyperbaton; in Diomedes, 93-94

Hyperbole; in Diomedes, 94-95

Hyponoia; and allegory, 5; in Bible, 30; and Homer, 3; in Philo, 9; in Plutarch, 6

Icon/imago; in Bede, 75; in Bible, 29-30; in Diomedes, 97; in Isidore, 72; in Macrobius, 13-14; in Plato, 10

Imago, see *icon*

Impersonation, see personification

Intentionality, 45, 82

Inversio; allegoria in Quintilian, 16

Irony; as applied allegory, 19; in Augustine, 47-48; in Bede, 74; in Christian literature, 85-86; in Diomedes, 95; in Greek grammarians, 119-26

Levels of meaning, xi-xii; in Augustine, 48-49; in Bede, 76-77; in Hugh, 80; in Nicholas, 77-78

Literal vs figurative, xi; in Augustine, 44-46, 58; in Philo, 8-9

Lying; in Augustine, 60-63

Metalepsis; in Diomedes, 91

Metaphor; in Diomedes, 89-90; in Greek grammarians, 131-41; succession of as allegory, 16

Metonymy; in Diomedes, 91; and personification, 5

Myth, see *fabula*

Narratio fabulosa; in Macrobius, 13

Neoplatonic allegorization, x, 3, 10-15, 18, 24

Obscurity, 16-17

Onomatopoeia; in Diomedes, 93

Parabola/parabole; in Bede, 75; in Bible, 33-42, 84; in Diomedes, 14, 97-98; in Greek grammarians, 150-58; in Isidore, 73; in Macrobius, 14-15; in Nicholas, 78-79; in Servius, 8

Paradigm, see *exemplum*

Paroemia/proverbium; and application, 22-23; in Bede, 75; in Bible, 33-39, 84; in Greek grammarians, 159; in Isidore, 72-73; in Quintilian, 17

Permutatio; allegoria in *Ad Herennium*, 16

Personification/impersonation, 25; *conformatio* (in *Ad Herennium*), 15; in Greek grammarians, 160-69, as *imago*, 14; in Plutarch, 10; prosopopoiia (in Quintilian), 15

Poetic coloring; in Isidore, 69-70; in Lactantius, 68, 70

Poetic fiction; in Augustine, 57; in Plutarch, 6, 9

Problema/propositio; in Bible, 35

Rationes (interpretations); Christian, 84; Christian view of pagan (in Arnobius, 66-67; in Augustine, 54-56; in Gnosticism, 64-65)

Religion and allegorization; in Augustine, 57-58; in Cicero, 5; in Plutarch, 6, 9

Res/facta and *verba*, ix, 81; in Augustine, 43, 53, 59; in Bede, 75-77

Riddle, see enigma

Sarcasm; as applied allegory, 19; in Diomedes, 96

Sequence, 55-56

Similitudo, see *homoeosis*

Stoic allegorization, x, 3-5, 25, 27

Suitable (appropriate) meanings; in Augustine, 45, 47-48

Symbol; in Demetrius, 7; in Philo, 9; in Plutarch, 7

Synecdoche; in Diomedes, 92-93

Terminology, xii; hyponoia and allegory, 5

Typos; in Bible, 32; in Isidore, 71

Vestigia; hints at meaning in Augustine, 44